Effective Teamwork

Effective Teamwork

Practical Lessons from Organizational Research

Third Edition

Michael A. West

Lancaster University Management School
Bailrigg, Lancaster

and

The Work Foundation
London

The British Psychological Society | BPS BLACKWELL

This edition first published 2012 by the British Psychological Society and John Wiley & Sons, Ltd
© 2012 John Wiley & Sons, Ltd.

First edition published by Blackwell Publishers 1994, second edition published by Blackwell Publishing 2003.
First edition copyright Michael A. West
Second edition copyright Michael A. West

BPS Blackwell is an imprint of Blackwell Publishing, which was acquired by John Wiley & Sons, Ltd
in February 2007.

Registered Office
John Wiley & Sons, Ltd, The Atrium, Southern Gate, Chichester, West Sussex, PO19 8SQ, UK

Editorial Offices
350 Main Street, Malden, MA 02148-5020, USA
9600 Garsington Road, Oxford, OX4 2DQ, UK
The Atrium, Southern Gate, Chichester, West Sussex, PO19 8SQ, UK

For details of our global editorial offices, for customer services, and for information about how
to apply for permission to reuse the copyright material in this book please see our website at
www.wiley.com/wiley-blackwell.

The right of Michael A. West to be identified as the author of this work has been asserted in accordance
with the UK Copyright, Designs and Patents Act 1988.

Library of Congress Cataloging-in-Publication Data

West, Michael A., 1951–
 Effective teamwork : practical lessons from organizational research / Michael A West. – 3rd ed.
   p. cm.
 Includes bibliographical references and index.
 ISBN 978-0-470-97498-8 (cloth) – ISBN 978-0-470-97497-1 (pbk.)
1. Teams in the workplace. I. Title.
 HD66.W473 2012
 658.4′022–dc23
                                          2011035195

A catalogue record for this book is available from the British Library.

This book is published in the following electronic formats: ePDFs 9781119966005; ePub 9781444355345;
eMobi 9781444355338

Set in 10/12pt Sabon by SPi Publisher Services, Pondicherry, India

1   2012

To: Rosa Hardy

for being a wonderful example of the supportiveness, courage and creativity that are essential for great teamwork

Contents

Acknowledgements   xi

Part 1   Team Effectiveness   1

1   Creating Effective Teams   3
    Task and Social Elements of Team Functioning   6
    Team Effectiveness   7
    Key Revision Points   12
    Further Reading   12
    Web Resources   12

2   Real Teams Work   13
    Why Work in Teams?   17
    Barriers to Effective Teamwork   21
    What is a Team?   27
    What do Teams do?   29
    How can we build Effective Teams?   31
    Conclusions   35
    Key Revision Points   37
    Further Reading   37
    Web Resources   38

Part 2   Developing Teams   39

3   Creating Teams   41
    Personality and Ability   43
    Teamwork Skills   49
    Diversity of Team Members   52
    Benefiting from Team Diversity   57
    Implications of Diversity   58
    Key Revision Points   59

| | *Further Reading* | 59 |
| | *Web Resources* | 59 |

4	Leading Teams	60
	The Three Team Leadership Tasks	61
	The Three Elements of Leading Teams	63
	Tripwires for Team Leaders	77
	Developing Team Leadership Skills	79
	Self-managing or Shared Leadership Work Teams	84
	Key Revision Points	85
	Further Reading	85
	Web Resources	86

5	Team Training	87
	The Stages of Team Development	89
	Types of Team Training Interventions	91
	Conclusions	101
	Key Revision Points	102
	Further Reading	102
	Web Resources	102

| **Part 3** | **Team Working** | **105** |

6	Setting Team Direction	107
	Team Objectives	107
	The Elements of Team Vision	113
	Strategy for Teams	115
	Key Revision Points	117
	Further Reading	117
	Web Resources	118

7	Team Playing	119
	Interaction	120
	Information Sharing	124
	Influencing and Decision Making	125
	Creating Safety in Teams	131
	Key Revision Points	133
	Further Reading	134
	Web Resources	134

8	Team Quality Management	135
	Groupthink	136
	Team Pressures to Conform	138
	Obedience to Authority	139
	Team Defence Mechanisms	139
	Commitment to Quality	141

Task Focus/Constructive Controversy 142
Encouraging Constructive Controversy in Teams 143
Conclusion 151
Key Revision Points 152
Further Reading 153
Web Resources 153

9   Creative Team Problem Solving 155
Team Innovation 156
Creative Problem Solving in Teams 160
Techniques for Promoting Creativity within a Team 162
Using Creativity Techniques in Team Meetings 166
Other Influences on Team Innovation 167
Key Revision Points 170
Further Reading 170
Web Resources 171

10   Team Support 172
The Emotional Life of Teams 174
Social Support 176
Support for Team Member Growth and Development 182
Balance between Home and Work Life 184
Social Climate 184
Conclusions 186
Key Revision Points 187
Further Reading 187
Web Resources 187

11   Conflict in Teams 188
Team Conflicts 188
Types of Team Conflict 189
Resolving Team Conflicts 189
Organizational Causes of Conflict 191
Interpersonal Conflicts 193
Difficult Team Members 195
Key Revision Points 198
Further Reading 198
Web Resources 198

Part 4   **Teams in Organizations** 199

12   Teams in Organizations 201
Introducing Team-based Working (TBW) 202
The Relationship between Teams and their Organizations 205
What do Teams need from their Organizations? 207
The Role of Human Resource Management (HRM) 209

What do Organizations require from Teams? 213
Bridging across Teams 216
Conclusions 219
Key Revision Points 219
Further Reading 220
Web Resources 220

13 Virtual Team Working 221
What is Virtual Team Working? 225
Advantages and Disadvantages of Virtual Teams 227
How to Develop Effective Virtual Team Working 228
Lifecycle of Virtual Teams 235
Conclusion 238
Key Revision Points 239
Further Reading 239
Web Resources 240

14 Top Management Teams 241
Task Design 243
Team Effort and Skills 245
Organizational Supports 248
Top Management Team Processes 251
Top Team Participation 254
Corporate Social Responsibility 255
Top Team Meetings 257
Conflict 262
CEO Leadership 263
Conclusions 266
Key Revision Points 268
Further Reading 268
Web Resources 268

References 269
Author Index 286
Subject Index 292

Acknowledgements

My thanks to the members of the research teams I have the privilege to be a part of, particularly Jeremy Dawson and Joanne Richardson, whose thinking and collaboration have influenced the preparation of this latest edition of *Effective Teamwork*. Lynn Markiewicz continues to inspire my thinking through her work in AstonOD and many of the examples of good practice either spring from her work in organizations or have been tested by her in challenging organizational settings. Thanks also to Lilian Otaye who patiently and kindly helped develop case studies, find useful web sites for readers and ensure a finished product. And to Ellie Hardy for so carefully proofreading and indexing to the high standards of an Oxford English scholar. And thanks to readers of previous editions who have offered useful suggestions for improvements.

Michael West
Lancaster University Management School,
and The Work Foundation
May 2011

Part 1

Team Effectiveness

In this first section of the book, we examine what effective teamwork means. The first chapter looks at what is required for effective teamwork, identifying two themes that run through the book. These are team task functioning and team socio-emotional climate. The chapter explains how effective teams take time to review their performance in these areas and to adapt accordingly. Ensuring the team is functioning well both as a task group and as a social group is vital to ensuring team effectiveness. Reflecting on these areas of teamwork regularly and making changes in objectives, strategies and team processes as necessary are vital for the long-term effectiveness of the team.

The second chapter focuses on the research evidence about whether teams work or not. Are teams effective in getting work done and does teamwork in organizations lead to improved organizational performance? Effectiveness includes the well-being and development of team members as well as the level of innovation in the team. The chapter reviews the research on the problems of team working to show the circumstances in which teams perform badly. However, the chapter also shows that teams outperform the aggregate of individuals working alone and are essential for the performance of many tasks in organizations. The key is knowing how to create the conditions for teams to work effectively – the subject of this book.

Effective Teamwork: Practical Lessons from Organizational Research, Third Edition.
By M. A. West. © 2012 John Wiley & Sons, Ltd. Published 2012 by John Wiley & Sons, Ltd., and the British Psychological Society.

1

Creating Effective Teams

Never doubt that a small group of thoughtful, committed citizens can change the world. Indeed, it is the only thing that ever has. (Margaret Mead)

Key Learning Points

- The basic conditions for effective teamwork
- The conditions for outstanding teamwork
- Team reflexivity and its importance in team functioning
- The two dimensions of team functioning – task and social reflexivity
- The five elements of team effectiveness
- The relationship of team reflexivity to team effectiveness
- The application of the reflexivity questionnaire to real teams

Our societies and communities face the fundamental challenge of how to enable people to combine their efforts and imaginations to work in ways that enhance quality of life through the achievement of our shared goals. The major challenges that face our species today require us to cooperate effectively in order to maximize the quality of life for all people while, at the same time, sustaining the resources offered by the planet? For thousands of years the most potent solution we have found has been teamwork. So why

Effective Teamwork: Practical Lessons from Organizational Research, Third Edition.
By M. A. West. © 2012 John Wiley & Sons, Ltd. Published 2012 by John Wiley & Sons, Ltd., and the British Psychological Society.

the need for a book on teamwork if we have been working in teams successfully for so long? Because the landscape of teamwork has changed fundamentally in the last 200 years. The growth of modern organizations has created a context in which teams no longer work in isolation. Teams must work together with other teams and with organizational systems and processes to achieve the goals we aspire to and overcome the challenges we face. This book offers guidelines for this new context, largely based on research evidence, for how to ensure effective teamwork and how to enable multi-team systems to operate in an integrated and effective way. More than that what the book offers is insights into how to create outstandingly effective teams – dream teams – teams that achieve more than their members imagined possible and which enable and inspire the success of other teams within their organizations. The book describes both the basic conditions for effective team working and the conditions that will produce dream teams.

The basic conditions for effective teamwork include having a real team whose membership is clear, which is of the right size, relatively stable in membership and working on a task that requires teamwork. The team must have an overall purpose that adds value and which is translated into clear, challenging team objectives. And the team needs the right people as team members with the required skills in the right roles. They must be enablers not derailers – people who support effective team working through their behaviours, not people who sabotage, undermine or obstruct team functioning.

In addition to these basic conditions, dream teams are characterized by transformational leadership that reinforces an inspiring and motivating team purpose focused sharply on the needs of the team's stakeholders (clients, customers, patients); that encourages all team members to value the diversity of its membership. Members have opportunities to grow and learn in their roles and there is a strong sense of continuous growth and development as a team. Dream teams have a high level of positivity, characterized by optimism and a healthy balance of positive and negative interactions. Members are open, appreciative, kind and genuine in their interactions with each other and eager to learn from each other. Team members believe in the team's ability to be successful and effective in their work (team potency). They are secure in their team membership and attached to the team because of the level of trust and support they encounter – and the fact that members appropriately back each other up in crises. And the team's relationship with the wider organization is engaged and supportive. The team actively builds effective inter-team relationships and members identify enthusiastically, not just with their team, but with the wider organization of which they are a part. Such dream teams, and teams of dream teams, enable effective communication and fruitful collaborations in which new ideas are shared and integrated, work load is shared, mutual support is provided and opportunities are exploited to their full potential. Later in the book, the reader will discover how to create these conditions.

Creating and sustaining effective teams requires persistent renewal and discovery of good practice. Moreover, teams vary in the tasks they undertake, the contexts they work in and their membership. And change is a constant: so teams must adapt to the changes that confront them within and outside their organizations. Both the variation between teams and the changing context of all teams requires flexible team members, flexible team processes and flexible organizations. And we have a wondrous capacity to encourage such flexibility. What we are able to do – and no other animal can – is to reflect upon our experiences and consciously adapt what we do to adjust to changing circumstances. And we can use this ability to learn to dance the dance of teamwork ever more effectively. Applied at team level, this is termed *team reflexivity*.

Team reflexivity involves:

- regular team reviews of the team's objectives including an assessment of their continuing relevance and appropriateness, as well as progress towards their fulfilment;
- team member vigilance for external changes that could affect the team's work;
- awareness, review and discussion of the team's functioning with a view to improving performance;
- creativity, flexibility and adaptability;
- tolerance of uncertainty;
- team members valuing the different perspectives, knowledge bases, skills and experience of team members.

Teams operate in varied organizational settings – as diverse as multi-national oil companies, voluntary organizations, healthcare organizations and the military – so we need to be cautious about offering one-size-fits-all prescriptions for effective teamwork. Within organizations too, teams differ markedly. Teams are often composed of people with very different cultural backgrounds, ages, functional expertise and personalities. Teams may span national boundaries, including members located in several countries. Differences in work patterns such as part-time, flexitime, contract working and home working all add further mixes to the heterogeneity of teams. As teams become more diverse in their constitution and functioning, team members must learn to reflect upon, and intelligently adapt to the constantly changing circumstances in order to be effective. In this book, it is proposed that, to the extent that team members collectively reflect on the team's objectives, strategies, processes and performance and make changes accordingly (team reflexivity) (West, 2000; Widmer, Schippers, and West, 2009), teams will be more productive, effective and innovative.

Task and Social Elements of Team Functioning

There are two fundamental dimensions of team functioning: the task the team is required to carry out, and the social factors that influence how members work together as a social unit. The basic reason for the creation of teams in work organizations is the expectation that they will carry out some tasks more effectively than individuals and so further organizational objectives overall. In fact, some tasks can only be undertaken by teams of people working together rather than individuals working alone – think of open-heart surgery, the construction of a car, catching an antelope on the savannah without the benefit of modern technology or weapons. Consideration of the content of the task, and the strategies and processes employed by team members to carry out that task, is therefore important for understanding how to work in teams. At the same time, teams are composed of people who have a variety of emotional, social and other human needs that the team as a whole can either help to meet or frustrate. Feeling valued, respected and supported by other team members will be a prerequisite for people offering their ideas for new and improved ways of ensuring team effectiveness. If we ignore either dimension in trying to achieve team effectiveness, we will fail to achieve the potential of team performance.

Research evidence now shows convincingly how important positive emotions, such as hope, pleasure, happiness, humour, excitement, joy, pride and involvement, are as a source of human strength (Fredrickson, 2009). When we feel positive emotions we think in a more flexible, open-minded way, and consider a much wider range of possibilities than if we feel anxious, depressed or angry. This enables us to accomplish tasks and make the most of the situations we find ourselves in. We are also more likely to see challenges as opportunities rather than threats. When we feel positive we exercise greater self-control, cope more effectively and are less likely to react defensively in workplace situations. The litany of benefits does not stop there. It spills over too into what is called 'pro-social behaviour' – cooperation and altruism. When we feel positive emotion we are more likely to be helpful, generous and to exercise a sense of social responsibility (for a review, see Fredrickson, 2009). The implications for teams are that by developing a team environment where people feel positive, we can encourage organizational citizenship – in other words the tendency of people at work to help each other and those in other departments; to do that bit extra which is not part of their job. And such citizenship makes a major difference between the most effective teams and the rest. The idea that we can create effective teams by focusing simply on performance and ignoring the role of our emotions is based on the false premise that emotions can be ignored at work. Positive relationships and a sense of community are the product and cause of positive emotions. We must work with human needs and capacities and potentials rather than against them if we are to create positive teams that succeed and at the same time, foster the health and well-being of those who work within them.

In order to function effectively, team members must actively focus upon their objectives, regularly reviewing ways of achieving them and the team's methods of working – 'task reflexivity'. At the same time, in order to promote the well-being of its members, the team must reflect upon the ways in which it provides support to members, how conflicts are resolved and what is the overall social and emotional climate of the team – or its 'social reflexivity'. The purpose of these reviews should be to inform the next steps by changing as appropriate the team's objectives, ways of working or social functioning, in order to promote effectiveness.

Team Effectiveness

So what does 'team effectiveness' mean? Team effectiveness can be seen as constituting five main components:

1   Task effectiveness is the extent to which the team is successful in achieving its **task-related objectives**.
2   **Team member well-being** refers to factors such as the well-being or mental health (e.g., stress), growth and development of team members.
3   **Team viability** is the likelihood that a team will continue to work together and function effectively.
4   **Team innovation** is the extent to which the team develops and implements new and improved processes, products and procedures.
5   **Inter-team cooperation** is the effectiveness of the team in working with other teams in the organization with which it has to work in order to deliver products or services.

Table 1 shows the two elements of teams, the task and social elements, drawn together in a two-by-two model to illustrate four extreme types of team functioning and the likely effects upon the five principle outcomes of team functioning: task effectiveness, team members' mental health, team viability, innovation and inter-team cooperation (such models are a simplification of reality but for our immediate purposes this model serves to illustrate some important points).

Type A, the *Resilient team*, represents a team which is high in both task and social reflexivity, that is, the extent to which the team reflects on and

Table 1   Four types of teams and their outcomes.

High Task Reflexivity	
Type D: Driven team	*Type A: Resilient team*
High short-term task effectiveness	High task effectiveness
Poor team member well-being	Good team member well-being
Short-term viability	Long-term viability
Moderate innovation	High innovation
High inter-team conflict	High inter-team cooperation
Low Social Reflexivity	**High Social Reflexivity**
Type C: Dysfunctional team	*Type B: Complacent team*
Poor task effectiveness	Poor task effectiveness
Poor team member well-being	Average team member well-being
Very low team viability	Short-term viability
Low innovation	Low innovation
High inter-team conflict	Moderate inter-team conflict
Low Task Reflexivity	

modifies its objectives, processes, task and social support strategies appropriately in changing circumstances. Such teams are likely to have good levels of well-being amongst team members, high task effectiveness, and sustained viability, that is, they have the capacity and desire to continue to work together. Because of the high levels of both task and social reflexivity they are able to adapt to changing circumstances and ensure sustained high performance. Consequently, they are also more likely to innovate and have the capacity to work effectively with other teams within the organization with which they have to work in order to deliver goods or services.

Type B, the *Complacent team,* is high in social reflexivity and low in task reflexivity. This is a team where there is a good deal of warmth, support and cohesion amongst team members, but where the ability to get the task done effectively is low. Team members do not dedicate time to reflecting upon the team's task objectives, strategies and processes and therefore do not confront their performance problems, learn from mistakes or adapt their task performance to ensure effectiveness. Therefore, while team members' well-being is good and they value their colleagues, the organization's satisfaction with team performance is low and team members experience the disappointment of membership of a failing or at best poorly performing team. As a result its viability is threatened. Even if team members wish to continue to work together over a period of time, the organization is likely to break the team up. In the longer term team members' well-being will be adversely affected by the low levels of competence experienced by team members in a team which is minimally task effective. We like to be successful and effective in our work. Staying in a poorly functioning team corrodes job satisfaction. Such a team, with a lack of performance focus, is unlikely to have the motivation to innovate. Despite their warmth, they will create a degree of irritation and dissatisfaction in the other teams they have to work with, because of their ineffectiveness.

Type C, the *Dysfunctional team*, is the worst scenario – a team that is low on both task and social reflexivity. Such teams fail to reflect on and change their functioning in either domain. They will not be viable in the long term since team members leaders will be dissatisfied with both the interpersonal relationships and with the team's failures to achieve. Frustration with the team's poor performance will cause organization leaders to intervene or disband the team. Interventions to promote both task and social reflexivity in the team should be immediate and sustained since team members will learn to function effectively both in the team of which they are currently members and in teams they are part of in the future. The lack of safety and effectiveness combine to mitigate against innovation and the team's performance creates high levels of conflict with the other teams that rely on them, because of their failure to deliver.

Finally team type D, the *Driven team*, is a team in which task reflexivity is high, but where the social functioning of the team is poor. Members are driven to focus on achieving task objectives as quickly as possible with minimum distractions. Task performance is generally good in the short term, but poor social functioning damages team viability and the well-being of members. Team members do not enjoy working in a team that they perceive as providing little social support and which has a poor social climate. Moreover, because the team does not feel safe, levels of innovation are low. The team fails to reflect on its health as a social entity, so little progress is made in improving the team's functioning as a social unit. In the long term, the team will fail to achieve its potential. Without a positive, supportive climate, levels of cooperation will be low and the team's capacity for creativity and innovation will be limited. In some circumstances (such as a short-term crisis) focusing on the task to the exclusion of all else might make sense but at some point there must be healthy reviews of social functioning. Support, backing up, enabling and coaching are vital team member behaviours in any team. Moreover, because they are driven, they are likely to come into conflict with the other teams with which they need to work, either because they become frustrated by the speed of delivery from other teams or because they are too concerned with their own team's performance and less concerned with findings ways of helping other teams.

These two aspects of team functioning, namely task and social reflexivity, have a direct impact upon the three principal outcomes of team functioning – task effectiveness, team members' well-being and team viability. In this book we examine these elements of team functioning and describe practical ways in which team reflexivity can be enhanced.

Research evidence drives the content of the book. We will challenge many assumptions about teamwork that the research evidence does not support by informing the reader on what research reveals about effective teamwork, rather than on what consultants and pundits guess makes for effective teamwork. I also offer examples from my experience of working with teams in a wide variety of settings and across many different countries.

Throughout the book, we will focus on answering the question: 'what makes teams effective?' in a way that will prove practically useful to you in working in or with teams, and will help you to develop them into fully functioning teams which are high in both task and social reflexivity.

Exercise 1   The team reflexivity questionnaire

How effectively does your team function?

To measure levels of task and social reflexivity in your team, ask all team members to complete this questionnaire without consulting each other about the answers. Add the scores for task reflexivity and social reflexivity separately, that is, add all team members' scores for the task element and then all team members' scores for the social element. *Divide both totals by the number of people completing the questionnaire.* At the bottom of this box are values against which you can determine whether your team's scores are high, low or average compared with the scores of other teams.

Instructions for completion:

Indicate how far each statement is an accurate or inaccurate description of your team by writing a number in the box beside each statement, based on the following scale of 1 to 7:

Very inaccurate						Very accurate
1	2	3	4	5	6	7

(a) **Task reflexivity**

1   The team often reviews its objectives. ☐

2   We regularly discuss whether the team is working together effectively. ☐

3   The methods used by the team to get the job done are often discussed ☐

4   In this team we modify our objectives in the light of changing circumstances. ☐

5   Team strategies are often changed. ☐

6   How well we communicate information is often discussed. ☐

7   This team often reviews its approach to getting the job done. ☐

8   The way decisions are made in this team is often reviewed. ☐

Total score ☐

(b) **Social reflexivity**

1   Team members provide each other with support when times are difficult. ☐

2   When things at work are stressful the team is very supportive. ☐

3   Conflict does not linger in this team. ☐

4   People in this team often teach each other new skills. ☐

5   When things at work are stressful, we pull together as a team. ☐

6   Team members are always friendly. ☐

7   Conflicts are constructively dealt with in this team. ☐

8   People in this team are quick to resolve arguments. ☐

Total score ☐

	(a) Task reflexivity	(b) Social reflexivity
High scores	42–56	42–56
Average scores	34–41	34–41
Low scores	0–33	0–33

As a team, you can discuss how to improve your functioning where it seems low for no good reason. Such a discussion can be a first step towards improving the extent to which the team reflects on its objectives, strategies, processes and social functioning in order to ensure it is a fully functional team.

Key Revision Points

- What are the basic conditions for effective teamwork?
- What are the conditions necessary for outstanding or 'dream' teams?
- What is team reflexivity and what is the difference between task and social reflexivity?
- What are the main elements of team effectiveness?
- How do task and social reflexivity affect team effectiveness?

Further Reading

Cameron, K.S., Dutton, J.E. and Quinn, R.E. (2003) *Positive Organizational Scholarship: Foundations of a New Discipline*, Berrett-Koehler, San Francisco.

Fredrickson, B. (2009) *Positivity*, Random House, New York.

Linley, P.A., Harrington, S. and Garcea, N. (eds) (2010) *Oxford Handbook of Positive Psychology and Work*, Oxford University Press, Oxford.

West, M.A. (2000) Reflexivity, revolution, and innovation in work teams, in *Product Development Teams* (eds M.M. Beyerlein, D.A. Johnson and S.T. Beyerlein), JAI Press, Stamford, CT, pp. 1–29.

Widmer, P.S. Schippers, M.C. and West, M.A. (2009) Recent developments in reflexivity research: a review. *Psychology of Everyday Activity*, 2, 2–11.

Web Resources

Reflexivity: http://reflexivitynetwork.com/index.php?option=com_content&view=article&id=47&Itemid=53 (last accessed 25 July 2011).

Team development: www.astonod.com (last accessed 25 July 2011).

Positivity: www.positivityratio.com/
www.cappeu.com/ (last accessed 25 July 2011).

2

Real Teams Work

There is no hope for creating a better world without a deeper scientific insight in the function of leadership and culture, and of other essentials of group life ... (Kurt Lewin, 1943)

Key Learning Points

- The difference between pseudo teams and real teams
- The organizational benefits of team working
- The drawbacks of working in teams – weaker effort, decision making and creativity
- Teams defined and types of teams
- Tasks for teams
- How to build an effective team
- How to measure team performance

Effective Teamwork: Practical Lessons from Organizational Research, Third Edition.
By M. A. West. © 2012 John Wiley & Sons, Ltd. Published 2012 by John Wiley & Sons, Ltd., and the British Psychological Society.

Case Study

18 carat or fool's gold: Team work and patient mortality in health care

The United Kingdom National Health Service employs in the region of 1.4 million staff whose responsibility is to provide high-quality and safe patient care. Every year a staff survey is carried out to elicit their views about their working conditions, their management and leadership, the quality of care they provide and the environment within which they work. They are asked 'Do you work in a team?' and typically each year around 90% of staff say 'yes' in response. Given the evidence on the importance of teamwork in health care for better patient outcomes, this might seem very encouraging. However, the survey asks three follow-up questions of those who indicate they work in a team: 'Does your team have clear objectives? Do you work closely together to achieve those objectives? Do you meet regularly to review your performance and how it can be improved?' These three questions tap the very basic dimensions of team working – shared objectives, interdependence and review meetings. Staff who answer 'no' to one or more of these questions are categorized as belonging to a pseudo team (around 50% of staff). Those who answer 'yes' to all three questions are classified as working in a real team (around 40%). There are therefore three groups: those who indicate they do not work in a team; those who work in real teams; and those who work in pseudo teams. The data reveal that the greater percentage of staff working in pseudo teams within a hospital or other healthcare organization, the higher the levels of injuries to staff at work (typically from needles, lifting and falls); the higher the level of witnessed errors that could harm patients or staff; the higher the levels of violent assaults from patients or their carers, relatives and friends; and the higher the levels of bullying, harassment and abuse from those same groups. The opposite relationships is observed in relation to the percentage of staff in the hospital working in real teams – fewer injuries, errors, violent assaults and cases of harassment, bullying and abuse. Moreover absenteeism is lower the greater the percentage of staff working in real teams. Most strikingly, there is a strong relationship with patient mortality. Having more real teams is associated with lower patient mortality and more pseudo teams are independently associated with higher mortality. The data show that 5% more staff working in real teams would be associated with a decrease of 3.3% in patient mortality (typically 40 deaths per year in each hospital). With 50% working in pseudo teams, the opportunities for improvement in mortality figures (assuming a causal relationship) are enormous and added across the entire National Health Service, truly staggering. (Further details of this work are available from the author at m.a.west@lancaster.ac.uk)

This case study reveals the importance of being clear about what we mean by teamwork – a topic we will explore in more depth in this chapter. Before we do that, we will consider the role of teamwork in human society and evolutionary history.

To live, work, and play in human society is to cooperate with others. We express both our collective identity and our individuality in groups and organizations (De Cremer, van Dick and Murnighan, 2011). Our identity comes from the groups of which we are a part – clubs, voluntary societies, professions, sports teams (playing or supporting), work organizations and political affiliations. We have, throughout our history, lived, loved, raised our young, and worked together in groups (Baumeister and Leary, 1995). Our common experiences of living and working together bind us with each other and with our predecessors. It is precisely because human beings have learned to work cooperatively together that we have made such astonishing progress as a species. By mapping the human genome we have discovered the underlying biochemical processes that make us what we are. And we have explored the beginnings and the outer limits of our universe. These extraordinary accomplishments have been accomplished largely by teams, and by teams of teams. When we work cooperatively we accomplish infinitely more than if we work individually. This is the principle of group synergy – that the contribution of the whole group is greater than the sum of its individual members' contributions. To push a large boulder up a hill is not manageable when we work alone – but we can achieve this when we work together. Throughout our history, we have worked in small groups and teams. It is only in the last 200 years that people have begun to work in the larger collectives we call organizations (prior to that only the religious and military were of any substantial size).

The growth of the modern organization, with its complex structures and competing goals of fostering innovation while exerting control over relatively large numbers of employees, has been astonishing in its rapidity. Yet most of us now take these entities for granted. In fact, they pose real challenges to us in our working lives. When we worked in small teams over very long periods of time in agricultural or craft settings, co-workers were intimately acquainted with each other's knowledge, skills and abilities. Team working was finely honed and developed over many years. Many of us today are members of multiple teams, interacting with other teams, and seeing a constant flux in team membership. Such conditions pose real challenges to effective working. And yet teamwork survives as an ideal way of working in organizations, partly because it is the way we have always worked successfully. But team working in many organizations is poorly developed – more fool's gold than 18 carat.

We face new demands in modern organizations that make cooperative work in teams both more vital and more challenging. To meet the pressures of the global marketplace, organizations are moving away from rigid, hierarchical structures towards more organic, flexible forms. Teams are developing and marketing products, solving production problems, and creating corporate strategy. Managers are experimenting with participation, high-commitment organizations, self-managing work teams, employee–management cooperation, and 'gainsharing' programmes (where employees have a share of the gains made as a result of the innovations they have implemented). These innovations involve the explicit use of teams to accomplish central organizational tasks. The team rather than the individual is increasingly considered the basic building block of organizations.

Teamwork is spilling out across organizational and national boundaries. Many manufacturers form teams with suppliers to boost quality, reduce costs and ensure continuous improvement. International alliances are becoming the accepted way to participate in the global marketplace. American and Japanese automakers and other traditional competitors have developed a wide variety of cooperative strategies. Increasingly, people with different organizational and national loyalties from diverse cultural backgrounds and with unequal status are asked to work together. And teams from commercial organizations are linking with those from universities to develop exciting, useful and radical innovations (West, Tjosvold and Smith, 2003). So why do we work in teams? Put simply it is because teams enable us to accomplish what would otherwise be impossible. Catching antelopes on the savannah 200 000 years ago or taking stones from the Preseli mountains in Wales to Stonehenge in southern England and erecting them in the famous circle required sophisticated teamwork; heart by-pass operations require tight interdependent working between surgeons, anaesthetists, surgical nurses and administrators; airline passengers rely on cockpit teams to deliver them safely to their destination. Every task that cannot be accomplished without people working interdependently in small groups is a compelling example of the value of teamwork (West, Brodbeck and Richter, 2004).

In hard-rock mining the introduction of team goals leads to a greater quantity of rocks mined. In work safety studies, the introduction of team goals and training sees an increase in safe work behaviour. When I finished my PhD at the University of Wales in 1977, I went to work in Oakdale Colliery for a year to pay off my student debts. Working in a coal-mining team demonstrated forcibly to me how the team managed safety effectively by exerting pressure to ensure we all worked in a way that minimized the likelihood of injury. In a study of timber harvesting the introduction of team goals led to a higher output rate; in restaurant services the introduction of team working for staff was associated with higher customer ratings of service quality, comfort and cleanliness; in an insurance company, increased compliance with a 24-hour reporting standard was found after the introduction of team working; and in truck loading and unloading, truck turnaround time was reduced after the introduction of a team goal (Weldon and Weingart, 1993). Studies in health care have repeatedly shown that better patient care is provided when health professionals work together in multidisciplinary teams (Borrill *et al.*, 2000). And it has been shown that the more real team working there is in hospitals, the lower the level of patient mortality (see, for example, West, 2002; West, Markiewicz and Dawson, 2006). There is evidence that when students work in cooperative groups rather than individually, they work harder, help less able group members, and learn more (Slavin, 1983). It is by working together and pooling our resources (knowledge, abilities, experience, time, money, etc.) that we can most effectively accomplish our shared goals. But we can go further in our understanding of the value of teams by considering the multiplicity of benefits they can offer in the modern organization.

Why Work in Teams?

- Teams are a very good way to *enact organizational strategy*, because of the need for consistency between rapidly changing organizational environments, strategy and structure. When organizations adopt team-based structures, there is less need for the ponderous hierarchies that slow organizational decision making because the team rather than the individual becomes the work unit. Team-based organizations, with their flat structures, can respond quickly and effectively in the fast-changing environments most organizations now encounter (Cohen and Bailey, 1997).
- Teams enable organizations to *speedily develop and deliver products and services* quickly and cost effectively. Teams can work faster and more effectively with members working in parallel and interdependently whereas individuals working serially are much slower. For example, in writing complex software for modern computer games, different teams can take responsibility for working in parallel on key elements of the overall program. Their separate contributions can then be combined to ensure quick delivery of the final product.

- Teams *enable organizations to learn* (and retain learning) more effectively. When one team member leaves, the learning of the team is not lost. Team members also learn from each other during the course of team working.
- Cross-functional teams promote *improved quality management.* By combining team members' diverse perspectives, decision making is more comprehensive because team members from diverse functional backgrounds question ideas and decisions about how best to provide products and services to clients. For example, in a team involved in developing cosmetics, the marketing specialist is likely to challenge decisions made by a chemist about product appearance, based on his or her knowledge of customer preferences. The chemist may be focused on the effectiveness of the product rather than its appearance. The perspectives of other team members around production processes, packaging, promotion and cost will all contribute to a more informed outcome. Diversity, properly processed, leads to high-quality decision making and innovation (van Knippenburg and Schippers 2007; West, 2002).
- Cross-functional design teams can undertake *radical change.* The breadth of perspective offered by cross-functional teams produces the questioning and integration of diverse perspectives that enables teams to challenge basic assumptions and make radical changes to improve their products, services and ways of working. In one organization I visited, teams were created out of all those involved in the servicing of military fighter planes. They then reduced the service time from six months to three weeks by pooling their diverse perspectives with the aim of achieving a huge increase in efficiency. *Time is saved* if activities, formerly performed sequentially by individuals, can be performed concurrently by people working in teams.
- *Innovation is promoted* within team-based organizations because of cross-fertilization of ideas. When we bring together team members with differing knowledge, skills and abilities that are relevant to the team's task, the process of sharing perspectives and knowledge challenges assumptions and opens up the space for exploration of new and improved ways of doing things. Whether in health care, manufacturing, oil and gas or any other area of industry, team working is associated with higher levels of innovation (Sacramento, Chang and West, 2006).
- *Flat organizations can be co-ordinated* and directed more effectively if the functional unit is the team rather than the individual. Setting objectives, aligned with organizational objectives, for seven teams each made up of seven members, is a lot easier than setting objectives for 49 individuals. One leader can oversee the work of seven teams but more like seven leaders are needed to oversee the work of 49 individuals. Consequently, fewer layers of management are needed where team working is widespread.

- As organizations have grown more complex, so too have their information-processing requirements. *Teams can integrate and link* in ways individuals cannot to ensure that information is processed effectively in the complex structures of modern organizations. Two product development teams can share information about engineering solutions for similar problems they face. Teams of teams engaged in the treatment of cancer (radiography, surgery, family doctors, palliative care and home-nursing teams) can coordinate care and communication with patients to ensure optimal treatment and support. Management teams at senior levels in organizations can communicate with their functional teams and support teams as a whole rather than via the director or senior manager HR, Finance, Production, Sales and, in matrix organizations, product teams can work together with support teams from HR, Finance, Sales, etc.). The potential for greater linkage and integration in team-based organizations is high and offers a distinct advantage over traditionally structured organizations. The potential, as we will see later in this book, is often not fulfilled because of poor inter-team linkages.

An analysis of the combined results of 131 studies of organizational change found that when comparing the results of 18 different organizational interventions including financial reward systems, diverse training and education interventions, those with the largest *effects upon financial performance* were team development interventions or the creation of autonomous work groups (see Macy and Izumi, 1993). When the full sample of studies was considered and overall performance (perhaps the best criterion) was used, the introduction of autonomous and semi-autonomous teams had the strongest effect size on overall firm performance ($r_{pbs} = 0.20, p < .05$; p. 279) out of all 18 interventions. A more recent analysis of 61 independent studies aimed to identify whether, and if so under what conditions, team working in organizations is related to organizational effectiveness (Richter, West and Dawson, 2011). Team working had a significant (though small) positive *relationship with organizational performance and staff attitudes.* Team working had a stronger relationship with performance outcomes if accompanied by complementary Human Resource Management (HRM) measures. Similar conclusions were reached in Applebaum and Batt's (1994) review of 12 large-scale surveys and 185 case studies of managerial practices. The authors concluded that team-based working leads to *improvements in organizational performance on measures of both efficiency and quality.* Cotton's (1993) review similarly reports 57 case studies that showed improvements on productivity following the implementation of self-directed teams, seven that found no change, and five that reported productivity declines. In a recent qualitative review of 31 survey-based quantitative studies linking teamwork to different indicators of organizational performance, Delarue *et al.* (2008) concluded that teamwork has a *positive impact on four different dimensions of performance outcomes* (operational, financial, attitudinal and behavioural outcomes). A number of other surveys have also reported links between team-based working and improvements in both labour productivity and quality (e.g., Mathieu, Gilson and Ruddy, 2006; Paul and Anantharaman, 2003; Procter and Burridge, 2004; Tata and Prasad, 2004). Positive effects of teamwork on productivity have been recorded in settings as diverse as US steel mills (Boning, Ichniowski and Shaw, 2001), the US apparel industry (Dunlop and Weil, 1996) and the Australian economy (Glassop, 2002). Zwick's (2004) study of German organizations showed that economic value increased after the introduction of teamwork. A core purpose of team-based working is to decentralize decision making to lower levels in the organization (Bacon and Blyton, 2000), and organizations that use self-managing work groups have been shown to be less hierarchical in structure and have a broader span of control (Glassop, 2002). Overall, research suggests that well-managed teamwork is likely to have a positive impact on organizational performance.

- *Change is effective* when multiple elements of change are made simultaneously in technology, human resource management systems and organizational structure, and team working is already present or a component of the change. The presence of teams appears to be an enabling factor in change processes, perhaps because teams can take responsibility for implementing agreed changes and can do so more effectively and consistently than individuals working alone.
- Staff who work in teams report higher levels of *involvement and commitment*, and studies also show that they have *lower stress* levels than those who do not work in teams (Richter *et al.*, 2011).
- *Creativity and innovation* are promoted within team-based organizations through the cross-fertilization of ideas (see West *et al.*, 2003). Where teams work effectively together with other teams within organizations, there is more sharing of good practice, more integration of differing perspectives, and more holistic understanding of team and organizational tasks. The combination of these factors produces many more ideas for new and improved ways of doing things and also the practical inter-team cooperation that enables the ideas to be put into practice.

Although team working can be effective for all the reasons listed above, it is not the case that the introduction of team working is inevitably successful. Simply relabelling a department in an organization as a 'team' does not lead to team working. It may well lead to decreased effectiveness, innovation and satisfaction. There are also some solid barriers to effective team working which team members must learn to overcome or avoid if they are to succeed in achieving synergy – the added advantage of working in teams over and above the outputs from individuals working alone (Brown, 2000).

Barriers to Effective Teamwork

Loss of effort

In the 1890s, French agricultural engineer Max Ringelmann explored whether individuals working alone were more effective than those working in teams. He instructed agricultural students to pull on a rope attached to a dynamometer and measured the amount of pull. Working alone, the average student could pull a weight of 85 kg. Ringelmann then arranged the students in teams of seven and instructed them to pull on the rope as hard as possible. The average pull for a team of seven was 450 kg. The teams were pulling only 75% as hard as the aggregated work of seven individuals pulling alone (for more details see Kravitz and Martin, 1986).

Subsequent research has involved teams solving cognitive problems such as how to transport sheep and wolves safely across a river in a single boat – although teams took longer than individuals, overall they were better at finding the correct solutions. Other tasks involved '20 questions' games. Here a particular object is selected and players have to guess the name of the object by asking up to 20 questions, to which they are given only a 'yes' or 'no' answer. Teams were slightly more effective than individuals in getting the correct solution within their 20 questions, but were much less efficient in terms of time use. Individuals took, on average, five person-minutes to come up with the correct solution. Teams of two took seven person-minutes (i.e., 3.5 minutes in real time) and teams of four, twelve person-minutes (three minutes in real time). There were no differences between teams of two and four in the likelihood of them getting correct answers (Shaw, 1932).

Why do these effects occur? They result from a phenomenon which psychologists call 'social loafing' (Rutte, 2003). Individuals sometimes work less hard when their efforts are combined with those of others, than when they are considered individually. Those whose work is difficult to identify and evaluate because of their roles in groups make less effort. This is not to say that all we have to do is single out those who 'socially loaf'. Rather, it is a characteristic of human behaviour that people may work less hard in teams than if they alone were responsible for task outcomes, especially if the task is not intrinsically motivating or they do not feel a strong sense of team cohesion.

The Ringelmann experiments have been replicated by other researchers. In one example, the person at the front of a rope was instructed to pull on the rope and was told that there were six people behind them also pulling. Each person pulling was blindfolded and so was unable to see what was going on behind them. In some cases the other 'pullers' simply stood behind the person at the front and made grunting noises suggesting that they were pulling when they were, in reality, making no effort. When individuals *believed* that they were in groups of seven pulling on the rope, they pulled with only 75% of the effort they made when they were working individually (Ingham *et al.*, 1974). In another devious experiment, the researcher instructed individuals to shout as loud as they could, either alone or, as they were told, in groups. They were blindfolded and given ear defenders to cut out visual and sound cues. When people believed they were shouting with others, they exerted only 74% of the effort that they made when they believed they were shouting alone – a phenomenon sometimes called 'free riding' (Latané, Williams and Harkins, 1979). The problem with free riding is that when it is discovered, other team members may feel like 'suckers' who are being taken advantage of, and they reduce their effort accordingly. Equality of workload in teams therefore affects how much effort team members exert on behalf of the team.

These difficulties present real problems for those working in teams and they challenge the common assumption that 'synergy' is the outcome of teamwork, that is, the idea that groups are more effective than the sum of the contributions of individual members. In such cases 1+1+1+1+1 does not necessarily equal five; in many cases1+1+1+1+1 may equal three or even less! Steiner (1972) proposed that group effectiveness is understandable if we separate out the *potential productivity* of groups, their *actual productivity*, and the gap between them. The gap, he asserted, was due to *'process losses'* such as coordination and communication problems. Below we identify some of the process losses that interfere with team productivity.

Poor problem solving and decision making

The social loafing explanation of poor group performance is helpful in understanding some of the difficulties faced by teams. However, it does not account for the fact that group decision making is sometimes inexplicably flawed. For example, Maier and Solem (1962) presented groups with mathematical questions. They deliberately formed some groups that had an individual in them who knew how to work out the answers. Surprisingly, they found that many of the groups still failed to come up with the correct solutions. Why should this be?

Although we tend to think of groups as somehow more reasonable and logical than individuals because a number of people can assess the wisdom of decisions and solutions, this perspective neglects important social processes that affect group or team decision making. One such process is the tendency of team members to agree with opinions expressed by those who are hierarchically senior to them in the group. In many healthcare teams for example, the opinions of the doctors in a meeting will have much greater influence than the opinions of nursing staff or receptionists. Team leaders particularly tend to have more influence over decisions regardless of whether their views are correct or incorrect (Zaccaro, Heinen and Shuffler, 2009). Moreover, dominant personalities within groups can exert a disproportionate

Box 1   Baseball or basketball teams?

In an interesting example of the importance of individual accountability for teamwork, researchers in the United States attempted to predict the performance of baseball and basketball teams at the end of a season from ratings of the abilities of individual team members. Each team member was given a score from 1 to 10 to denote overall ability within their professional sport. These were then added together and used to predict the eventual performance of their teams over a whole season. In one sport the aggregated ratings of the individual abilities of team members predicted team performance with 90% accuracy, while in the other sport, they predicted with only 35% accuracy.

Which do you think was which?

(The answer to this question is given over the page along with an explanation for the finding.)

influence over group outcomes. Studies of jury decision making have shown that it may be the person who talks most who has most influence over the jury verdict (McGrath, 1984).

Overall, research suggests that group decision making in experimental settings is generally superior to that of the average member of the group, but often inferior to that of its most competent individual. In the real world of organizations the situation is more complex so it is difficult to demonstrate quite such clear findings. Though the situation is somewhat different the pitfalls of group decision making are not.

Low creativity

Every day in thousands of organizations around the world, people come together in meetings and undertake group idea-generation exercises, usually called 'brainstorming'. Early studies comparing the effectiveness of brainstorming individually or in groups involved creating 'statisticized' and 'real' groups. Statisticized groups (groups consisting of people who never actually work together, but whose performance is based on the statistical addition of their individual efforts) consisted of five individuals working alone in separate rooms who were each given a five-minute period to generate ideas for uses for an object (such as a brick or a paper cup). Their results were aggregated at the end and any redundant ideas due to repetition by different individuals were taken out. Real groups of five individuals worked together for five minutes generating as many ideas as possible and withholding criticism. The statisticized groups produced an average of 68 ideas, while the real groups produced an average of only 37 ideas (Diehl and Stroebe, 1987). Many subsequent studies have confirmed that individuals working alone produce more ideas when they are aggregated than individuals do when working together in groups. But perhaps the quality of ideas produced by groups will be better than the quality of ideas produced by individuals. However, the research does not support this conclusion either. Most measures indicate that individuals working alone produce ideas rated by external evaluators as of a higher quality (i.e., in numbers of good ideas), and there is no research evidence suggesting that groups produce superior quality ideas. Individuals working alone produce a greater quantity of ideas and ideas of at least as good quality as in brainstorming groups (Paulus *et al.,* 2006).

Why should groups fail to produce the synergistic outcomes that we expect of them in brainstorming groups? The explanation appears to be that when people are speaking in brainstorming groups other individuals are not able to speak and so are less likely to put ideas forward. Moreover, they are busy holding their ideas in their memories, waiting for a chance to speak, and this interferes with their ability to produce other ideas. This 'production blocking' effect is only one of several problems with group brainstorming. Another problem is social comparison processes whereby individuals judge the level of creativity required by the contributions of others and the presentation of relatively mundane ideas initially can lead to subsequent ideas mirroring this level of mundanity. People may also feel inhibited from offering what they see as a relatively ordinary idea after a particularly creative idea has been offered by another group member. Finally, the first idea offered may bias all group members' thinking in the direction of that idea, limiting the range of potential ideas they might offer.

Baseball or basketball teams?

The result (see page 00)
It was possible to predict baseball team scores with 90% accuracy since team performance is much more dependent upon individual performance in batting and pitching. Basketball involves passing, coordination and team strategies for success. Individual accountability is greater in baseball therefore and this makes it easier to predict team performance.

Accepting the fact that production blocking and other factors can inhibit the performance of brainstorming groups, there are three important reasons for working in team settings when proposing new ideas and new ways of doing things. The first is that those who make up teams in 'real life' as opposed to laboratory settings have valuable experience of the particular domains of the team's work. For example, in a primary healthcare team, there are people with nursing, medical and social work backgrounds. Together they bring a broad range of relevant experience to the team's deliberations. It is important that team members are involved in the brainstorming process, so that this wide experience is available as a resource. The second reason for brainstorming in teams is the importance of participation. Involving all those affected by organizational change in the process of change is vital in order to gain commitment and reduce resistance (Heller *et al.*, 1998). Working in brainstorming teams, especially where the teams are focusing on ideas for change, encourages commitment to that process. Finally, many team members argue that it is just more fun to brainstorm in teams, and that humour and laughter are outcomes which themselves can spur creativity. Indeed, with the right rules in place (separate generation of ideas from evaluation, ensure that the group stays focused on the idea-generation task, build on others' ideas) group brainstorming productivity increased by up to 79% (Paulus *et al.*, 2006).

Notwithstanding these arguments, it is clear from the research that we can alter the mechanics of the process to overcome the production blocking effect. Team members should brainstorm individually to generate their own ideas before bringing them to the team. Then each member should have the opportunity to present all of his or her ideas to the team before evaluation and selection takes place.

Is the picture of less effort, poor decision making and low creativity as bleak in teams as suggested here? An answer to this question emerges from an analysis of 78 studies of individual versus group performance undertaken by Karau and Williams (1993). They found the social loafing effect in 80% of the studies but, intriguingly, they found the opposite effect in some. In a small number of studies, group productivity was *greater* than would have been predicted based on knowledge of individual group members' capabilities. This phenomenon, in contrast to 'social loafing' is called 'social labouring'. Instead of experiencing process losses, these groups experienced 'process gains'. Further analysis reveals that if the team's task is important to them and team members feel the group is significant to them, then the group displays the social labouring effect, demonstrating productivity beyond their calculated potential productivity. Other research suggests that evaluations of the group's performance and the national culture of team members both play a significant role.

What Karau and Williams' analysis revealed is that most research studies had used trivial team tasks such as clapping, shouting or finding creative uses for a brick. There was little true teamwork involved since group members did not have to coordinate or build on each other's work. Consequently, participants probably had low task motivation. More complex team tasks that required coordination or integration of members' contributions seemed to produce higher levels of team member motivation and process gains. In one study, teams had simple or complex crossword puzzles to solve. On simple puzzles, there was no difference between the observed and predicted performance of groups based on a knowledge of how well individuals in the groups could do these puzzles. But on the complex puzzles the groups reliably exceeded their predicted performance. Further research showed that the ability of partners in teams may affect performance also and produce process gains. When team members were told they were working with a relatively low ability partner on a brainstorming test (for example), they often worked hard to 'make up for' the weaker member. There is evidence too that the less able may raise their performance to a level close to that of the highest performing team member when the discrepancy between their abilities is not too large (Stroebe, Stroebe and Zech, 1996). One implication for education is that if learning is set up as a cooperative process (with students working together towards a group goal) then a mix of abilities in student groups may raise the level of performance of both the group and of the less able individuals.

The review also showed that in groups with a strong identity, social labouring and process gains were usual. Worchel *et al.* (1998) conducted an experiment in which groups had to make paper chains with either another group present or alone. Worchel and colleagues had first checked the ability of the individuals involved in the task in order that they could calculate the potential productivity of the groups. Half of the groups were kitted out with identical coloured coats and given a team name to increase the sense of group identity. In this case (strong identity) and in the presence of another competing group, they far exceeded their potential productivity.

We should also be cautious about simply transferring laboratory findings, which are based on ad hoc groups, into practical settings. For example, ad hoc groups (e.g., in collective problem solving) reach a maximum of process loss in their first and second task trial (one or two task trials are the norm in laboratory settings), but these are substantially reduced or even eliminated when subsequent task trials are allowed for (e.g., Brodbeck and Greitemeyer, 2000). In applied settings the majority of groups perform tasks repeatedly. Thus, the process losses seen in ad hoc laboratory research are likely to be irrelevant in many practical settings.

The role of culture is also hugely significant, since most of the studies were carried out in the individualistic cultures of the United States and Western Europe. In Eastern cultures, which tend to be more collectivist (people strive more to achieve group rather than their individual goals), the social loafing effect is less marked. Earley (1993) had Israeli (also a collectivist culture) and Chinese trainee managers do an office simulation task in groups and found that they worked harder in groups than they did alone in contrast to the typical social loafing phenomenon seen in Western research. Even in relation to leadership of teams, there is huge variation in what different cultures expect of their leaders (Chhokar, Brodbeck and House, 2007).

It is clear therefore that the motivational value of the team task, the sense of identity in the team, and the national culture can all influence dramatically whether working in teams leads to productivity gains or losses.

So far on this journey into teamwork, we have seen that there is clear evidence of the value of team working for organizational performance, but we have also seen that in relation to the critical areas of effort, decision making quality and creativity, teams may be worse than the aggregate of individuals (especially in experimental research) or considerably better. This book offers to explain this paradox and to show how we can harvest the benefits of teamwork and avoid the drawbacks. To begin to do this we must first understand what we mean by 'team', what teams do and how to build an effective team. It is to these three questions that we now turn.

What is a Team?

- Many terms describe groups of people working within organizations (e.g., project groups, work groups, quality improvement teams) and the way they work (self-managing, self-directed, self-regulating, semi-autonomous, autonomous, self-governing or empowered teams). This can lead to confusion within organizations when team-based working is being discussed and implemented. So what is a work team? Work teams are groups of people embedded in organizations, performing tasks that contribute to achieving the organization's goals. They share overall work objectives. They have the necessary authority, autonomy and resources to achieve these objectives.
- Their work significantly affects others within or outside the organization. Team members are dependent on each other in the performance of their work to a significant extent; and they are recognized as a group by themselves and by others. They have to work closely, interdependently and supportively to achieve the team's goals. They have well-defined and unique roles. They are rarely more than 10 members in total (though, as we shall see, size is a big issue in understanding the success and failures of teams). And they are recognized by others in the organization as a team.

What does this mean in practice? First, members of the group have shared objectives in relation to their work. Second they have genuine autonomy and control so that they can make the necessary decisions about how to achieve their objectives without having to seek permission from senior management. They have both responsibility and accountability. This usually means budgetary control as well. Necessarily, they are dependent upon and must interact with each other in order to achieve those shared objectives. They have an organizational identity as a work group with a defined organizational function (e.g., a primary healthcare team: doctors, nurses and receptionists). Finally, they are not so large that they would be defined more appropriately as an organization, which has an internal structure of vertical and horizontal relationships characterized by sub-groupings. In practice, this is likely to mean that a team is smaller than 15 members (and ideally should be no bigger than six to eight members) and larger than two people.

The definition of teamwork I find most useful is:

> A team is a relatively small group of people working on a clearly defined, challenging task that is most efficiently completed by a group working together rather than individuals working alone or in parallel; who have clear, shared, challenging, team level objectives derived directly from the task; who have to work closely and interdependently to achieve these objectives; whose members work in distinct roles within the team (though some roles may be duplicated); and who have the necessary authority, autonomy and resources to enable them to meet the team's objectives. (Woods and West, 2010).

There are multiple types of teams in organizations. But they can be grouped usefully into five types (Woods and West, 2010):

- Strategy and policy teams; for example, management decision-making teams; university committees setting standards on teaching quality; politicians at cabinet level deciding on how to reduce carbon emissions in the nation's cars.
- Production teams; for example, manufacturing assembly teams in a mobile phone producing company; production process teams in an aluminium smelting company; bottling teams in a brewery; teams in a garden nursery that grow plants and display them ready for sale.
- Service teams; for example, teams that service photocopiers in client organizations; radiography teams in hospitals; advice centre teams for a computer sales organization; healthcare teams in primary care.
- Project and development teams; for example, research teams; new product development teams; software development teams; problem-solving teams trying to determine the cause of defects in a carbon fibre coating system.
- Action and performing teams; for example, surgical teams; negotiation teams; cockpit crews in commercial airliners; ambulance teams; fire-fighting teams; lifeboat crews; football teams; string quartets and rock bands.

Key dimensions on which they differ include:

- degree of permanence – project teams have a defined lifetime that can vary from weeks to years. An engineering team working on the development of a new steel processing plant may be together for years, whereas many accident and emergency teams in hospitals are together for only hours.
- emphasis on skill/competence development – surgical teams working on complex operations such as neurosurgery must continually develop their skills, whereas top management teams often place little emphasis (perhaps wrongly as we shall see in Chapter 12) on their skill development.
- genuine autonomy and influence – customer call centre teams may have little autonomy and influence whereas top management teams have considerable discretion and are powerful.
- level of task from routine through to strategic – short-haul airline flights involve crews in routine tasks whereas a top management team in a multinational organization may consider which country they will locate their $10 billion manufacturing operation.

Implicit in this exploration of types of teams is that there are certain tasks that are best performed by teams and others that are best performed by individuals or groups of individuals working serially or in parallel. The second learning objective of this chapter is to understand what tasks are best performed by teams.

What do Teams do?

The only point of having a team is to get a job done, a task completed, a set of objectives met, whether it is catching a wildebeest for meat, performing surgery on a patient with heart disease, or pushing a large boulder up a hill. Building teams simply to have teams, and without specifying the team task, is like setting the table for guests but not cooking any dinner! It is also likely to damage organizational functioning and encourage conflict, chronic anger and disruption in the organization.

The tasks that teams perform should be tasks that are best performed by a team. Painting the hull of a super-tanker does not require painters to work interdependently and in close communication over decisions. Each of those involved in the painting simply needs to know which is their section of hull. Navigating the tanker out of a port is likely to require teamwork as is doing a refit on the engines. Similarly, football and hockey teams are called teams since they have to work interdependently, to communicate constantly, to understand each other's roles, and to collectively implement a strategy in order to achieve their goals (literally).

What tasks are best performed by teams rather than individuals? The following dimensions can be used to analyse the appropriateness of tasks in organizations for teamwork:

- *Completeness,* that is, whole tasks – not simply putting the studs on the car wheels but assembling the whole transmission system plus wheels.
- *Varied demands* – the task requires a range of skills that are held or best developed by a number of different individuals.
- *Requirements for interdependence and interaction* – the task requires people to work together in interdependent ways, communicating, sharing information, and debating decisions about the best way to do the job.
- *Task significance* – the importance of the task in contributing to organizational goals or to the wider society. A lifeboat team in a rural coastal area with busy shipping lanes and a health and safety team in a high-risk industry are likely to be highly intrinsically motivated by the significance of their tasks.
- *Opportunities for learning* – providing team members with chances to develop and stretch their skills and knowledge.
- *Developmental possibilities for the task* – the task can be developed to offer more challenges to the team members, requiring them to take on more responsibility and learn new skills over time. The shop floor manufacturing team might develop responsibility for direct interaction with customers over product lead time (the time from ordering to delivery of products) as well as pricing of products.
- *Autonomy* – the amount of freedom teams have over how to do their work, from something as mundane as when to take breaks, through to making decisions about new products or new staff. We will examine the issue of autonomy in depth because it is an area failure in the introduction of team working.

Creating teams and then failing to give them the freedom and authority to make the decisions that allow them to accomplish their tasks in the most effective way is a little like teaching someone to ride a bicycle, giving them a fancy road-racing bike and then telling them they can only ride it in their bedroom. Yet in many organizations I see precisely this – teams are created but they are not given the power to make decisions, implement them and bring about radical change. Moreover, the number of layers in the organizational hierarchy barely changes. Consequently, expectations are not met and team members lose faith in the concept of teamwork other than as a comfortable idea to do with how we can all be supportive of each other. The degree of autonomy of the team reflects the team's influence over:

- The formulation of goals – what and how much it is expected to produce;
- Where to work and number of hours (when to work overtime and when to leave);
- Choice about further activities beyond the given task;
- Selection of production methods;
- Internal distribution of task responsibilities within the team;
- Membership of the team (who and how many people will work in the team);
- How to carry out individual tasks.

A lifeboat team charged with responsibility for saving people in stricken vessels is likely to rate each of the dimensions (completeness, varied demands, requirements for interdependence, task significance, opportunities for learning, task development, and autonomy) very highly. A group of people responsible for typing the correct postcodes onto wrongly addressed envelopes in the postal service is likely to rate them all very low.

How can we build Effective Teams?

How can teams at work overcome some of the problems that have been identified so far such as social loafing and poor decision making or not having an appropriate task?

Salas *et al.* (2009) suggest that there are five core components of teamwork. These are: (1) *leadership,* which incorporates the search for and structuring of information to help the team perform its task; the use of information to solve problems; the management of team members; and the management of resources (e.g., IT). Leadership may also be shared when the leadership function is transferred between members for particular tasks, depending on who has the knowledge, skills and abilities to best enable the team to perform a particular task; (2) *adaptability,* which is the team's ability to adapt its performance processes in response to changes or cues in the environment; (3) *mutual performance monitoring* between team members to ensure teamwork is on track; (4) *'backup behaviour'* – team members supporting each other when they have a workload problem; and (5) *team orientation,* which refers to the team's robustness in maintaining effective teamwork even under pressure or stress. These components are facilitated by three coordination mechanisms: (1) *shared mental models* are knowledge structures or representations of the team's work, processes or environment that are shared or distributed (to a greater or lesser extent) throughout the team and enable them to work in a compatible way; (2) *closed-loop communications* whereby a message is sent by team members, received by other team members and followed up by the sender to ensure the message was appropriately received and interpreted; and (3) *mutual trust*, which exists when team members can rely on each other to do what they say they do and they support each other in their shared endeavour. This analysis leads to clear recommendations for building effective teams including clear and effective leadership; encouraging scanning of the team's environment and adaptation to it; monitoring and giving feedback on each other's performance; backing each other up; developing a shared understanding of the task, each other's roles and the environment; communicating effectively and thoroughly; and building trust by ensuring all members are reliable and supportive.

An additional set of guidelines focuses on the tasks the teams perform and how feedback is managed (see Cohen and Bailey, 1997; Guzzo, 1996):

Teams should have intrinsically interesting tasks to perform.
People will work harder if the tasks they are asked to perform are intrinsically interesting, motivating, challenging and enjoyable. Where people are required to fit the same nut on the same bolt hour after hour, day after day, they are unlikely to be motivated and committed to their work. Where teams have an inherently interesting task to perform there is generally high commitment, higher motivation and more cooperative working. This therefore calls for very careful design of the objectives and tasks of work teams (see Chapter 2).

Individuals should feel they are important to the fate of the team.
Social loafing effects are most likely to occur when people believe that their contributions to the team are dispensable. For example, in working with primary healthcare teams, my colleagues and I have found that some nurses and receptionists feel their work is not highly valued. One way that individuals can come to feel that their work is important to the fate of the team is by using techniques of *role clarification* and *negotiation*. These are described more fully in Chapter 8. By careful exploration of the roles of each team member, together with the identification of team and individual objectives, team members can experience and demonstrate to other team members the importance of their work to the success of the team overall.

Individuals should have intrinsically interesting tasks to perform.
Individual tasks should be meaningful and inherently rewarding. Just as it is important for a team to have an intrinsically interesting task to perform, so too will individuals work harder, be more committed and creative if the tasks they are performing are engaging and challenging. For example, a researcher sitting in on team meetings and observing team processes is more

motivated and has a more creative orientation towards the task, than the researcher who is required to input the data from questionnaires onto a computer.

Individual contributions should be indispensable and evaluated.
Research on social loafing indicates that the effect is considerably reduced where people perceive their work to be indispensable to the performance of the team as a whole. Equally important, however, is that individual work should be subject to evaluation. People have to feel that not only is their work indispensable, but also that their performance is *visible* to other members of the team. In laboratory settings, where team members know that the products of their performance will be observed by other members of the team, they are much more likely to maintain effort to the level which they would achieve normally in individual performance. For example, when individuals are told that each team member's shouting will be measured to assess individual contribution to the overall loudness of the team, the classic social loafing effect does not occur. We could measure a doctor's performance by such things as: the number of patients seen; the quality of clinical interactions with patients; patient satisfaction with the general practitioner; the number of home visits completed; the quality of clinical interactions during home visits; prescribing practices; and the quantity and quality of communications with other team members.

There should be clear team goals with in-built performance feedback.
For the same reasons that it is important for individuals to have clear goals and performance feedback, so too is it important for the team as a whole to have clear team goals with performance feedback. Research evidence shows very consistently that where people are set clear targets to aim at, their performance is generally improved (Locke and Latham, 1990). However, goals can only function as a motivator of team performance if accurate performance feedback is available. For example, in the case of IT support teams, there should be performance feedback at least annually on all or some of the following indices:

- customer satisfaction with the quality of support given;
- effectiveness of innovations and changes introduced by the team in improving customer care;
- quality of technical support given in the team;
- quality of team climate and how well team members feel they have worked together;
- quality of relationships with other departments such as Sales, R&D, Finance and HR;

- financial performance and productivity;
- efficiency of the team in reducing customer waiting times;
- improvement in customer access to support and guidance.

The more precise the indicators of team performance, the more likely a team is to improve its performance and inhibit the effects of social loafing.

Exercise 2   Measuring the effectiveness of your team's performance

1   Identify all those teams or important individuals who have an interest or 'stake' in your team's work: These might include:

- management
- customers
- service receivers
- other teams/departments in your organization
- those in other organizations
- the general public
- you and your team colleagues.

2   Identify the criteria of effectiveness each of these 'stakeholders' might use to evaluate your team's effectiveness. Taking those listed under (1) above, these might include:

- meeting the organization's objectives
- providing quality goods on time and giving good 'after-sales service'
- providing a helpful, timely, excellent and considerate service
- giving useful information
- cooperating effectively
- producing goods or services of value to society, in an ethical way
- having a good quality of working life and experiencing a sense of growth and development.

(These criteria can be made much more detailed for your team and each stakeholder will probably have a number of other criteria.)

3 Give a rating from 1 *(not at all important)* to 7 *(of great importance)* to each criterion. If possible ask other team members to do the same. This can be useful for identifying areas of agreement and disagreement.

4 Give a rating from 1 *(not at all effective)* to 7 *(highly effective)* on each criterion in terms of how well you feel the team is achieving on each criterion. Again, if possible, your colleagues should go through a similar rating process. This exercise will give a simple but clear indication of how well you feel the team is achieving in each area. By subtracting the 'effectiveness' score from the 'importance' score you will also get a good indication of areas where action appears most urgently needed to improve performance. Best of all is to ask the stakeholders themselves to rate the importance and effectiveness of the team's performance on these measures.

Conclusions

The effectiveness of teams is dependent upon a number of psychological factors that can inhibit or improve performance.

- Subtle processes such as social loafing, hierarchical effects, and personality differences can dramatically inhibit team performance.
- Within organizational settings, teams are usually put together and allowed to function without attempts being made to ensure effective functioning.
- The most important elements of team management are specifying team objectives, individual roles and objectives and ensuring clear leadership.
- At the same time there must be regular clear and accurate feedback to the team on its performance over time in order to promote team effectiveness.

Team performance is complex and we need practical guidelines based on scientific and applied understanding of team processes to ensure optimum team functioning. These guidelines are to be found in the remaining chapters of this book.

Case Study

Students in Mrs. Rickshaw's Student Success class are required to do a half-hour team presentation on a topic of their choice. Mrs. Rickshaw randomly assigns students to teams. Students have approximately four weeks to research and prepare, including two hours of class time. Marks are given based on an instructor evaluation of the presentation combined with a peer evaluation by their team members.

Jane, Robert, Danny, Sharon and Liz were assigned to Team 3. During their first team meeting they introduced themselves and began to decide on a topic. After 45 minutes, they were still trying to settle on a topic. They finally settled on Money Management; however the instructor informed them that another team had already chosen that topic but Conflict Management was still available. During the last 15 minutes of class time, Robert tried to convince the group that they should present a role-play of conflict. Sharon wanted to do research and give a more detailed, informational presentation. Jane was excited by the role-play idea and suggested they make a video presentation of their own play-acting. Danny fell asleep some time before the topic was chosen and Liz sat quietly listening to the arguments of her teammates. At the end of the class no work division had occurred but the team agreed to meet in a study area at 4:15 on the following Monday.

After waiting for Danny until 4:30, the team decided to start without him. Jane announced she had to leave in twenty minutes because she had to pick up her child at the day care by 5:00. Robert was ready to start script writing but Sharon wanted to discuss the content of their presentation and assign research – thinking they could write the script once they were knowledgeable. Liz just listened quietly. An argument ensued, and Jane had to leave before a decision was reached. The next meeting was to be held during their class time the next week.

Before the next meeting, Robert convinced Jane that a role-play was the way to go, and together they put together a draft script, working hard to make the skit funny and entertaining. Robert confronted Danny and warned him to attend the class meeting or he wouldn't get a part in the play. In the meantime, Sharon picked up six books from the library and printed four articles from the Internet. She prepared an outline detailing various aspects of conflict management. Liz just worried about her role in the whole project.

At the class meeting, all team members were present. Robert informed the group that he and Jane had decided to do a skit, and they had a script all ready. Then he began to assign parts to his teammates. Sharon was incensed and insisted the script was short on content and demanded that they re-build the script around her outline. Robert said he wanted no part in a boring presentation.

Danny did not show up to the remaining team meetings. Liz agreed to do a small part in the play. Jane promised to gather props and costumes. Sharon stubbornly insisted on preparing an informational presentation. She would have liked to have this integrated into the role-play but Robert would not agree to change his script. They planned a practice of the role-play during their math class on the morning of October 16, the day of their presentation.

On the morning of October 16, Danny did not come to school and Liz forgot to bring the props. The practice ended up being more of an argument session. Danny showed up just before Student Success was to start and said "You mean it's today?!" Liz was very nervous and felt very sick. She wasn't sure she could do her part. The presentation began with Sharon reading her lengthy introduction and then the skit began. The skit was five minutes in length. The whole presentation left the other class members confused and it ran twelve minutes instead of the required thirty.

Source: http://www.oncourseworkshop.com/interdependence001. htm (last accessed 1 August 2011)

What went wrong and how could it have been prevented?

Key Revision Points

- What are the main benefits of working in teams?
- What are the main drawbacks of working in teams?
- What are the defining characteristics of a team?
- Describe the types of teams in organizations.
- How do they differ?
- Which kinds of tasks are appropriate for teams and which are not?
- How can we build effective teams?

Further Reading

De Cremer, D., van Dick, R. and Murnighan, K.K. (2011) *Social Psychology and Organizations*, Routledge, London.
Kozlowski, S.W.J. and Ilgen, D.R. (2006) Enhancing the effectiveness of work groups and teams. *Psychological Science in the Public Interest*, 7, 77–124.

Mathieu, J., Maynard, M.T., Rapp, T. and Gilson, L. (2008) Team effectiveness 1997–2007: a review of recent advancements and a glimpse into the future. *Journal of Management*, 34, 410–476.

Paulus, P.B., Nakui, T. and Putnam, V.L. (2006) Group brainstorming and team-work: some rules for the road to innovation, in *Creativity and Innovation in Organizational Teams* (eds L. Thompson and H.S. Choi), Lawrence Erlbaum, Mahwah, NJ, pp. 69–86.

van Knippenburg, D. and Schippers, M.C. (2007) Work group diversity. *Annual Review of Psychology*, 58, 515–541.

West, M.A., Tjosvold, D. and Smith, K.G. (eds) (2003) *The International Handbook of Organizational Teamwork and Cooperation*, John Wiley & Sons, Ltd, Chichester.

Web Resources

Twelve Tips for Team Building: How to Build Successful Work Teams, at http://human-resources.about.com/od/involvementteams/a/twelve_tip_team.htm (last accessed 1 August 2011).

http://www.nwlink.com/~donclark/leader/leadtem.html (last accessed 1 August 2011). The information here gives you a picture view on teams and aspects of team development.

Part 2

Developing Teams

Part 2 explores the processes of creating teams, leading teams effectively and training teams to work effectively together. Chapter 3 explores the question of who should be in the team and starts from the premise that team working is about the team task – a task that needs a group of people working together to coordinate their efforts and skills for success. That means identifying the skills needed to complete the task first and foremost. After that, we can consider how personality mix might affect team performance, and how gender and age diversity, functional background diversity (engineers, chemists, managers) and culture diversity will influence team processes and performance. The chapter explains how to ensure that the mix of people leads to innovation and effectiveness rather than conflict and failure.

Chapter 4 explores the key role of leadership in teams distinguishing between three related tasks for the leader – providing direction, managing the team's performance and coaching members to success. Some of the tripwires for team leaders are identified and practical guidance for becoming an outstanding team leader is presented.

Chapter 5 considers the issue of team training and how we can intervene to promote team success. The gap between practice and evidence is described showing that many team training interventions have limited effectiveness. Well-designed team training does lead to improved team performance and the chapter explains what is required to provide training that shapes a team's success.

Effective Teamwork: Practical Lessons from Organizational Research, Third Edition.
By M. A. West. © 2012 John Wiley & Sons, Ltd. Published 2012 by John Wiley & Sons, Ltd., and the British Psychological Society.

3

Creating Teams

Many times a day I realize how much of my own outer and inner life is built upon the labours of my fellow men, both living and dead, and how earnestly I must exert myself in order to give in return as much as I have received. (Albert Einstein)

Key Learning Points

- In creating teams, it is important to focus on task-related skills
- The ability of team members is a good predictor of team performance
- The complex relationships between functional, personality and demographic mixes and teamwork processes and outcomes
- The skills for working in teams and how they affect team processes and performance
- How to benefit from diversity in teams

When you play in a great team, it doesn't matter how good the players are individually, it's how well you play together and understand each other's styles and moves. It's really about intuitive ways of playing off each other.

The talent in the team is amazing. Individually they are outstanding but for some reason they just can't make it happen together. I think there are maybe too many prima donnas in the team.

Effective Teamwork: Practical Lessons from Organizational Research, Third Edition. By M. A. West. © 2012 John Wiley & Sons, Ltd. Published 2012 by John Wiley & Sons, Ltd., and the British Psychological Society.

It's about finding the magic mix, that blend of skills and experience that combines maturity, energy, determination and creativity. It's like a ballet when it happens. Beautiful to behold!

These quotations from players in sports teams could come as easily from members of work teams and they show we must think carefully about how we create teams. Team members are often recruited to the team because they work in the same location or work in the same department or the team leader thinks they are hard workers or the team leader likes them. These should not be the primary reason for selecting people to work in a team. Of course it makes sense to seek hard-working or collegial people to be part of our team. Consider why teams exist. They exist because there is a task that requires a group of people to work interdependently together to accomplish it. Imagine the task of pushing a large boulder up a hill. No individual working alone will be successful. It will require a group of people coordinating their efforts and all pushing in the right direction to be successful. In selecting people for this team, we would want people with the right abilities or skills – notably strength, stamina and coordination abilities. If the task is to run a lifeboat the team leader would look for some members with navigation skills, some with helmsman skills, some with first-aid skills and some with mechanical skills. Probably all would need to have experience of working on boats. For a top management team in a manufacturing organization, directors look to appoint managers for production, human resource management, finance, R&D and marketing, and to appoint people with outstanding skills in these areas.

The point of creating a team is to get a task done that can only be done by a team. The first step is therefore identifying the task and then to identify the skills needed to perform that task. If task identification and clarification and team skill needs are not identified at the outset, the team is unlikely to be successful. Few team leaders follow these guidelines in setting up teams. Mathieu and Schulze (2006) showed that teams with high levels of task-related knowledge perform better and plan their work over time more effectively than other teams.

Where consultancies make their money, however, is in advising team leaders about the personal characteristics of team members, though, as we will see, there is little evidence to vouch for the value of their products and services. Nevertheless it is reasonable to argue that we should consider the extent to which candidates have the personal characteristics necessary to work effectively as part of a team. Since it is unlikely that all are well-suited to teamwork, some personal characteristics and preferences might be considered in the recruitment of team members. There are also specific skills of team working just as there are skills associated with any complex behaviour; do candidates have the skills to work in a team and are they good at using them? The third quotation indicates we also need to ponder on the mix of people in the team. If we have a team of talented, creative, temperamental individualists working together on a problem, the team will probably fail. Or, if the team is made up of dominant leaders, hostility is likely to be the main team outcome.

The context of work teams dictates consideration of diversity, including visible attributes such as gender and age, as well as less obvious aspects of diversity such as values, skill, social status, background, education, and (hugely important in our multicultural world), societal culture. How do we make judgements about the 'magic mix' our interviewee above referred to? And is diversity a good thing in teams or should we be looking to avoid the inevitable process losses diversity produces? We explore these questions in this chapter.

But the first issue to address is how to select the right team members and with the right mix? These two questions will occupy the rest of this chapter. We begin by exploring ability, then personality, skills of teamwork, skill diversity and finally demographic diversity. The results of this exploration reveal some surprising discoveries.

Personality and Ability

For individual jobs, general mental ability is one of the best predictors of job performance (Schmidt and Hunter, 1998). Not surprisingly, team members' overall ability predicts team performance. This was demonstrated in one study of military crews (Tziner and Eden, 1985), which showed that people of high ability contributed most to performance when all the other crewmembers were also high in ability. In the last chapter, we pointed to some research that suggests mixed-ability teams may perform better than high-ability teams on a learning task. Nevertheless, overall the evidence is clear in suggesting that teams composed of members high in ability will perform better than would be predicted by the sum of their abilities (Devine and Philips, 2001) particularly on unfamiliar tasks. What seems particularly important is that in teams with high average levels of cognitive ability, the team's workload should be equally distributed to ensure good team learning (Ellis *et al.*, 2003).

What of personality? The 'Big Five' model of personality (Barrick and Mount, 1991) offers a robust personality model that we can use to analyse mix of personality in teams and the effects on team performance. The model describes five dimensions of personality:

Openness to experience – New ideas, experiences and imaginings
Conscientiousness – Competence, order and self-discipline
Extraversion – Positive emotions, gregariousness and warmth
Agreeableness – Trust, straightforwardness and tender-mindedness
Neuroticism – Anxiety, self-consciousness and vulnerability.

Research suggests that teams composed of members with high average levels of conscientiousness, extraversion, openness to experience and agreeableness perform best (Bell, 2007). It is not surprising that certain personality dimensions are linked to effective teamwork, but what is enlightening is the discovery that the particular dimensions that emerge as important depend on the type of task (English, Griffith and Steelman, 2004). In interdependent teams where individual contributions to team success are easily recognized and rewarded, hard-working and dependable team members are most successful (Mount, Barrick and Stewart, 1998). Other team members see these conscientious individuals as valued team members because they can be relied upon to perform their part of the work. Conscientiousness is particularly important in team settings because hierarchical control is reduced, so there is a need for self-discipline (Barrick *et al.*, 1998). Such self-discipline is particularly important if team-based rewards are used in the organizations (i.e., compensation is based on performance of the entire team) because team member pay is dependent on the successful performance of each and every team member. Teams composed of conscientious team members perform at a high level, particularly on productivity and planning tasks.

However, teams with high levels of extraversion are better at decision making than at planning and performance tasks, probably because their warmth and optimism helps them in persuading others to accept their decisions. For teams requiring creative decisions or innovation, openness rather than conscientiousness or extraversion are most important. In teams requiring creative output, openness is also an important characteristic.

There are a number of models of personality mix for teamwork that are popular in business and it is appropriate to subject them to scrutiny based on research evidence to see how they stand this test. For example, some organizations try to achieve compatibility within teams based on the *cognitive styles* of members, by using the Myers-Briggs Type Indicator assessment instrument (a questionnaire measure of cognitive style) (Myers and McCaulley, 1985). This widely used measure describes four dimensions: Extraversion – Introversion, Sensing – Intuition, Thinking – Feeling, and Judging – Perceiving. The first criterion defines the source and direction of energy expression for a person. The extrovert has a source and direction of energy expression mainly in the external world while the introvert has a source of energy mainly in the internal world (E for external or I for internal). The second criterion defines the method of information perception by a person (S or N). Sensing people believe mainly information they receive directly from the external world; intuitive people believe mainly information they receive from the internal or imaginative world (S for sensing vs N for intuition). The third criterion defines how people process information. Thinking people make decisions mainly based on logic; Feeling people make decisions based on emotion (T or F). The fourth criterion defines how people implement the information they have processed. Judging people organize their life events and act strictly according to their plans; Perceiving people are inclined to improvise and seek alternatives (J or P). The different combinations of the dimensions describe each person as being of one of sixteen types. Thus people will often identify themselves to other team members as INFJ or (in my case) as ENFP. There are some problems with this approach in general since classifying people as either/or types does not make empirical sense except at extremes – I score equally on both T and F but am classified as F. And the reality is that people behave in different ways in different situations; simplifying personality in this way, therefore takes an already overarching and simple concept and simplifies it even further to the point, potentially, of meaninglessness. Of course the approach is popular precisely because it does simplify our understanding. Much is made of the value of combinations of these types in teams and there is a healthy branch of consultancy activity selling the technology for deriving ideal combinations. However, there is no compelling body of rigorous research evidence presently available showing a relationship between compatibility of Myers-Briggs types and team performance.

Schutz's (1967) theory of fundamental interpersonal relations orientations (FIRO) seeks to explain how personal attributes of team members affect team performance. Schutz sees three basic human needs expressed in group interaction: needs for inclusion, control and affection. The theory proposes that groups composed of people with compatible needs (high initiators of control and high receivers of control, for example) will be more effective than groups composed of those with incompatible needs. Compatible groups have a balance of initiators and receivers of control, inclusion and affection. In an incompatible group, for example, some members may want more affection than others are able to provide. Although some research has shown that compatibility on the dimensions of control and affection predicted time to task completion in teams of managers working in a laboratory setting, there is a good deal of research showing no relationship between compatibility and group performance (e.g., Hill, 1982). Indeed, Hill (1982) found that incompatibility on FIRO-B (a measure of a person's fundamental personal relations orientation) was associated with higher productivity in teams of systems analysts! Perhaps what this research reveals is that the imperatives of doing the job in teams at work, override issues of personal compatibility, and that when we need to get a job done (working in an accident and emergency department of a children's hospital) we adapt to each other's differences and do not let issues of compatibility influence our effectiveness. One message of this book is that if we create the right conditions for team working, good relationships follow, while the reverse is not necessarily the case (Mullen and Copper, 1994).

Another popular approach to team personality issues is Belbin's Team Roles Model (Belbin, 1993). Belbin suggests that there are nine team personality types and that a balance of these team personality types is required within teams (see Box 2). Belbin argues that a balance of all nine team roles is required for a team to perform effectively. Individuals usually incorporate several of these team role types in their personality profiles and so, within teams of only three or four individuals, there may nevertheless be primary and secondary team role types which cover the nine areas of team role functioning. However, again there is simply no body of rigorous research evidence to support these predictions and the instruments developed to measure the team role types (Belbin, 1981, 1993) do not appear to have good psychometric properties (Anderson and Sleap, 2004; Furnham, Steele and Pendleton, 1993). Scales have low internal consistencies and very high inter-correlations. It is likely that the Team Roles Inventory taps the 'Big Five' measures of personality and thus reflects some of the findings about personality types and team functioning described above. The model, however, is one that many managers and consultants find immensely practical in helping them to think through the dynamics of their teams and consequently many millions of pounds, dollars and euros are spent every year on assessing team role types and attempting to create compatibility. The evidence does not support this approach and in general the search for compatibility may miss the point. When we need to catch an antelope on the savannah or work together in a complex and demanding situation, the salient issue is not how compatible we are but how well we work as a team to deploy our individual skills collectively in pursuit of our shared aims.

Box 2   Belbin's team role theory

Based on research with over 200 teams conducting management business games at the Administrative Staff College, Henley, in the United Kingdom, Belbin identified nine team types. Almost always people have a mix of roles and will have dominant and sub-dominant roles. Likely Big Five dimensions that underlie the team roles are appended to these descriptions:

Coordinator

The coordinator is a person-oriented leader. This person is trusting, accepting, dominant and is committed to team goals and objectives. The coordinator is a positive thinker who approves of goal attainment, struggle and effort in others. The coordinator is 'someone tolerant enough always to listen to others, but strong enough to reject their advice'. The coordinator may not stand out in a team and usually does not have a sharp intellect. *Extraversion*

Shaper

The shaper is a task-focused leader, who abounds in nervous energy, who has high motivation to achieve and for whom winning is the name of the game. The shaper is committed to achieving ends and will 'shape' others into achieving the aims of the team. He or she will challenge, argue or disagree and will display aggression in the pursuit of goal achievement. Two or three shapers in a team, according to Belbin, can lead to conflict, aggravation and in-fighting. *Neuroticism*

Plant

The plant is a specialist idea-maker characterized by high IQ and introversion while also being dominant and original. The plant takes radical approaches to team functioning and problems. Plants are more concerned with major issues than with details. Weaknesses are argumentativeness and a tendency to disregard practical details. *Openness to experience*

Resource investigator

Resource investigators are people who are never in their rooms, and if they are, they are on the phone. The resource investigator is someone who explores opportunities and develops contacts. Resource investigators are good negotiators who probe others for information and support and pick up other people's ideas and develop them. They are sociable, enthusiastic, and good at liaison work and exploring resources outside the team. Their weaknesses are a tendency to lose interest after initial fascination with an idea, and they are not usually a source of original ideas. *Extraversion*

Company worker/implementer

Implementers are aware of external obligations, are disciplined, conscientious and have a positive self-image. They are tough-minded and practical, trusting and tolerant, respecting established traditions. They are characterized by low anxiety and tend to work for the team in a practical, realistic way. Implementers figure prominently in positions of responsibility in larger organizations. They do the jobs that others do not want to do and do them well: for example, disciplining employees.

Implementers are conservative, inflexible and slow to respond to new possibilities. *Conscientiousness*

Monitor evaluator

According to the model, this is a judicious, prudent, intelligent person with a low need to achieve. Monitor evaluators contribute particularly at times of crucial decision making because they are capable of evaluating competing proposals. The monitor evaluator is not deflected by emotional arguments, is serious-minded, slow in coming to a decision because of a need to think things over, and takes pride in never being wrong. Weaknesses are that they may appear dry and boring or even over-critical. They are not good at inspiring others. Those in high-level appointments are often monitor evaluators. *Neuroticism plus conscientiousness*

Team worker

Team workers make helpful interventions to avert potential friction and enable difficult characters within the team to use their skills to positive ends. They keep team spirit up and allow other members to contribute effectively. Their diplomatic skills together with their sense of humour are assets to a team. They have skills in listening, coping with awkward people and being sociable, sensitive and people-oriented. They are indecisive in moments of crisis and reluctant to do things that might hurt others. *Agreeableness*

Completer finishers

The completer finisher dots the i's and crosses the t's. He or she gives attention to detail, aims to complete and to do so thoroughly. They make steady effort and are consistent in their work. They are not so interested in the glamour of spectacular success. Weaknesses, according to Belbin, are that they are over-anxious and have difficulty letting go and delegating work. *Conscientiousness*

Specialist

The specialist provides knowledge and technical skills that are in rare supply within the team. They are often highly introverted, anxious and are self-starting, dedicated and committed. Their weaknesses are single-mindedness and a lack of interest in other peoples' subjects. *Neuroticism*

Teamwork Skills

When we create teams we should think beyond the relatively unchangeable aspects of the person such as their personality and think more of their motivation, knowledge and skills for working in teams. This includes their preferences for working in teams; whether they have an individualist or collective approach to working with others; their basic social skills such as listening, speaking and cooperating; and their team-working skills such as collaboration, concern for the team and interpersonal awareness.

Social skills

Social skills include:

- Active listening skills – listening to what other people are saying and asking questions)
- Communication skills – planning how to communicate effectively taking into account the receiver, the message and the medium
- Social perceptiveness – being aware of others' reactions and understanding why they react the way they do
- Self-monitoring – being sensitive to the effects of our behaviour on others
- Altruism – working to help colleagues
- Warmth, positivity and cooperation
- Patience and tolerance – accepting criticism and dealing patiently with frustrations (Peterson *et al.*, 2001).

Such skills are likely to be particularly valuable to the performance of teams and could therefore be among the criteria for selecting team members.

Knowledge, skills and attitudes (KSAs) for teamwork

In teamwork settings, employees need the abilities to perform the job as individuals as well as the abilities to work effectively in a team because both are important for team performance (West and Allen, 1997). Stevens and Campion (1994, 1999) propose that effective team functioning depends on teamwork abilities, focusing on team members' knowledge of how to perform in teams that extends beyond the requirements for individual job performance. Based on the literature on team functioning, they identified two broad skill areas (interpersonal KSAs and self-management KSAs), consisting of a total of 14 specific KSA requirements for effective teamwork

Table 2   Stevens and Campion's Knowledge, Skills and Abilities for team working.

I Interpersonal Team Member KSAs

A Conflict resolution	1 Fostering useful debate, while eliminating dysfunctional conflict
	2 Matching the conflict management strategy to the cause and nature of the conflict
	3 Using integrative (win–win) strategies rather than distributive (win–lose) strategies
B Collaborative problem solving	4 Using an appropriate level of participation for any given problem
	5 Avoiding obstacles to team problem solving (e.g., domination by some team members) by structuring how team members interact
C Communication	6 Employing communications that maximize an open flow
	7 Using an open and supportive style of communication
	8 Using active listening techniques
	9 Paying attention to non-verbal messages
	10 Warm greetings to other team members, engaging in appropriate small talk, etc.

II Self-management Team KSAs

D Goal setting and performance management	11 Setting specific, challenging and acceptable team goals
	12 Monitoring, evaluating and providing feedback on performance
E Planning and task coordination	13 Coordinating and synchronizing tasks, activities and information
	14 Establishing fair and balanced roles and workloads among team members

Source: Stevens and Campion, 1999 (Reprinted with permission from xxx).

(see Table 2). Stevens and Campion (1994) developed a 35-item multiple choice test in which respondents are presented with challenges they may face in the workplace and asked to identify the strategy they would most likely follow. They found that team members' scores on this test were significantly related to team performance in several studies (Cooke *et al.*, 2003; Hirschfield *et al.*, 2005; McDaniel *et al.*, 2001). Regardless of their task specialism or their preferred team role, there are certain attributes that *all* team members ideally will demonstrate if the team is to achieve its goal. We should create teams of people who have all or most of the KSAs described by Stevens and Campion and/or train all team members to develop these KSAs.

Exercise 3   Knowledge, skills and attitudes for teamwork

Complete the questionnaire below to assess your own KSAs for teamwork.

You should identify areas where your teamwork performance is not adequate (when you indicate 'very little') and aim to improve your KSAs in these areas. A better measure is to ask your team colleagues to rate you (or all members of team) on these dimensions, so you have more objective feedback on your KSAs.

Communication	*A great deal*	*Very little*
I understand and use communication networks – making sufficient contact with colleagues	☐	☐
I communicate openly and supportively	☐	☐
I listen actively and non-evaluatively	☐	☐
There is a consistency between my verbal and non-verbal behaviour	☐	☐
I value and offer warm greetings and small talk with colleagues	☐	☐

Goal setting and performance management

I help establish clear and challenging team goals	☐	☐
I monitor and give supportive feedback on team and individual performance	☐	☐

Planning and coordination

I help to coordinate activities, information and working together between members	☐	☐
I help to clarify tasks and roles of team members and ensure balance of workloads	☐	☐
I respond positively and flexibility to feedback from team members	☐	☐

Collaborative problem solving

I identify problems requiring participation of all team members in decision making	☐	☐

I use appropriate ways of involving team members in decision making	☐	☐
I explore and support proposals for innovation in the team	☐	☐
Conflict resolution		
I discourage undesirable conflict	☐	☐
I employ win–win rather than win–lose negotiation strategies	☐	☐
I recognize types and sources of conflict and implement appropriate conflict resolution and reduction strategies	☐	☐

Diversity of Team Members

How similar to or different from each other should team members be? If all have very similar backgrounds, views, experiences and values, team members are likely to pass through the norming and storming phases quickly, establish good relationships and perform their jobs effectively. Where team members are very dissimilar to each other, they are likely to find that early interactions, particularly during norming and storming, are characterized by intense conflict as members try to understand each other, and agree on the objectives, leadership and roles in the team. Over time though, their greater diversity of perspectives will offer a broad range of views and knowledge, which will in turn produce better decision making, more innovation and higher levels of effectiveness. But such synergy will be achieved only with a high level of effort to ensure effective, integrated team working. In practice, how can we create teams that are appropriately diverse?

One perspective on this comes from the attraction-selection-attrition model (ASA) (Schneider, Goldstein and Smith, 1995), which proposes that teams attract people similar to existing team members, they select such people, and those who are dissimilar are likely to leave the team. Another theory (similarity–attraction theory; Byrne, 1971) proposes that we are attracted to those who are similar to us and, thus, contrive to organize, and evaluate, our social worlds accordingly. The tendency of team members and team leaders will therefore be to create homogeneous teams. Is this a helpful tendency in relation to team effectiveness and innovativeness?

In order to answer this question, Susan Jackson (1996) advocates distinguishing between *task-related diversity* (such as organizational position or specialized technical knowledge), and *relations-oriented diversity* (such as age, gender, ethnicity, social status and personality) (see also Maznevski, 1994). A more recent review (Mathieu *et al.*, 2008) distinguishes between functional, personality and demographic diversity. We consider these in turn.

Functional diversity

When teams form or when new team members are recruited, leaders and team members strive to appoint people who will have the skills to enable the team to accomplish its task. In the case of an R&D team in pharmaceuticals, the team will need a number of chemists, a marketing specialist, a finance specialist and probably a specialist in the product area.

Beyond this though, is the question of how much diversity to encourage. Does the team recruit chemists with the skills in the specific product area or do they broaden the range of skills available to the team by bringing in some with experience in cosmetics as well as medicines, since there may be some valuable cross-fertilization from these apparently unrelated areas? Should we aim to build teams by specifying quite narrowly the range of skills absolutely necessary for the task and bring together people with very similar backgrounds and experience? Or should we specify broadly the range of skills required but hope to attract team members with differing and even unusual skills and experiences?

One narrow approach to answering these questions is 'skill mix', defined as the balance between trained and untrained, qualified and unqualified, and supervisory and operative staff within a service area as well as between different staff groups. Optimum skill mix is achieved when the desired standard of service is provided, at the minimum cost, which is consistent with the efficient deployment of trained, qualified and supervisory personnel and the maximization of contributions from all staff members. A skill-mix review involves discovering what activities need to be carried out within the team; who is currently doing them; the skill level of people doing them; the minimum level of skill required to do them and the potential for combining tasks in new ways to create in some cases new roles and staff groupings. This orientation to selecting for teams therefore focuses on the identification of particular technical skills required by the team that are not already supplied, or are supplied at higher cost, by others in the team.

Another approach suggests that diversity should be developed within teams because of effects on innovation. For example, in a study of 100 primary healthcare teams, Carol Borrill and colleagues (Borrill *et al.*, 2000) found that the greater the number of professional groups represented in the team, the higher the levels of innovation in patient care. Groups that contain people with diverse *and* overlapping knowledge domains and skills are particularly creative (Dunbar, 1997). Wiersema and Bantel (1992) found that strategic management initiatives were more likely to be made by top management teams whose members had a high level of diversity in their educational specialization. The biggest ever study of these issues was undertaken by a UNESCO-sponsored international research group which set out to determine the factors influencing the scientific performance of 1222 research teams (Andrews, 1979). They assessed diversity in six areas: projects; interdisciplinary orientations; specialities; funding resources; R&D activities; and professional functions. The results showed that diversity and the extent of communication both within and between research teams had strong relationships with scientific recognition of their teams, R&D effectiveness, number of publications, and the applied value of their work. There is some evidence (Bunderson and Sutcliffe, 2002) that functional diversity is more problematic, the narrower the specialisms of team members. Where team members each have a broad range of skills, information processing and performance are enhanced.

Diversity of functional backgrounds may also influence team performance as a result of the higher level of external communication that team members initiate, precisely because of their functional diversity. Varied links favour innovation through the incorporation of diverse ideas and models gleaned from different functional areas. And research does show that the greater a team's functional diversity, the more team members communicate outside the team's boundaries and the higher their levels of innovation (Ancona and Caldwell, 1992).

All well and good. But diversity also has a down side. When diversity begins to threaten the group's safety and integration, then creativity and innovation implementation will suffer. For example, when diversity reduces group members' agreement about team objectives, teams will fail. The challenge is to create sufficient diversity within the team without threatening their shared view of their task and their ability to communicate and work effectively together. Where diversity is very low, the group pressures will be towards conformity rather than integration. Where diversity is very high, there is unlikely to be adequate agreement in the team about its task, ways of working and roles; consequently communication and coordination of efforts will be problematic continually. Thus the research team composed of a statistician, Marxist sociologist, quantitative organizational psychologist, social constructionist and political scientist may be so diverse that they are unable to develop a coherent and innovative programme of research to discover under what circumstances nursing teams on hospital wards acknowledge and discuss medication errors. This is not to suggest that the less diverse a group is, the better integrated and safer it will be for its members. On the contrary, it is likely that members only learn integrating skills and discover safety through the effective management of diversity. Where the group is homogeneous then there will be strong pressures for conformity. Where the group is heterogeneous there will be pressures to manage (via group processes) the centrifugal forces of diversity that could lead to the disintegration of the group and could also threaten individual members (others' differing perspectives threatening one's own beliefs for example). We only discover a solid sense of safety through the management of apparently threatening environments. The child who explores her environment is more confident than the child who never strays from her mother.

One resolution to this problem is to suggest that diversity of knowledge and skills will be beneficial for team performance and innovation if, and only if, group processes minimize process losses due to diversity, such as disagreements, misunderstandings and suspicion arising from diversity of perspectives (West, 2002). Groups composed of people with differing professional backgrounds, knowledge, skills and abilities, will be more innovative than those whose members are similar, because they bring usefully differing perspectives on issues to the group (Paulus, 2000). Their divergence of views offers multiple perspectives and the potential for constructive debate. Diversity also contributes to the magnitude of the team's total pool of task-related skills, information and experience. If the differences in information and perspectives are worked through in the interests of effective decision making and task performance rather than on the basis of motivation to win or prevail, or because of conflicts of interest, this in turn will generate good performance and high levels of innovation (Paulus, 2000; Tjosvold, 1998).

Personality diversity

There is little clear evidence about the effect of diversity in personality on team performance (another reason for being suspicious of engineering team personality using models such as Belbin's Team Roles, MBTI (Myers-Briggs Type Inventory) and FIRO-B). Some research finds that diversity in extroversion and emotional stability relates positively to team performance; others show that Big Five dimension diversity predicts poorer outcomes (Mathieu *et al.*, 2008). However, diversity in time urgency (perceptions of deadlines, time awareness and the speed with which tasks must be performed) appears to reliably predict relationship conflict in teams (itself a predictor of poor performance) (Landy *et al.*, 1991). Not surprising really!

Demographic diversity

As I experience the cultures and practices of a range of organizations, it is remarkable to observe how much they vary in their variation. Some companies, such as a large construction company I work with, is dominated by white, male, British, 30 to 50 year olds. Others have a wide range of employees, with more than 40% coming from countries other than the

United Kingdom, and with a wide range of ages, tenure in the organization and a balance of genders. This leads to great variation in the structure of teams in relation to demographic and other 'relations' differences (such as how diverse the team is in time of team membership). What do we know about relations diversity?

In teams composed of people of very different ages, people are more likely to leave than in teams homogeneous with respect to age. Moreover, in top management teams, we found that age-diverse teams ran companies that were subsequently less profitable (West, Patterson and Dawson, 1999). Other research suggests the opposite (Kilduff, Angelmar and Mehra, 2000). There is some emerging evidence too that age diversity and team innovation may have a U-shaped relationship: very high or very low diversity in age being associated with low levels of innovation. Moderate diversity was linked to relatively high levels of innovation (for a review see Webber and Donahue, 2001).

In our work with teams, my colleagues and I have carefully examined differences between teams with varying gender mixes. The results suggest that the more women there are in a team (excluding women-only teams) the more positively do all team members report the team's functioning. This may be because women focus more on the participation and involvement of their colleagues, whereas men are more likely to focus on the task (Carli and Eagly, 2011). Moreover, men are more likely to interrupt women in team meetings and to pay less attention to their contributions (West, Borrill and Unsworth, 1998). Putting team processes aside however, reviews generally suggest that diversity in gender is detrimental in terms of both relationship conflict and team performance (Mathieu *et al.*, 2008).

In top management teams of manufacturing companies, Malcolm Patterson, Jeremy Dawson and I found that the longer the teams had been together, the more profitable their companies subsequently were (West, Patterson and Dawson, 1999). And there is increasing evidence from studies in a variety of sectors in the United States that shows that the longer teams are together, the better they tend to perform (Hackman, 2002; Wageman *et al.*, 2008). This makes sense, since the longer they work together, the more they come to have a clear understanding of each other's styles of working and strengths. Teams in which the members have very dissimilar tenure in the team, not surprisingly report that their teams are less effective.

We live in a global village where international travel and communication have become the norm. Societies too are increasingly multicultural, and organizations and teams must mirror the diversity in the communities they serve in order that they can understand and respond to the needs of the clients they serve. Does cultural diversity enable or hinder team performance? This is not a simple question to answer but in one of the very few longitudinal studies in this area, Watson, Kumar and Michaelsen (1993) found that groups that were heterogeneous with respect to culture, initially performed, on a series of business-case exercises, more poorly than culturally homogeneous groups. As group members gained experience with each other over time, however, performance differences between culturally homogeneous and heterogeneous groups largely disappeared. This is exactly what my colleague Felix Brodbeck has found in studies of multicultural groups in Aston Business School.

What emerges from much research into cultural diversity is that decision making is improved in groups with members from both collectivist cultures (such as China or Japan) and those from individualist cultures (such as the United Kingdom and the Netherlands). The former tend to adopt dialectical approaches to decisions, seeing both sides of every argument. The latter tend to take more extreme decisions on issues, adopting clear 'yes' or 'no' positions. By combining these two orientations, there is more comprehensive processing of decision issues in multicultural groups representing both collectivist and individualist cultures (Leung, Lu and Liang, 2003).

Overall, the research on cultural diversity suggests that the norming and storming phases in culturally diverse teams are extended, but that if these teams can learn to work with and integrate their differing perspectives, they are more effective and innovative than more homogeneous teams. The devil is in the discovery of how to learn to work and integrate their differing perspectives and this is the subject of most of the rest of this book!

Benefiting from Team Diversity

Daan van Knippenburg has undertaken a comprehensive analysis of team diversity research and developed a sophisticated approach to resolving many of the challenges and contradictions. Starting with an authoritative review of the literature (van Knippenburg and Schippers, 2007) he identified two main theoretical approaches to understanding team diversity. The first, the information/decision-making perspective, proposes that diversity is an informational resource for teams. Greater diversity of people offers more information – broadening the pool of task-relevant information, knowledge and perspectives available to the team. This in turn increases problem solving, decision quality, creativity and innovation. From this perspective then diversity is good for performance. The second approach, the social categorization perspective, takes diversity as a source of inter-group bias where team members differentiate 'us' and 'them' (engineers vs chemists; men vs women). This social categorization leads to inter-group bias with team members having less liking for, trust in, and cooperation with dissimilar others. Diversity, from this perspective, disrupts performance. Van Knippenburg argues that both approaches are well supported but that there is the possibility of helpful resolution. He proposes a Categorization-Elaboration Model (van Knippenberg, De Dreu and Homans, 2004). Diversity is seen by members as an informational resource and members learn to elaborate the informational diversity on offer: exchanging, processing and integrating task-relevant information. The leader must encourage and coach members to elaborate information exchange, particularly where tasks are complex since this will enable more effective decision making. The leader must also reduce social categorization processes that produce inter-group bias by building a strong and proud identity for the team. In particular, and most encouraging, leaders can increase the benefits of diversity while reducing the disadvantages by encouraging all team members to appreciate the benefits of diversity for team functioning (what are called 'diversity beliefs). Van Knippenburg and colleagues have shown that when team members believe in the value of diversity, diversity is more likely to have positive effects in terms of team processes and team performance (van Knippenberg, Haslam and Platow, 2007).

Implications of Diversity

Creating teams involves assembling the range of skills required for task completion. It also involves thinking through what types of behaviours, attitudes, skills and abilities are going to be required to ensure team effectiveness. We need to consider whether prospective team members have the basic team-working skills (communication, conflict management) that are required for effective team performance. Teams should also have a sufficient level of diversity in members' functional backgrounds, life experience, cultures and work experience to ensure a variety of perspectives is taken in their work and decision making. This diversity will translate into effectiveness and sparkling innovation, but only if team members can learn to manage their differences as a valuable asset rather than as a threat to their individual identities. This means having diversity beliefs that focus on the benefits to team performance of diversity. Teams of like-minded clones will experience a comfortable existence but will be ineffective and creatively stagnant in the long term.

Team leaders should be selected, in part, for their ability to deal with these team composition effects – that is, their ability to enhance the positive effects of heterogeneity and reduce its negative effects. This requires the ability to mobilize team members under a common banner. Strategies may include: the articulation by the leader of clear team-based goals, the use of socialization tactics that focus on what team members have in common, and the benefits of their differences, and the development of mentoring relationships (Anderson and Thomas, 1996). Team leaders must do this while clarifying the differentiation among roles that provides team members with a sense of their unique contribution to the team. Above all, they need to facilitate the exploration and integration of diverse and often conflicting viewpoints, in ways which enable teams to derive synergistic benefits from their diversity. It is these strategies and skills we turn to in the next chapter.

Key Revision Points

- What are the key stages in selecting people for teams?
- What personality types are associated with effective team performance?
- Does complementarity of personality types predict team effectiveness?
- What are the main areas of knowledge and skills that are necessary for effective teamwork?
- How does diversity of functional backgrounds affect team effectiveness, innovation and the relations among team members?
- How do age, gender and cultural diversity affect team working?
- How can we best ensure teams benefit from diversity rather than being disadvantaged?

Further Reading

Bell, S.T. (2007) Deep-level composition variables as predictors of team performance: A meta–analysis. *Journal of Applied Psychology, 92,* 595–615.

Mathieu, J., Maynard, T.M., Rapp, T. and Gilson, L. (2008) Team effectiveness 1997–2007: A review of recent advancements and a glimpse into the future. *Journal of Management, 34,* 410–476.

van Knippenburg, D. and Schippers, M.C. (2007) Work group diversity. *Annual Review of Psychology, 58,* 515–541.

Wageman, R., Nunes, D.A., Burruss, J.A. and Hackman, J.R. (2008) *Senior Leadership Teams: What It Takes To Make Them Great,* Harvard Business School Press, Boston.

Web Resources

http://ezinearticles.com/?The-Five-Stages-of-Team-Development—A-Case-Study &id=3800957 (last accessed 6 August 2011).
This is a summary of the five stages of team development.

http://www.kent.ac.uk/careers/sk/teamwork.htm (last accessed 6 August 2011). An interesting exercise on team-working skills and roles people play in meetings.

http://en.wikipedia.org/wiki/Group_development (last accessed 6 August 2011). A useful and accurate summary of academic approaches to understanding group development.

4

Leading Teams

Drive, ability, and constitution come together to make leaders ... the most successful are able to conjure visions through their words and infect others with their confidence ... they inspire trust by showing they share people's values and concerns ... these qualities don't just apply to the good guys: many of the greatest villains in history were charismatic. (Nicholson, 2000, p. 108).

Key Learning Points

- Creating a positive team environment
- The three central tasks of the team leader
- The skills of leading teams
- The skills of managing teams
- The skills of coaching team members
- The tripwires that confront team leaders
- How to develop team leadership skills
- Transformational versus transactional leadership

Team leaders influence coordination, creativity, knowledge sharing, problem management, actions, affective tone (positive or negative climate), efficacy, empowerment, potency and commitment to the team and the organization (Burke *et al.*, 2006). Team leaders also affect the overall performance of the team (Ahearn *et al.*, 2006; Chen *et al.*, 2007). What the research reveals

Effective Teamwork: Practical Lessons from Organizational Research, Third Edition.
By M. A. West. © 2012 John Wiley & Sons, Ltd. Published 2012 by John Wiley & Sons, Ltd., and the British Psychological Society.

is that team leader functions distil down into task-focused activity and people-focused activity. Burke *et al.* (2006) showed that person-focused leadership – specifically transformational behaviour and consideration behaviour – correlated with team effectiveness significantly (0.34 and 0.25). Overall, it is important that leaders create a positive emotional environment for effective team working. When people feel positive emotions they are more creative, altruistic and cooperative – precisely the behaviours required for teams performing complex tasks. And leaders exercise a major influence on the emotional climate of teams (Sy, Cote and Saavedra, 2005). What does this mean for leaders? First they have to model optimism – not starry-eyed idealism but realistic and encouraging optimism. Team leaders must have confidence, enthusiasm and a balanced optimism if they are to encourage those they lead and to create similar climates within the team. This also requires leaders to tackle relationships in the team discoloured by long-term anxiety or anger. Transient arguments or concerns are an inevitable, and often necessary, part of team working. It is the long-term unresolved anxieties and angers that leaders should confront, creatively deal with and enable those in the team to leave behind. It also means encouraging good humour, positive feedback, confidence and enthusiasm through socialization of new team members, through the messages given by the leaders about the wider organization and through the modelling of relationships with other teams and departments across the organization. Discouraging the use of aggressive emails is one small step. Encouraging celebrations of success and appreciation of contributions is vital.

This is not to imply that team leaders must become bouncy, extroverts (unless that is their natural orientation) irritating their co-workers by pinning a permanent false smile on their approach to work and team members. Rather, as Barbara Fredrickson (2009) points out, positivity means being appreciative (particularly of team members' contributions), open to ideas, learning and others; curious to learn about difference, new and improved ways of doing things and effective team-working practices; kind in dealing with colleagues; and above all real and genuine in interactions with colleagues at work.

Within the context of creating a positive emotional environment team leaders have three core tasks. Grasping the fulfilment of these is the key, along with positivity, to the team leader's success.

The Three Team Leadership Tasks

The team leader has three overall tasks to perform: to create the conditions that enable the team to do its job; to build and maintain the team as a performing unit; and to coach and support the team to success (see Hackman, 2002 for an extended exploration of these three tasks).

First, creating the right conditions means ensuring that the team has a clear task to perform (and one that is best done by a team) and making sure the team has the resources it needs to do its work. This means that sometimes the leader has to fight to ensure the team gets the necessary budget, accommodation, IT equipment or other tools to do its job effectively. The team leader does not need to be wonderfully bountiful in this since that encourages waste and inefficiency. But the leader should be adamant and unapologetic about arguing for the resources the team needs to get its job done. It is also important for the team's members to be clear about who is and isn't in your team – the boundaries of the team. Some healthcare teams are composed of core members who work together every day and have others who join the team for perhaps half a day every two weeks (such as medical oncologists in breast cancer care teams). In a warm but misguided attempt to ensure inclusion, leaders often include these visitors as team members and try to involve them in the team as much as possible. It is better to designate people clearly as either core team members or peripheral team members. The team is its core members. The peripheral members work with the team from time to time but cannot operate as full team members because they are simply not together with the others enough. Creating inappropriate expectations about the team's boundaries is a recipe for conflict. Moreover, as we discussed earlier, teams should not exceed six to eight members.

Second, in order to build and maintain the team as a performing unit the leader must ensure that the team is composed of members with the necessary skills and abilities (see Chapter 3 on creating teams). And the team must be sufficiently diverse. A team of people who are simply clones of the leader will be neither effective nor innovative. The leader must also develop team processes that help the team to perform effectively by nurturing good decision making, problem solving, conflict management and the development of new and improved ways of working together. Good team working does not occur naturally. It takes practice. Following one world cup, promoters formed a team from the very best players of all the sides to tour Europe to play exhibition matches. They lost every game they played. Why? Because they were excellent individually but had not learned to work as a team. The leader's job is to encourage the team to practise teamwork so they do learn to work as a team.

The third task of the team leader is to coach and support the team to success. Team coaching involves direct interaction with team members helping them coordinate and work effectively towards task accomplishment. It means intervening to help the team do its work successfully by giving direction and support. What does the team leader as coach have to do? The team leader has to learn to be sensitive to the mood of the team and to how well members are interacting and communicating with each other. The leader must pay attention to these processes and intervene to encourage

Box 3 Team leadership differs from traditional leadership

Traditional leaders tend to be directive rather than facilitative and advice giving rather than advice seeking. They seek to determine rather than integrate views and play a directive rather than supportive role. Effective team leaders share responsibility for the team and encourage team members to take responsibility when things are not going well: 'Well, what do you think are the problems here and how should we go about solving them?' They are less likely to exercise control over the final choice when decisions need to be made: 'OK, so we need to make a choice now. What should it be?' They will tend to manage the team as a whole (like a sports team in its performance) rather than simply managing the individuals. This means focusing on issues like the general mood in the team – is it anxious, stressed, optimistic or confident? Team leadership differs most clearly from traditional leadership in that the leader focuses on the team as a whole rather than on just the individuals, and shares responsibility for the team's functioning with the team.

more meetings between particular members, encourage more exchange of information, or shape a supportive approach to suggestions made by team members. The leader's task also includes helping team members develop their skills and abilities. This means taking time to review what it is they want to achieve, what skills each needs to develop, and creating learning opportunities for them (this could be formal training, visits to other organizations, or learning on the job).

So how can the team leader accomplish these three tasks? In order to answer this question, it is helpful to distinguish between three broad elements of the team leader's role: leading, managing and coaching.

The Three Elements of Leading Teams

Leading is long term, focused on strategic direction and requires thought about issues of people management, power and control; managing involves medium-term planning and clarification of objectives; while coaching is the day-to-day business of close interaction with team members. These three approaches to ensuring team effectiveness are all essential components of the team leader's work. Below we discuss each of these leadership elements in turn, beginning with the skills of leading teams.

Leading the team

Leading refers to the process of making appropriate strategic interventions in order to motivate and give direction to the team. The team leader encourages team members to work as a team in a collaborative, supportive way and with a developing sense that the team has the ability and potency to accomplish its tasks. Leading involves intuition, fine judgement and risk. It also demands confidence and even charisma.

Leading involves creating a real team rather than a team in name only. When managers are asked about the extent of team working in their organizations, they sometimes respond 'We're all one big team here' and this may be in organizations of hundreds through to thousands of people! It is heartening when there is a positive and supportive atmosphere in organizations but that is not the same as team working. Leading a team means creating the conditions that will produce team success. Leading means creating a compelling direction for the team's work, designing the team in a way that enables it to perform effectively, ensuring the organizational supports are there to enable the team to do its work, and timing leadership interventions carefully. This takes training – in other words, leaders have to practise their leadership skills to develop them. A little like developing running skills by training regularly.

Leading involves clearly communicating a compelling direction for the team's work. This is not a democratic process. If it is simply left to team members to work out, it is possible they will get lost in uncertainty or the confusion of trying to meet multiple aims – the leader's role is to provide overall direction (if the team is highly competent it may make sense for the leader to ensure the team collectively develops a sense of direction and we discuss the concept of shared leadership at the end of this chapter). Consider the elements of the direction this pensions team in a financial advisory organization pursues:

> We aim to provide a service that surprises clients who come to get advice on their pensions. We will achieve that by focusing on what they really need and offering a variety of attractive options in ways that make sense to them. We will do this by working in a team that is supportive, professional and committed to making the work experience of every member positive and stimulating.

The vision their leader paints for the team is *challenging* and therefore energizes team members' motivation. We respond best to clear and challenging, rather than 'do your best', goals (Locke and Latham, 1990, 2002). So the vision is also *clear*, since this orients team members and ensures that their work efforts contribute to the team's purpose. Finally, achieving the vision is *consequential* – team members see the value of the vision for clients and for themselves, so they are fully engaged in trying to ensure the vision becomes reality. As a result, they contribute their knowledge, skill and creativity to the achievement of the vision.

Leading means designing or sculpting the team in a way that enables it to perform effectively. How can leaders learn to sculpt their teams? They have to practise shaping the task, the authority of the team, the team size, the mix of members, and its tenure. This means designing *the task* to be one that can be performed only by a team working together (such as catching antelope on the savannah). The task must be challenging: it will demand a high variety of skills, represent a whole piece of work, and be important for the organization or the wider society. Team leaders give their teams clarity about the *authority* they have to do the work (and the limits of this authority) and give them clear, helpful feedback on team performance. *Team size* will be as small as possible to get the task completed and no more than six to eight members. Team leaders will therefore think about whether the task could be accomplished without loss of quality for customers, by having fewer team members. The team will also be *diverse* in terms of members' experience, skills and functional specialties; diverse in demographic characteristics such as age, gender and culture; and members will be good team workers – they will have the necessary team-working *knowledge, skills and attitudes*. They will stay together long enough over the course of their work that they can learn to dance the dance of teamwork beautifully together – sufficient *tenure* for success. Every six months team leaders should review these dimensions of design and think about whether some redesign of their teams is needed. By practising these design elements (just like a sculptor or an engineer) leaders will become more and more expert in their team leadership. They will make some mistakes of course, but without mistakes from time to time they cannot develop their skills.

Leading involves winning the organizational supports that enable the team to be successful. This means ensuring appropriate rewards, the right training for people to work in teams and do their jobs well, the necessary resources to do the job (e.g., IT equipment, suitable office space), and the information about organizational performance and strategy the team needs to be sure it is making the right contribution to the organization. It means ensuring there is all the support the team requires from the organization to enable successful performance and the well-being and growth of team members. Capable team leaders are vigorous in influencing others in the organization to ensure their teams can do their work effectively.

Leading requires timing interventions appropriately to help the team succeed. Teams are most responsive to leader interventions at the beginning of their life, when they have reached a half-way point in their work, when they reach a natural break in their work, or when the 'product' has been

Box 4   The essence of effective leadership

The essence of effective team leadership is articulating a clear vision and aligning the team around the vision and strategies to achieve it. It means that the leader should communicate enthusiasm, optimism and excitement about the team's work. The essence of effective leadership is also helping team members to develop their relationships with each other by encouraging them to appreciate each other, and helping them to learn how to confront and resolve differences constructively and creatively. Growth and development is a powerful human motivation so team leadership requires the leader to aid team members to coordinate their activities together, continuously improve their work and performance, and develop their capabilities. Leaders can contribute to this by encouraging them to be flexible in their approach to the team's work (e.g., by experimenting with different ways of working), by objectively analysing team processes, and collectively learning about better ways to work together. A good team leader will also represent the interests of the team, protecting its reputation, helping to establish trust with other teams, departments and senior managers, and helping to resolve conflicts creatively between the team and these groups. The leader will also ensure that the team has an identity – celebrating the team's successes, marking departures and arrivals of team members warmly and with rites of passage, all contribute to this sense of identity. We fashion our identities from the groups we belong to in and out of work and we need to feel proud of them. The leader plays a key role in this. Much of this requires that leaders have the courage to go against the way things are done in many organizations to offer a better service to clients and to create an environment that is a positive, healthy and affirming home for team members. Most of all good leadership is about kindness, because that is at the heart of any successful community or team. Indeed recent research has focused on the concept of servant leadership in teams showing it is related to both team potency and team effectiveness (Hu and Liden, 2011). Servant leadership is described by seven team leader behaviours: behaving ethically, emotional healing, putting team members first, helping team members grow and succeed, empowering, creating value for the community, and conceptual skills.

produced or a performance period has ended (Gersick, 1988, 1989). When a team is getting on with its work and is engaged in the process of doing the job intensively, it is generally a bad time for leader interventions since it disrupts the effectiveness of the group.

Managing the team

The second element of the team leader's role is managing: making sure team members are clear about the objectives of the team, their roles in the team and their objectives. Managing a team involves ensuring that team objectives, team members' roles and team structures have been established and are regularly reviewed, and also making certain that formal feedback about team performance is given to team members. Managing involves ensuring team members are clear about how well they are performing.

Managing the team means setting clear shared team objectives. The team has to negotiate its specific objectives linked to the overall compelling direction the leader has set. The leader must ensure that there is a high degree of fit and consistency between organizational objectives, team direction and team objectives. A statement of those objectives must be laid down in a form that makes the work of the team clear both to itself and to others within the organization, and enables the success of the team to be evaluated.

Managing the team means clarifying the roles of team members. The team leader must manage by ensuring that the role of each team member is clear to all. It is important that each team role is, in part at least, unique to that person, important to the team's work, and contributes to the achievement of team objectives.

Managing the team means developing individual roles. For effective team functioning, individual roles and tasks should be seen by team members as meaningful, whole pieces of work, giving them opportunities for growth and development and the exercise of skills (Hackman and Oldham, 1976). In order to maintain motivation, enthusiasm and commitment, people need intrinsically interesting tasks to perform which offer them opportunities for challenge, creativity and skill development. Managing involves helping team members to set goals every year which stretch their skills, require new learning and are intrinsically interesting.

Managing the team means evaluating individual contributions. The team leader plays a central role in ensuring that individual contributions to overall team objectives are evaluated formally so that people have clear feedback on their performance. Such feedback is usually given on an annual basis, though more frequent feedback is valuable.

Individuals also require regular, constructive feedback about their performance if they are to grow and develop in their jobs. Traditionally this has taken place via the annual appraisal or review interview in which the individual's superior gives feedback on the year's performance. As flatter structures lead to larger spans of control and each employee's contact network becomes ever wider, this is an increasingly ineffective means of giving team members the feedback they need. Moreover, it is consistent with a team philosophy that the team should appraise team members not the team leader (West and Markiewicz, 2003). The mechanics are straightforward: team members are asked to rate each other team member's skills and performance, and feedback is collected (usually via a questionnaire) from the team leader and all team members. The questionnaire usually assesses performance against predetermined competencies, including team-working skills. Answers are then analysed and feedback is given to the individual.

This approach improves team communication processes; extends ownership and involvement; and enhances the concept of team feedback. The approach can give team members information about the perceived value of their:

- contribution to the output of the team, measured against predetermined targets derived from the team's overall goals;
- performance in their team role;
- contributions in the areas of communication, goal setting, giving feedback to other team members; planning and coordination; collaborative problem solving; conflict resolution; innovation, and supportiveness;
- contribution to the team climate or how the team works.

There are a number of ways of providing team member feedback:

- the team leader collects team members' views on predetermined dimensions, collates the information and gives feedback to the individual;
- at the time of the team performance review, the team also discusses individual performance, sometimes with the help of a facilitator from outside the team;
- a sub-group of the team is delegated to consider individual aspects of performance and give feedback to individuals on that area only.

The important principles are that the process should help individuals clarify their work objectives, help them to feel valued, respected and supported, and help them identify the means to achieve any desired personal growth.

Managing the team means providing feedback on team performance. Considerable performance benefits result from the provision of clear, constructive feedback to teams, though this is often an area which team members report is neglected. Team members may get feedback on their performance but team performance is rarely evaluated systematically. In a team-based organization considerable attention should be devoted to the development of performance criteria against which teams can be measured. Teams can be evaluated in relation to:

Team outcomes – the team's performance, be it producing parts, treating patients, or providing customer service – likely to be best defined and evaluated by the 'customers' of the teams.

Team viability – the team's sustained ability to work well together. If some team members end up not wanting to work with another team member again, the team's performance has not been functional.

Team member growth and well-being – the learning, development and satisfaction of team members. In well-functioning teams, members learn from each other constantly.

Team member mental health and engagement – the well-being and flourishing of team members that result directly from their work in the team.

Team innovation – the introduction of new and improved ways of doing things by the team. This is an excellent barometer of team functioning. Teams, by definition, should be fountains of creativity and innovation since they bring together individuals with diverse knowledge, orientations, skills, attitudes and experiences in a collective enterprise, thus creating the ideal conditions for creativity.

Inter-team relations – cooperation with other teams and departments within the organization. Teams must not only be cohesive; they must also work effectively with other teams and departments to deliver goods or services. Otherwise team cohesion may simply reinforce the steel walls of traditional silos within the organization, undermining collective efforts to achieve organizational goals.

Managing involves the team leader offering observations about the performance of the team of course, but also providing feedback from objective, quantitative and qualitative data wherever possible. It must involve feedback from those affected by the team's work. For example, from customers (both external and internal). In a primary healthcare team, the manager might seek feedback in one or more ways: patient satisfaction surveys with the practice; patient satisfaction surveys with clinical interviews; feedback from relatives and carers on the supportiveness of the practice; and feedback from local hospitals on the efficiency of the practice.

Managing means reviewing group processes, strategies and objectives. Task reflexivity is the extent to which a team openly and actively reflects upon and appropriately modifies its objectives, strategies and processes in order to maximize effectiveness. Teams should regularly take time out to review the methods, objectives and procedures they are using and modify them as appropriate. Chris Argyris, an American organizational psychologist, has coined the term 'double-loop learning' to describe the difference between how teams and organizations assess whether they are doing things right, versus whether they are doing the right things. Argyris (1993) argues that many organizations only consider how efficient they are, that is, whether they are doing things right. For example, a manufacturer of metal springs might be spending time focusing on whether the correct amount of tension exists within the springs that are being

---

Box 5　The fallacies and wisdom of team leadership

Smart and brilliant leaders sometimes act foolishly and with disastrous results. Robert Sternberg (2003) has identified four faulty beliefs that can lead to foolishness in leaders, sometimes with disastrous consequences:

The egocentrism fallacy: They believe it's all about them and so only take into account their own interests and needs rather than those of all team members when making important decisions.

The omniscience fallacy: Leaders may well know a lot about some things but it is a mistake for them to assume they know a lot about everything. Otherwise, why have a team?

The omnipotence fallacy: Leaders think that they are all powerful and can do what they want, regardless of the legitimacy or morality of their actions in their own or team members' eyes.

The invulnerability fallacy: Leaders sometimes think they can get away with whatever they want to do, that they will not be caught out, and, even if they are, they will be able to get themselves out of it. Team members are aware of and vigilant in relation to the team leader's behaviour. Leaders are particularly prone to falling victim to these fallacies because the higher up they go in the status hierarchy, the more people are respectful, unquestioning and seek their approval. Wisdom does not necessarily go with the territory.

Wisdom, in contrast, is defined as '… the use of intelligence and creativity towards a common good through balancing one's own interests, other people's interests and infusing moral and ethical values' (Sternberg, 2003, p. 5).

---

produced in order to achieve a bigger market (doing things right) rather than developing a completely new type of spring for the changing market (doing the right things). Double-loop learning involves going a step beyond and asking whether the organization or team is doing the right thing. For example, it may be that the production of wireless networking devices is not the right thing to be doing in a highly competitive market and that the manufacturer should change to become a service organization, providing cloud networking.

Managing the team requires the leader to ensure there is a high degree of double-loop learning or reflexivity within a team. This could involve regular

---

Box 6   Favouritism

Team leaders typically behave in a way which communicates there is an in-group and an out-group within the team. In-group members are those the leader perceives as more competent and likable. Out-group members are those the leader has most difficulty getting on with and who the leader thinks are less competent. The team leader will tend to explain the success of in-group members in terms of their ability, and their failures to circumstances beyond their control; with out-group members the leader does the opposite. On reflection, leaders recognize that they spend markedly less time talking and meeting with out-group members. What they probably do not realize is that all team members would be able to tell who is 'in' and who is 'out'. This builds resentment and undermines team effectiveness. Leaders must practise spending more time with those team members whose competence they are least confident about or who they find less agreeable to be with. They should train them and develop their relationships with them by using coaching skills and so build one all-encompassing in-group in the team (Graen and Scandura, 1987).

---

reviews of team objectives, methods, structures and processes. As a minimum, in complex decision-making teams, reviews should take place at least every six months where the team discusses successes over the previous period, difficulties encountered, and team failures.

It is usually the responsibility of the team manager to set up 'time out' from the team's daily work to enable these review processes to take place. While some doubt the wisdom of taking time out from a team's busy work to conduct such reviews, there is strong evidence that teams which do this are far more effective than those which do not (Hackman and Morris, 1975; West, 2000). Often in our work with the top management teams of hospitals in the United Kingdom, we have found that teams under most pressure are those which are working least effectively and which are consequently least prepared to take time out to review their strategies and processes. It is as though they are running so fast on a treadmill, they are not aware of the opportunities that stepping off affords them, either to go in a different direction or to travel not on a treadmill but on an escalator! They have become busy fools.

Coaching the team

Coaching is the facilitation and management of day-to-day team processes, involving listening rather than administering. Whereas managing focuses on monitoring, giving feedback and communicating information about the wider organization, coaching is a less formal process in which the coach listens, supports and offers advice, guidance and suggestions to team members. Hackman and Wageman (2005) introduced a theory of team coaching that outlines three core ways in which leaders can coach their teams:

- motivating team members by increasing commitment and a sense of identity, and reducing social loafing;
- encouraging effective task performance strategies by minimizing unimportant work and ensuring effective coordination and task focus;
- ensuring members' knowledge and skills are used and developed effectively.

Below we will echo many of these themes. Coaching is the day-to-day work the leader undertakes to help the team achieve its objectives and its potential by giving frequent and specific support, encouragement, guidance and feedback. It is the process of facilitating the individual and collective efforts of members of a team. Think of the football coach on the side of the pitch during the game; this is similar to the coaching role of the team leader. The concept of coaching is based on the idea that there should be both guidance in appropriate directions, and the creation of conditions within which team members can discover for themselves ways of improving work performance. Coaching requires the basic skills of listening, recognizing and revealing feelings, giving feedback and agreeing goals. We will explore each in detail below.

Listening is the principal skill of team coaching and has four elements: active listening, open listening, drawing out, and reflection.

(a) *Active listening.* Active listening means putting effort into the listening process. All too often I am aware, when meeting with team members, how easy it is for me to be nodding, looking interested and concerned, but actually to be far away thinking about a previous meeting or, say, a conversation about a theatre production with my daughter. Active listening means giving active attention to the team member you are with here and now, as well as interpreting what they are saying, that is, listening between the words. It takes continuous practice (practising mindfulness is a powerful way of becoming a good active listener, leader and team coach) (Kabat-Zinn, 2004).

(b) *Open listening.* Open listening is listening with an open mind; suspending judgement to let the individual work through an idea. The team leader should not assume he or she knows the answer before the person has presented their problem or told their story. Listening with an open mind involves suspending judgement until the person has had an opportunity to explore the issue thoroughly or to explain the problem issue fully. The best strategy for problem solving is to spend most of the time clarifying the problem before trying to generate solutions. It is clearly not a productive course of action to generate solutions to the wrong problems! *The team leader should therefore encourage team members to explore problems fully rather than offering solutions.* This is tough to practise in reality. For example, in working with hundreds of team managers across Europe who have role-played team coaching, I have found the major challenge they experience is with the temptation to solve problems too quickly. Coaching involves waiting until team members have clarified for themselves what the nature of the problem might be and giving them the opportunity to discover a solution for themselves. That enables learning rather than dependence. It may be appropriate in certain leadership situations to solve problems for team members but it is not part of the coaching model.

(c) *Drawing out.* A major part of listening, involves encouraging team members to talk about their ideas, feelings and aspirations. This is helped considerably by asking 'open' questions, such as: Why? How? and Who? The purpose is to enable team members to elaborate and articulate their own exploration of a particular problem or issue which they are consulting the team leader about. Closed questions are characterized by whether 'yes' and 'no' answers can be given in response to them, such as: 'Is spending too much time at work causing you problems at home?' An appropriate open question in that situation might be: 'How is your current workload causing problems for you?' Again, most aspiring team coaches too readily identify the nature of the problem in their questioning. When a team member tells the leader that he is spending too much time at work, the leader may make the mistake of asking what appears to be an open question, but is in fact a closed and leading question such as: 'Why are you having difficulties prioritizing your work?' What a more effective team coach could ask is: 'Why do you think this is happening?' 'What sorts of pressures do you feel you are currently under?' 'How do you feel about it?'

(d) *Reflective listening.* Reflective listening involves re-stating your understanding of what a team member has said to you. Essentially it involves summarizing their previous statements, for example: 'So you're saying despite enjoying your work, you feel you want to have more freedom to define and pursue new projects on your own?' Again, this interpretation should not be the team leader's definition of the nature of the problem; it should be a genuine attempt to re-state and summarize the information given by the team member. This is a very powerful form of coaching which enables team members to explore particular issues in their team-work more thoroughly. Reflective listening is powerful for the following reasons:

- It ensures that you listen actively to what the team member is saying.
- It communicates to the team member your genuine desire to understand what he or she is saying.
- It gives you the opportunity to correct your misunderstandings.
- It enables you to be confident that you have correctly understood what the team member is saying.
- It builds mutual empathy and understanding.

You may be concerned that simply re-stating information offered by team members will appear to be an empty, parrot-like process. Research on interaction processes has demonstrated that such summarizing statements normally encourage others to elaborate further on the information already given, rather than simply affirming the correctness of what was said. Exploration is facilitated rather than curtailed by reflective listening.

Recognizing and revealing feelings. If a team leader is to facilitate team members' work and experiences, the whole person must be encompassed and not just those parts of them that are perceived as comfortable to deal with. It is sometimes appropriate and necessary to spend time exploring and clarifying the feelings of team members if team leaders are to perform their tasks effectively. This also demands revealing one's own feelings within limits and being comfortable and clear about doing that. Team leaders will be the object of frustration or anger from time to time and will themselves occasionally feel frustrated and angry with team members. Dealing with those feelings in an appropriate way, and at the right times, is an important part of coaching.

What I am not suggesting is that team leaders should explore every nuance of team members' emotional reactions and frustrations. Where there are major 'feelings' issues team members should be given an opportunity to express and explore those feelings. Team members who are feeling overloaded and frustrated with their colleagues may need some space to express that frustration before they are able to analyse the balance of tasks and priorities currently facing them. It is often the case that by focusing on feelings, the facts emerge, whereas when the focus is on facts, the feelings often remain hidden and unexpressed in the short term (in the long term they may be expressed inappropriately such as in an explosive outburst). The expression of emotions has a useful impact not just on people's immediate well-being but also on their ability to deal with similar stresses in the future.

Leaders should express their emotions in a constructive non-blaming way: 'I'm feeling frustrated because after our last team meeting I promised the customer we would deliver the order by tonight, and it is looking as if we may not be able to do that. I feel embarrassed about letting them down and frustrated because we agreed we were able to achieve this with ease. Can we discuss as a team what has gone wrong and what we can learn from this?' Such expressions are much more likely to be accepted if 95% or more of a team leader's emotional expressions are warm, positive and encouraging. The task of a team leader is to create a positive and enthusiastic emotional climate, since this will enable the team to be creative and cooperative in its work.

Giving feedback. Feedback is a word that is widely used in organizations but often misunderstood and rarely practised. Feedback involves giving clear reactions to specific behaviours in a sensitive and constructive way. When Nigel Nicholson and I conducted a survey of over 2000 British managers we found that most criticized their managers for not giving them positive feedback about their work (Nicholson and West, 1988). When we then asked them to analyse their own time use we found that they put giving positive feedback to their own team members almost at the bottom of their list of activities!

Giving feedback means being specific and focusing on team members' behaviour and the consequences of their behaviour. For example:

> I noticed that you stopped the group from reaching agreement about the inclusion of that set of questions in the marketing survey because you had a sense that they were not appropriate. This was in the face of some frustration from other team members. However, the consequence was that a much better set of questions was achieved and will provide us with more useful information as a result.

In this instance, feedback focuses on a particular example of behaviour and the positive consequences of it. Feedback is not about patting people on the head and giving them 'smiley faces'. That can be patronizing and implies the team coach has a parental type of power over the individual. Rather, feedback should be aimed at consolidating and improving performance within the team.

Feedback is most effective in changing and strengthening behaviour when it follows immediately after the behaviour. Within organizations feedback is often withheld until the annual appraisal meeting. This has very limited impact on behaviour. The team leader (and indeed all team members) should provide feedback for team members on a daily or hourly basis.

Positive feedback is much more effective in changing behaviour than negative feedback. It is better to ensure a very strong balance of positive against negative feedback (95% to 5% is getting to the right sort of balance). But because we are quicker to recognize the discrepancies between actual and desired behaviour in the workplace, the balance is often inappropriately in favour of negative feedback. This is a consequence of our normal reaction to our environment. We tend to see discrepancy when what we expect and what actually occurs do not match. Consequently the team leader has to be alert and attentive to spot the constant examples of consistency – when there is a match between expectations and reality – rather than discrepancy, and then to provide feedback as a result.

Agreeing goals. The number one task of a team leader is to constantly ensure the team and its members are clear about the team's direction, its objectives and individual team members' goals. It is a fundamental principle of work behaviour that goal setting has a powerful influence on performance (Locke and Latham, 1990, 2002). The role of the team leader must involve helping team members clarify and agree goals. If, for example, a team member is concerned about workload, part of coaching should be to facilitate a shared agreement about goals between the team leader, the other team members and the concerned individual. Making sure there is a fair balance of workloads among team members is vital for team effectiveness as we saw earlier in our discussion of social loafing. Equally, ensuring that no one is so overloaded that they are unable to cope is the team leader's (and all team members') responsibility.

Box 7 summarizes the key leadership functions under the headings of setting direction, managing team operations and developing team leadership skills broadly similar to the three themes of leading, managing and coaching teams.

Box 7   Team leadership functions (adapted from Zaccaro, Heinen and Shuffler, 2009).

Direction setting: environmental scanning, sense making, explaining, planning, goal setting.

Managing team operations: staffing, developing norms and communication, establishing performance expectations, monitoring performance, giving feedback, aligning teamwork with external changes, winning resources, acting as ambassador for the team, protecting the team.

Developing team leadership skills: developing expertise, coaching direction setting, coaching planning and role assignment, coaching collective information processing.

These then are the three main tasks for team leaders: leading, managing and coaching. By blending these activities appropriately in their performance, leaders will very powerfully shape their team's success. This is a recipe for team potency, team effectiveness, team innovation and team member well-being. Followed carefully and mindfully, these prescriptions will ensure outstanding team success. There are also some hidden tripwires to be aware of.

Tripwires for Team Leaders

Richard Hackman (1990, 2002) has identified five hidden tripwires that can cause team leaders to fail:

Call the performing unit a team, but really manage members as individuals. There are two approaches to managing team members. One involves the leader assigning individual responsibilities within a team and coordinating individual activities so that the sum of team members' efforts combines to form the whole team product. The second strategy is to assign a team task and give team members responsibility for determining how the task should be completed. Hackman argues that a mixed model, where people are told they are a team but are treated as individuals, with individual performance appraisal and individual rewards, confuses team members and leads to team ineffectiveness. Individual performance is rewarded with bonuses but team performance is given no attention. Similarly, the careers of individual team members are managed separately and sometimes even in competition with one another. Consequently team working is inhibited since team members are likely to compete to achieve their individual goals rather than to cooperate with one another towards achieving shared goals.

> To reap the benefits of teamwork, one must actually build a team. Calling a set of people a team or exhorting them to work together is insufficient. Instead, explicit action must be taken to establish the team's boundaries, to define the task as one for which members are collectively responsible and accountable, and to give members the authority to manage both their internal processes and the team's relations with external entities such as clients and co-workers. (Hackman, 1990, p. 495)

'*Fall off the authority balance beam*'. Exercising authority in teams creates anxiety for team members and for team leaders. Inappropriate ways of resolving that anxiety are sometimes to exercise excessive leadership and sometimes to exercise too little. Leadership involves exercising authority in some areas and withholding it in others; or conversely, giving autonomy in some areas but withholding it in others. Team leaders should be unapologetic about exercising authority to ensure that direction is achieved for the team's work, since this is such a fundamental contributor to team effectiveness. At the same time teams should be given the authority, within obvious boundaries, to determine the means by which they achieve their ends. Ensuring that the team has set itself a clear direction empowers rather than disempowers the team. One can 'fall off the authority balance beam' by giving a team too much autonomy or leeway by not providing sufficient direction; the result is that the team wallows in uncertainty and lacks motivation and commitment. Alternatively, the team leader can exercise too much authority and prevent the team from operating as a team altogether. A typical mistake is giving a team too much authority early in its life when direction is needed and then intervening too heavily later when the team is not performing well.

Simply assemble a large group. Where group composition is unclear or vague and where structures and responsibilities have not been worked out, team members may fall victim to the kinds of process losses such as social loafing and free-rider effects that were described earlier. Hackman argues that three important elements are necessary to ensure a suitable structure for a team. First is a *well-designed team task* which represents a meaningful and motivating piece of work accompanied by a sufficient degree of autonomy for team members to be able to conduct the work successfully and get direct feedback about the results of their efforts. Second is a *well-assembled team* which should be as small as possible while enabling the team to get the job done efficiently and which has the appropriate mix of skills and resources within the team. Third, the team should have *clear, explicit and unambiguous information* about the extent and limits of its authority and accountability so that team members do not stray into areas beyond their scope or make decisions which are not appropriate for them to make.

Specify challenging team objectives but skimp on organizational support. Teams in organizations are sometimes given 'stretch' objectives which require them to achieve ever more challenging targets. This can be very useful in improving performance and giving team members a sense of challenge. But if organizations give inadequate organizational resources then teams will be unlikely to get their work done. The key resources are:

- a reward system that recognizes and rewards excellent team performance not just individual performance;
- an educational system within the organization that provides the necessary training in skills to enable the team to achieve its objectives;
- an information system that provides the team with the kinds of data which will enable them to achieve their objectives and in an adequate form;
- and the material resources which will enable them to get the work done, such as money, computing equipment, congenial space, staff, etc.

These systems and resources are described in more detail in Chapter 11 (see also West and Markiewicz, 2003).

It is my own observation that in many organizations there is little thought given to how teams rather than individuals can be rewarded or how teams can be provided with the resources and information that they need. This is despite the fact that team-based organizations are becoming much more the norm within both the public and private sectors. There is also very little training given to people for working in and managing teams. Leaders must therefore exercise upward and lateral influence to ensure that appropriate support systems are available for their teams.

Assume that members already have all the competencies they need to work well as a team. Team leaders have to make process interventions to improve the effectiveness of teams from time to time. The point at which they intervene is very important also. Team leaders must take the time to coach and help team members and the team as a whole through periods of difficulty as well as through periods of success, and it is a mistake to assume that team members are competent to deal with new challenges as they come up. Team leadership involves constant awareness of the processes in teams and active intervention to improve them at appropriate times. Teamwork is not blind democracy but a constant learning about how to dance more creatively and effectively together.

Developing Team Leadership Skills

At least once a year team leaders should ask their team members to give them feedback on how well they are accomplishing their leadership tasks:

- 'To what extent have I provided a clear direction for your work?'
- 'Are you excited and motivated by the work we do?'
- 'Does the team task really require a team to do it?'
- 'To what extent does the task stretch us and require us to use our skills to full effect?' 'How could the work we do be made more challenging and motivating?'
- 'To what extent do I give enough authority to you for you to get on and be successful as a team?'
- 'To what extent do I give you sufficient information about how well the team is performing?'
- 'Do I time my interventions to help the team work well appropriately or do I come across as interfering?' [always ask for examples]
- 'Do we have enough team members to do the job effectively?'
- 'To what extent do we have the resources, information, accommodation and training to accomplish our task?'
- 'To what extent are you satisfied with the rewards you get as a team for the work you do (rather than individual rewards)?'

Box 8   Emotional intelligence (EI): Developing self-awareness

Your emotional intelligence (EI) determines your success as a leader (Goleman, 2002). EI has four elements: self-awareness, self-management (learning to control your impulses), social awareness (empathy) and managing relationships. How can you develop self-awareness, the first and most important element of emotional intelligence?

1   Start to keep a diary of how you felt during the course of each working day, noting your overall mood, how you felt when talking with specific team members, or during team meetings. Note when you felt emotionally positive and negative and why.
2   Read through the diary at the end of each week and look for any patterns in the flow of your feelings so that you can become more aware of the patterns of your emotions.
3   Practise mindfulness each day also (Kabat-Zinn, 2004). Try to catch yourself ten times a day and note how you are feeling. In other words, just like an athlete, train your self-awareness.
4   Take time out once each day for 20 to 30 minutes' quiet reflection. You can do this by closing your office door to others and blocking phone calls. Or you can take a walk alone to give you the peace and stillness to reflect.
5   Consider, learning meditation and practising once or twice a day (Batchelor, 2001). First thing in the morning and before your evening meal or last thing at night are good times (or even on train journeys or flights). When you awaken in the night, filling the space with meditation enables you to practise, rest and not worry about getting back to sleep. Meditation automatically develops your self-awareness.
6   As you arrive at work each day, note how you feel: are you optimistic, confident, enthusiastic or down, anxious or angry? Choose to be optimistic and confident rather than negative – quietly confident and optimistic is fine!
7   Remember, your job as a manager and leader is to help those you lead by not indulging your moods. So practise being positive in your approach to life and work, by being enthusiastic and optimistic, and – most important – encourage good humour and laughter.
8   Think positive and you will feel positive (Seligman, 1998).

The answers provide feedback on team leadership skills, indicating areas that need developing. Seeking such feedback takes courage, but team members regard feedback seeking as a sign of competence and ability rather than weakness in their leaders (Ashford and Tsui, 1991).

Other approaches to leadership development include training emotional intelligence and nurturing a transformational style of leadership.

Transformational team leadership

Two dominant styles of team leadership are transformational and transactional (Howell and Avolio, 1993; Yukl, 1998). *Transformational leadership* is defined as leadership that inspires followers to trust the leader, to perform at a high level, and to contribute to the achievement of organizational goals. Bass (1985) describes transformational leadership as having four key components:

- *Idealized influence*: leaders behave in admirable ways so that followers tend to identify with them (e.g., they display conviction; they portray role-modelling behaviours consistent with a vision; they appeal to the commitment and loyalty of followers on an emotional level as well as rational level).
- *Inspirational motivation*: leaders articulate a vision which is appealing and inspiring to followers (e.g., this provides meaning for the work task; they set high standards and communicate optimism about the achievability of the vision).
- *Intellectual stimulation*: leaders stimulate and encourage creativity in their followers (e.g., challenge assumptions, take risks, ask followers for their ideas and for suggestions on how to develop them into practice).
- *Individualized consideration*: leaders attend to each follower individually (e.g., by acting as a mentor or coach, and by listening to their concerns and paying attention to their needs, including their skill and career development needs).

The theory contrasts two styles of behaviour called transformational and *transactional leadership*. Transactional leadership motivates followers by exchanging rewards for high performance and noticing and reprimanding subordinates for mistakes and substandard performance. Transactional leadership consists of three dimensions underlying leaders' behaviour:

- *Contingent reward*: leaders set up constructive transactions or exchanges with followers; for example, clarifying expectations, establishing rewards in order to motivate and shape their performance. Other examples include exchanging rewards for appropriate levels of effort, or responding to followers' self-interests as long as they are getting the job done.

- *Active management by exception*: leaders monitor follower behaviour, anticipate problems, and take corrective action before serious difficulties occur
- *Passive management by exception*: leaders wait until the followers' behaviour has created problems before taking action.

Transformational and transactional behaviours are not mutually exclusive and research suggests that effective leaders use both styles. However, the most effective leaders use the transformational approach more since it increases follower motivation and performance more. Passive management by exception is negatively related to effectiveness. Both contingent reward and transformational leadership are positively and relatively strongly related to leadership effectiveness (Judge and Piccolo, 2004).

Another category, *laissez-faire leadership,* represents the absence of leadership. It differs from passive management by exception, where at least some influence is exerted. In effect, this involves leaving staff to manage themselves and make their own decisions regardless of their competence or of the need to structure the task. It is strongly negatively related to effectiveness (Judge, Piccolo and Illies, 2004).

Overall, the research evidence suggests that transformational leadership is effective and that a combination of transformational leadership and contingent reward is powerful in producing desirable outcomes such as effectiveness (productivity, profitability), innovation, employee commitment and engagement, and employee well-being. These are important lessons for team leaders and are consistent with the principles of leading, managing and coaching described earlier.

Team leaders can develop their transformational leadership learning to be optimistic (not unrealistic), and expressing positive emotions in the form of enthusiasm, excitement, appreciation, pleasure, contentment and celebration rather than negative emotions such as anger, anxiety, discontent and irritation. Bring positive energy to work and those around you will be affected by your energy. Moodiness is particularly damaging. Transformational leadership also involves stimulating team members by painting for them an attractive, compelling picture of what they can accomplish and the means to accomplish it. This requires thinking through what it is the team is trying to achieve, developing wise and effective plans for success, and then communicating, discussing and selling these plans to your team. They will have an increased awareness of their tasks, the importance of them to the organization and will be motivated to achieve the goals and to performing their tasks well. Moreover they will be motivated to work for the good of the team and the organization and not just their own personal gain or benefit.

Box 9   Fitting leadership style to the situation

Another way of thinking of team leadership is in terms of four overall styles: directive, achievement-oriented, supportive and facilitative. The first two are primarily transactional and the last two more transformational. Choosing one depends partly on your own personality but it should also be appropriate for the situation. This is a combination of the task the team has to perform (how clear and predictable it is) and the strength of the team members in skills, motivation and confidence.

Choose a directive, transactional style, set goals and give guidance and rewards as appropriate when the task your team members must perform is not clear or straightforward and they do not have a high level of skill or confidence in the task.

Select an achievement-oriented (transactional) style by setting challenging goals and communicating your expectations that your team members will perform at the highest level. Reward for achievement. Use this style when the task is very clear, and your team members have a high level of skill, ability and motivation for the task.

A supportive (transformational) style that involves showing concern for followers is more appropriate when the task is very clear and predictable but the team members have a low level of skill, ability, confidence or motivation.

Finally a participative (transformational) style, which is characterized by the leader consulting with team members before making decisions, is most appropriate when the task is unclear and complex, but the team members have a high level of skill relevant to the task and are highly motivated.

You will transform your team members too by devoting a good part of your considerable energy to thinking through how to help them develop their knowledge, skills, abilities, and careers, and discussing and planning this with them. By doing this you focus them on their own development, increase their skills and confidence, and satisfy one of the basic human needs – the need to grow, develop and discover through engaging with our environments. And of course, that means they are likely to perform to a much higher level and to be more satisfied in their work as a consequence.

A word of warning about charisma and self-esteem: charismatic leaders who are motivated primarily by their own needs for self-advancement and simply use team members to help achieve their own ends are precisely those who most spectacularly derail in organizations (and in history). They are the equivalent of religious cult leaders who are more concerned with using followers to confirm their self-image and beliefs, rather than to help their followers. Check that your decisions are designed to meet the needs of your clients and your team members first and foremost.

What all leaders must develop, if they do not already possess this quality, is humility. Personally this means we have to be aware of our own inadequacies and the strengths of others and that our power should not lead us to assume that we can behave in inconsiderate, arrogant or insensitive ways. An old Zen prescription for all, and it applies particularly to leaders, is 'keep don't know mind; only keep don't know mind'.

Self-managing or Shared Leadership Work Teams

Much of the discussion in this chapter has implied that leadership, management or coaching is the remit of one member of the team. It is certainly more convenient to describe management and leadership in this way, but it is important for the leader to be aware that every member of the team should take responsibility for managing, coaching and leading. If team members evade their own responsibilities for direction, support, influencing and authority in the team, it is likely that the team will be less effective. Managing meetings, for example, is the responsibility of each person in the team. When a team member sees the team going in what they think is an inappropriate direction, it is his or her responsibility to speak up if team effectiveness is to be maximized (for a good discussion of leader-centric versus team-centric leadership, see Zaccaro, Heinen and Shuffler, 2009). Research in this area reveals that shared leadership is increasingly accepted as an idea (Bennett *et al.*, 2003), though it is called a variety of names (emergent, shared, distributed and lateral (Day, Gronn and Salas, 2004)). The research evidence suggests that shared leadership is positively related to team performance generally (Carson, Tesluk and Marrone, 2007; Mathieu *et al.*, 2008).

This chapter has examined team leadership and it is clear there is no simple prescription for managing or leading teams. Being democratic or authoritarian, supportive or directive, hands-off or hands-on are all necessary elements of the role of those leading the team. Much depends on the time in a team's life, the stage of the projects it is pursuing, the organizational context within which it is working, the individual personalities and skills of team members, and the personality of those delegated to be team leaders (see Kozlowski *et al.*, 2009 for an extensive discussion of some of these contingencies).

Team leadership is the responsibility of all team members and that responsibility should not be abrogated in situations where one person is designated as team leader. The promise of effective managing, coaching and leadership is that the skills and abilities of diverse individuals can be moulded together to produce excellent team performance, in which the ideal of synergy is created in practice. As those who have worked in successful teams will know, the consequences in terms of personal satisfaction, the sense of competence and collegiality are enhanced considerably, and the sense of being part of an effective dynamic unit is indeed a rewarding one.

Key Revision Points

- What does a team leader focus on to ensure team success?
- What are the three main tasks of the team leader and why are they so important?
- How does traditional leadership differ from team leadership?
- What does leading a team involve and how does this differ from managing and coaching a team? How does it affect the performance of the team?
- What are the main tasks involved in managing a team and why are they important for team effectiveness?
- What are the main skills involved in coaching a team and why are they important for team effectiveness?
- What are the main tripwires confronting team leaders and how can they be avoided?
- What is the difference between transformational and transactional approaches to leading teams?
- In what situations are directive, achievement-oriented, supportive and participative styles of team leadership most effective and why?
- What is shared or emergent leadership and how can this be nurtured in a team

Further Reading

Bryman, A., Collinson, D., Grint, K. *et al.* (2011) *The Sage Handbook of Leadership*, Sage, London.

Burke, C.S., Stagl, K.C., Klein, C. *et al.* (2006) What types of leadership behaviors are functional in teams? A meta-analysis. *Leadership Quarterly*, 17, 288–307.

Goleman, D., Boyatzis, R. and McKee, A. (2002) *The New Leaders: Transforming the Art of Leadership into the Science of Results*, Little, Brown, London.

Hackman, J.R. (2002) *Leading Teams: Setting the Stage for Great Performances*, Harvard Business School Press, Boston.

Hu, J. and Liden, R.C. (2011) Antecedents of team potency and team effectiveness: an examination of goal and process clarity and servant leadership. *Journal of Applied Psychology*, 96(4), 851–862.

Kozlowski, S.W., Watola, D.J., Jensen, J.M. *et al.* (2009) Developing adaptive teams: A theory of dynamic team leadership, in *Team Effectiveness in Complex Organizations: Cross-disciplinary Perspectives and Approaches* (eds E. Salas, G.F. Goodwin and C.S. Burke), Routledge, London, pp. 113–155.

Nohria, N. and Khurana, R. (eds) (2010) *Handbook of Leadership Theory and Practice,* Harvard Business Press, Boston.

Sy, T., Côté, S. and Saavedra, R. (2005) The contagious leader: Impact of the leader's mood on the mood of group members, group affective tone, and group processes. *Journal of Applied Psychology,* 90, 295–305.

West, M.A. (2004) *The Secrets of Successful Team Management. How to Lead a Team to Innovation, Creativity and Success,* Duncan Baird Publishers, London.

Yukl, G. (2008) *Leadership in Organizations,* 7th edn, Prentice Hall, London.

Zaccaro, S.J., Heinen, B. and Shuffler, M. (2009) Team leadership and team effectiveness, in *Team Effectiveness in Complex Organizations: Cross-disciplinary Perspectives and Approaches* (eds E. Salas, G.F. Goodwin and C.S. Burke), Routledge, London, pp. 83–111.

Web Resources

http://www.businessballs.com/action.htm(last accessed 8 August 2011).
A brief description of John Adair's action-centred leadership model.

http://www.teal.org.uk/et/page5.htm (last accessed 8 August 2011).
What makes a good team leader?

http://www.leader-values.com/Content/detail.asp?ContentDetailID=57 (last accessed 8 August 2011).
An interesting article on coaching teams by David Clutterbuck.

5

Team Training

Start the day with a raft building and racing team-building event designed to get you thinking, communicating and working together. The competitive theme continues with the afternoon paintballing activities. Here resource management is introduced with a limit of 500 included paintball rounds per individual. Teamwork, leadership and good communication skills are required to win the day. Points are accumulated throughout the day. (Combat Games Ltd, 2002, www.paintball-games.co.uk)

We trained hard, but it seemed every time we were beginning to form up into teams, we would be reorganized. I was to learn later in life that we tend to meet any new situation by reorganizing, and a wonderful method it can be for creating the illusion of progress while producing confusion, inefficiency and demoralization. (From *Petronii Arbitri Satyricon AD 66.* Attributed to Gaius Petronus, a Roman General who later committed suicide)

Key Learning Points

- The stages of team development
- The effect of team training on team effectiveness and team member attitudes
- The seven main types of team training

Effective Teamwork: Practical Lessons from Organizational Research, Third Edition. By M. A. West. © 2012 John Wiley & Sons, Ltd. Published 2012 by John Wiley & Sons, Ltd., and the British Psychological Society.

- How to run team training sessions
- Topics to be covered in away days
- Role clarification and negotiation

Parallel to the development of the team as a principal functional unit of organizations has come the development of a myriad of team training interventions offered by consultants, popular books and personnel specialists. However, reviews of the effectiveness of team training interventions have shown that, while they often have a reliable effect upon team members' attitudes to one another, there is little impact upon team task performance (Tannenbaum, Salas and Cannon-Bowers, 1996).

The most recent review (Salas, Nichols and Driskell, 2007) compared the effectiveness of three types of team training. Cross training describes an intervention whereby team members rotate positions during training so that they can learn about each other's roles and develop an understanding of the knowledge and skills required. Team coordination and adaptation training describes an intervention whereby team members learn to adapt their coordination strategies and communications to increase effectiveness, specifically by reducing the amount of communication needed for effective task performance. Finally, guided team self-correction training involves team members in identifying team problems and developing effective solutions. By pooling the data from seven studies (involving 695 team members from 178 teams), the researchers were able to test which of these three approaches was most effective. Cross training appeared to have no effects on performance; self-correction small to moderate effects, with team coordination and adaptation having the strongest (but still only moderate) effects on team performance. The researchers say that this intervention aims to help team members learn about their performance by anticipating and discussing potential problems, especially during idle periods. It is a form of reflexivity (described in Chapter 1) involving reflecting on objectives, strategies and processes and adapting them accordingly.

Overall, it is clear, however, that most team training interventions appear to have limited impact on performance. How do we reconcile the contradiction between the increase in the number of team training interventions offered and the lack of evidence justifying their effectiveness?

Many team training interventions focus on team relationships and cohesiveness, and are based on the mistaken assumption that improvements in cohesiveness lead to improvements in team task performance. In the few interventions which have focused primarily on task issues there does appear to be some improvement in task-related performance, though not consistently so. In this chapter therefore, a clear distinction is drawn between team task processes and team social processes.

Teams exist to do a job, to perform a task. Some 200 000 years ago it was catching antelope on the savannah. Today it may be providing postal services for a rural area or healthcare for an inner city community. Whether team members like each other is much less relevant to their catching the antelope than whether they are clear about each other's roles. They need to understand which team members will drive the herd across the plain, which will identify the beast to target, and which team members will hide behind the rocks ready to leap out and spear the target beast. Moreover, they have to share an understanding of the implicit strategy here. Whether they feel warm and friendly towards one another is largely irrelevant to their success in catching the antelope and so having enough food for the community to survive.

Teams that are successful become more cohesive – our liking increases for those with whom we experience success (Mullen and Copper, 1994). Cohesive teams are not necessarily successful. Cohesive teams may collude not to work hard in an organization; or they may be more concerned with everyone agreeing and being warm to one another than with vigorously debating how to give the best service to customers. Success breeds cohesion. Failure lowers morale (Worchel, Lind and Kaufman, 1975).

We need to clarify the type of team training intervention required when working with teams and then identify very specific objectives, rather than assuming that a general intervention will have generally beneficial effects. Many team training interventions are based on the expectation that a day or two of team building will lead to dramatic improvements in team functioning. It is equivalent to hoping that one session of psychotherapy will change a person's life dramatically. The evidence suggests that it is continual interaction and effort which lead to improvements in functioning rather than any 'quick fix'.

Before we do so, we will examine how teams develop over their lifespan since this helps to provide the context for understanding how to build effective teams. The issues to consider at the outset of a team's life are very different from those during the mature performing stage. Understanding how to create teams requires us to understand that team processes vary according to the stage of their development and that their beginnings require particular consideration (see Kozlowski *et al.*, 2009). Like any life form they develop and change, and what is significant at one point in their lives is replaced at other points by new influences.

The Stages of Team Development

The best-known and most widely used model of team development (Tuckman and Jensen, 1977) suggests five stages: forming, storming, norming, performing and adjourning. Each of these stages has characteristic interpersonal relations and task activities (according to the authors' review of previous studies of groups and teams).

Forming: There is often considerable anxiety at the forming stage. Team members ask testing questions which reflect their concern about roles – particularly the nature of the leadership role – and about the resources available to the team. Individuals within the team seek out information about other team members, particularly their backgrounds and experience in the type of work that the team will undertake. They are likely to be anxious about external expectations of the team, and to request information about rules and regulations that will affect the team's working methods. At this early stage, team members may be rather guarded in the information they divulge. Their early judgements of one another will therefore be based on limited information. The most important task at this stage is to ensure that team goals are clearly stated and agreed. It helps too if the team is optimistic about its likely performance. Team optimism was shown to be an important predictor of team outcomes when teams are newly formed (West, B.J., Patera and Carsten, 2009).

Storming: During the storming stage, conflict emerges between individuals and sub-groups. The choice, authority and/or competency of the leader are challenged, and individuals resist attempts by the leader to control team processes. Members question the value and feasibility of the team task. Hidden tensions surface during this stage. Individuals may react strongly and opinions may become polarized. This stage can also see an emerging honesty and openness within the team as they work through conflicts. The team leader must build positively on this to gain shared commitment to the team goals, to build trust, begin the definition of team roles and to establish conflict resolution strategies for the team.

Norming: During norming, conflicts are resolved and the team begins to address the task with positive cooperation. Plans are made and work standards are established. Norms or agreed rules and ways of working emerge regarding team and individual behaviour. Team members more readily communicate their views and feelings; networks for mutual support emerge. During this stage the team leader should allow the team to take more responsibility for its own planning and team processes, perhaps allowing team members to make mistakes and encouraging the team to reflect upon them. It is important to ensure that norms are established which meet the needs of the organization since teams could develop norms which are destructive to effective functioning (e.g., it's acceptable to be late or not to turn up for team meetings).

Performing: Team members begin to see successful outcomes as their energies focus constructively on the joint task. They settle into an effective team-working structure, within which individual members feel comfortable, and begin to work together more flexibly. The team leader can usually withdraw from day-to-day involvement, a change that is acknowledged and accepted by team members. At this stage, systems of regular review should be established to ensure that the team continues to be effective and responsive to its environment.

Adjourning: Not all teams go through the final adjourning stage as a team, but at various times of its life, key members will leave or major projects will be completed or curtailed. It is important that the effects of such changes on the life of the team should be acknowledged: teams may revert to earlier stages of development depending on their levels of maturity, their stability and the scale of the change. What many teams quite naturally do at the end of their work is to celebrate the transition with a meal together, party or outing. Such celebrations and formal leave takings are an important ritual, recognizing the significance of the team as a social and task unit, and providing a positive closure to the team's life, enabling members to move on. Such rituals are important in human society and should not be neglected in organizational settings – their symbolic and therefore emotional significance punctuate satisfactorily for its members the work of the team.

Not all teams will fit neatly into Tuckman's sequence of team development. A team might go back and forth, revisiting stages to deal with them gradually at different levels. Team leaders can encourage teams by introducing an effective team-development process and ensuring that the team task is clear; that conflicts are processed with satisfactory (and ideally creative) consequences; that team members' roles are clear; that positive norms are established; that the team performs well; and that it disbands constructively and in a timely fashion when its task is complete.

Another model of team development suggests that 'groups and individuals attune their rates of work to fit the temporal conditions of their work situations, and that such attunement, once established, persists to some degree even when surrounding temporal conditions have changed' (McGrath and Kelly, 1986, p. 100). Gersick (1988, 1994) found that teams go through cycles of inertia and change, and that temporal milestones (such as the halfway point in a team's life and the occurrence of specific events, such as errors or conflicts) can initiate change in the work rate and work pattern of teams. Habitual routines in some teams changed at the midpoint in their work and towards the end of a project. Interventions in teams to promote more effective working are particularly valuable at the outset of the team's work, at the midpoint and shortly before the end of the team's work.

Types of Team Training Interventions

Team-building interventions can be divided into seven main types, each requiring a very different approach. Before beginning an intervention a team should therefore satisfy itself about the type of team-building intervention required.

Team start-up

This type of team building is specific to a team which is just beginning its work and which requires clarification of its objectives, strategies, processes and roles. The beginning of a team's life has a significant influence on its later development and effectiveness, especially when crises occur. Start-up interventions can help create team ethos, determine clarity of direction and shape team working practices. Many of the issues which should be dealt with in a start-up intervention were covered in Chapters 1 and 2. They include:

- Ensuring the team has a whole and meaningful task to perform;
- Clarifying team objectives;
- Ensuring that each team member has a whole, meaningful and intrinsically interesting task to perform;
- Ensuring that team members' activities can be evaluated;
- Ensuring that team performance as a whole is monitored and that team members are given regular and clear feedback on individual and team performance;
- Establishing a means for regular communication and review within the team (Guzzo, 1996).

It is ambitious to introduce established procedures in all areas of a team's functioning at its inception. Rather, effort should go in to determining: the overall task and objectives for the team; clarifying objectives and inter-related roles for team members; building-in performance feedback for individual team members and the team as a whole; and establishing mechanisms for regular communication and review of all aspects of team functioning.

Regular formal reviews

Formal reviews usually take the form of 'away days' of one or two day's duration during which the team reviews objectives, roles, strategies and processes in order to maintain and promote effective functioning.

As in any other area of human activity, regular review of functioning can lead to greater awareness of strengths, skills, weaknesses and problem areas, and future functioning being improved. Whether for individuals, couples, families, teams or organizations, there is value in stepping back from on-going day-to-day processes, examining areas of activity and reflecting upon the appropriateness of existing ways of doing things. Within work teams, regular away days are a useful way of ensuring a team's continuing effectiveness. Indeed there is much evidence that teams which take time out to review processes are more effective than those which do not.

When should a team take time out for an away day? When a team is involved in completing its work effectively and busy with task-related issues, an away day to review activities can be disruptive. A good time to schedule an away day is when a team has completed a major component of its work. However, if away days are regularly established, for example, on a six-monthly basis, then these need not interfere with the team's normal functioning since they are expected and can be used to deal with specific issues identified by the team. Away days should be of at least one full day's duration since there is usually more to talk about than is anticipated. Two days is ideal for most teams, but in some cases, this may be perceived as a luxury.

There is great advantage in conducting away days in comfortable locations away from the team's normal working environment. I have conducted team-building sessions for BP Oil Europe in the luxurious Brussels Sodehotel in Belgium. The drawback was that the hotel was located a mere 200 metres from BP Oil Europe's headquarters and team members would sometimes 'slip out' to attend to an 'urgent' matter of business. It is therefore wise to hold team sessions well away from the demands of the place of work to avoid such interruptions. At the same time, there is much to be said for the kind of comfort and facilities provided in hotels and conference venues. Having a good supply of flip charts, pens, paper, post-it notes, good food and pleasant surroundings can make the team work enjoyable and pleasurable, especially for those who are reluctant to attend initially. Both the financial commitment and the time invested in a well-conducted, focused away day is more than amply remunerated by the returns in performance which accrue.

All team members should attend away days and, where possible, a facilitator should be commissioned. Facilitators enable team leaders and other team members to focus on the content of the day, without being distracted by responsibility for the processes. Also, a facilitator can some-times provide an outside view of processes and comment on apparent diversions or blockages. Facilitators should be chosen with care. They should have experience of team interventions and be knowledgeable about team processes. Ideally the facilitator will be a psychologist who can provide evidence of team development work in other organizational settings and who would be prepared to give the names of contacts in organizations who could vouch for the effectiveness of their intervention work. The facilitator should have a good knowledge of the relevant research literature on teams at work. He or she should also be able to advise on how to evaluate the effectiveness of the interventions. For qualified facilitators highly skilled in developing effective teams contact info@astonod.com.

Away days must be carefully planned, but with a sufficient degree of flexibility to allow emerging topics to be dealt with appropriately. Having a well-structured programme of activities is essential for a productive away day. It is useful to have a mix of individual work, pairs work, syndicate work, and whole group work. Individual work is often necessary to enable team members to clarify their thoughts and reactions to various issues before being exposed to the melting pot of the whole group. Pairs work is an invaluable way of ensuring that all team members are encouraged to be active in the process of reviewing activities. It is also much less threatening for some team members than working in larger groups. Syndicate work involves small sub-groups of the team working together and this can encourage team members who do not normally work together to share their knowledge and expertise. Finally, whole group work is valuable in ensuring that the whole team has ownership of outcomes. It also minimizes suspicions about any secret deals and political manoeuvrings which might be taking place.

What topics or what content should be dealt with? There is little value in trying to cover every topic in one day. Changing behaviour is extremely difficult and trying to change complex teams in one session is nigh impossible. Away days should focus on a limited range of topics, such as objectives and communication. One indication that an away day intervention has attempted to cover too many areas is when the end of the day is rushed and action plans are ill-specified and badly formulated.

Topics to be covered in an away day can include:

- Team successes and difficulties in the previous six-month or one-year period and what can be learned from them
- A review of team objectives and their appropriateness
- The roles of team members
- Quality of team communication
- Team interaction frequency
- Team meetings, how valuable they are and what needs to be changed to improve them
- Team decision-making processes
- Excellence in the team's work
- Support for innovation
- Team social support
- Conflict resolution in the team
- Support for personal growth and development.

Box 10 Dealing with a known problem

Wendy was the Assistant Team Leader in a voluntary organization's personnel department. She wanted a team-building workshop because of problems of team divisiveness and hostility. After background briefing to a facilitator on the history of the team, its tenure and its composition, the facilitator gave questionnaires to team members which included questions asking them to indicate what they saw as the major barriers to team functioning. Examination of the responses revealed a strong sense of dissatisfaction with Wendy as a leader. Most team members described her as being overly directive, bureaucratic and inclined to have favourites. A number of team members also felt that she was guilty of talking behind their backs about their 'poor performance'. This, they claimed, had led to bad feeling on the part of both Wendy's favourites and those seen as her victims. Wendy was in her first management position and felt uncertain and anxious, which may have contributed to her directive style and tendency to reward and punish inappropriately.

A day was set aside for a team-building intervention to examine the team processes. Wendy failed to turn up, phoning in to say she was ill. Nevertheless, the team decided to address the issue and discussed how they should function on that day, given the complication of Wendy's non-attendance. It was generally agreed that back-biting and gossiping behind Wendy's back would merely accentuate the overall problem. Ground rules were therefore established and the team worked on ways of generalizing these ground rules for the day and how they might be applied to the team's functioning overall in the longer term, including areas such as respecting confidentiality, dealing with issues openly, not making personal attacks and developing strong respect and support. It was agreed these should become the ground rules for the team generally. The team also identified some ambiguity about Wendy's role, vis-à-vis the role of the team leader. It was decided that this should be addressed in separate meetings between team members, the team leader and Wendy herself in order to clarify her role and draw on her strengths and skills so that she could be more supportive to team members. Team members agreed to set up a time also to brief Wendy fully on the work of the day and to outline suggested solutions.

Addressing known task-related problems

In order to deal with specific known problem issues the team must take time out to define carefully the task-related problem it is confronting. Then the team develops alternative options for overcoming the problem, and action plans for implementing the selected way forward.

Where a specific problem can be identified and team members are satisfied they have correctly identified the nature of the problem and not simply a symptom of a deeper unresolved team issue, it is useful to take time out for focused intervention. The content and process of the intervention depends very much on the nature of the problem. If it is to do with objectives, participation, commitment to excellence, or support for innovation, then the exercises described in Chapters X to X of this book can be used. If it concerns the social elements of team functioning, the material described in Chapter X should be employed. In some circumstances, however, the nature of the problem will require a facilitator to help the team.

In this example, a known problem was handled by a team in ways which led to improvement in team relationships and functioning. It was an indication of the success of the day that the whole team, including Wendy, decided subsequently to set up regular away days for the team in the future.

Sometimes the problem need not concern internal team functioning. One team I worked with was responsible for the production of springs used by the Ford Motor Company. They were experiencing problems with rejection rates from Ford who informed them that the quality of their springs was not up to the standards required. A team meeting was set up to learn techniques of total quality management and continuous improvement from an expert. This led to changes in team objectives, strategies and processes which had a dramatic impact on quality. The team was subsequently promoted far up the list of Ford's accredited suppliers.

Identifying what the problems are

Here the intervention focuses on the diagnosis of task-related problems. After the agreed identification of the nature of specific problems the team goes on to use appropriate strategies to overcome them in future.

When a team is functioning ineffectively, but it is unclear what is causing the problem, three alternatives are possible. The first involves group discussions to explore and clarify the nature of the problems. As indicated earlier, the amount of time spent exploring and clarifying problems is disproportionately more valuable than the time spent trying to solve them. Extended group discussions examining problem areas can lead to good problem identification. A second alternative is for team members to offer their ideas individually and privately about the nature of the problem in response to open-ended questions on short questionnaires. The third approach is to employ the Team Climate Inventory (a questionnaire measure for examining team functioning – see Anderson and West, 1998) or the more comprehensive ATPI (Aston Team Performance Inventory; see www. astonod.com). These questionnaires, which have been used by many thousands of teams, are well validated and have excellent reliability. They can be used effectively as diagnostic instruments to identify problems in team functioning and as an aid to identifying techniques associated with particular team problems. All members of a team should complete the questionnaire if the exercise is to be effective.

Crew Resource Management (CRM) Training

Crew Resource Management training (CRM) was introduced as a team development strategy in the 1970s following several serious incidents in the US aviation industry including the crashes of United Airlines Flight 173 at Portland and Eastern Airlines Flight 401 in the Florida Everglades. In the first case, the crew failed to realize they were running out of fuel while they focused on a landing gear problem and in the second they failed to notice they had not deactivated the autopilot when trying to sort out a malfunction of the landing gear indicator system.

CRM was developed with the aim of training cockpit crews to use resources effectively – people, information and equipment. It has subsequently been extended to a variety of settings (medical settings particularly) including air traffic controllers, surgical teams and off-shore oil teams. The purpose of CRM training is to present trainees with important information about the task, illustrations of effective and ineffective performance, opportunities for practice, and helpful and timely feedback after practice (Salas *et al.*, 2006a). The expectation is that such training will increase the effectiveness of these teams, many of which work in critical industries such as transport, medicine, energy and chemicals.

One of the leading researchers into teamwork in the United States, Eduardo Salas, has identified the key teamwork skills that CRM can and should focus on (Salas *et al.*, 2006b):

- Communication – ability of team members to send and receive accurate information and feedback.
- Briefing /Mission analysis and planning – ability of team members to plan actions and strategies and ensure tasks are completed effectively.
- Backing up – ability of team members to anticipate each other's support needs and shift resources and workloads to ensure effectiveness.
- Mutual performance monitoring – ability of team members to monitor each other's performance, intervene as appropriate and give feedback.

- Team leadership – ability to set direction, manage team processes and coach the team.
- Decision making – ability of team members to make sound judgements on the basis of information available.
- Task-related assertiveness – ability of team members to influence team task decisions by appropriate interventions.
- Team adaptability – team members' ability to adapt to changing circumstances and demands.
- Shared situation awareness – ability of team members to use information to develop a common understanding of the environment in which the team operates.

Does CRM work? Evaluations of CRM (Salas *et al.*, 2006a) suggest that while trainees evaluate CRM positively, there is little evidence for its effectiveness as a team intervention. This is because there are too few studies, CRM interventions vary widely in content and evaluation criteria, and researchers must improve their evaluation designs. Salas and colleagues offer a checklist for improving CRM training based on our knowledge of team working, the psychology of learning and the training evaluation literature (Salas *et al.*, 2006c).

Social process interventions

Social interventions focus on interpersonal relationships, social support, team climate, support for growth and development of team members, and conflict resolution. They aim to promote a positive social climate and team member well-being.

Team social process interventions should be employed where a team has unsatisfactory answers to one or more of the questions listed in Exercise 3.

Interventions should focus on one area rather than attempting to accomplish change in all. If, for example, the main problem is a lack of social support in the team, one solution might be to train team members in simple co-counselling techniques where individuals undertake to give a partner in the team a set period of time – say half an hour or an hour every month – to discuss work-related problems. It is a mutual contract where both team members are provided with equal time at the same session and ensures that all team members get regular support. The basic techniques of co-counselling can be taught at an intervention or on a course.

If the problem relates more to support for growth and development the team might spend a day identifying each other's skill training or personal development needs and then action plan for how they could best provide the support to enable these needs to be met. General social climate problems can be addressed by asking team members to agree to simple behavioural

Exercise 3 Satisfaction with team social processes

	Yes, very definitely	Yes, but only somewhat	No, but only somewhat	No, definitely not
Does the team provide adequate levels of social support for its members?	1	2	3	4
Does the team have constructive, healthy approaches to conflict resolution?	1	2	3	4
Does the team have a generally warm and positive social climate?	1	2	3	4
Does the team provide adequate support for skill development, training and personal development of all its members?	1	2	3	4

Have the whole team discuss team scores on this questionnaire and discuss whether there is a need to improve any of those areas of team social functioning.

rules for improving team functioning, such as arranging regular and varied social events. Again action planning and agreed contracting arrangements within the team can promote the likelihood that good intentions will be carried through. Finally, if the problem relates to a failure to resolve conflicts in a timely fashion, conflict-resolution techniques based on the principles of assertiveness and ethical negotiation can be introduced (De Dreu and Van de Vliert, 1997; Fisher, Ury and Patton, 1999).

Exercise 4   Role negotiation exercise

Team members use mutual influence and negotiation in order to change team behaviours and improve team functioning.

Step 1
Each team member lists his or her objectives and principle activities on a piece of flip-chart paper.

Step 2
Each piece of flip-chart paper is hung on the wall around the room and team members examine each role.

Step 3
Under three headings on a piece of paper, each team member writes down what behaviours they would like that person to do less, do more, or maintain at the present level in their working relationship. For example, a personal assistant receptionist might indicate that they want the senior manager they work with to keep them informed more fully of plans for the coming month, in order that they are up to date with the manager's movements. The receptionist may ask the manager not to check so often that paperwork has been completed, since it feels like controlling rather than trusting their role. Finally he or she may ask the manager to sustain these attempts to improve communication but also to involve the personal assistant by seeking her views concerning the manager's work where appropriate.

Each person signs their name after their requests for more, less or maintained behaviour.

Step 4
Pairs of individuals within the team then meet to examine the end result. The two negotiate together in order to reach agreement about the various requests. This is a highly participative step in the exercise and some teams may need help in managing the negotiation, especially if a particular pair is having difficulty reaching agreement.

Through role negotiation, the needs of individual roles are met more effectively and the functioning of individual members is dove-tailed more into the objectives and needs of the team as a whole. This is a very powerful exercise which can enhance team functioning considerably, overcoming many of the problems of process loss and coordination described in Chapter 1.

Role clarification and negotiation

One potential problem in teams is lack of clarity about team roles. To address this, team members can undertake the following exercise in role clarification and negotiation.

Conclusions

The blanket approach to team training employed in many organizations is unlikely to be effective for most teams. Those wanting to intervene in teams should ask 'What intervention is most appropriate, for which teams, and at which point in time?' Then the following checklist can be used to ensure appropriate focus for the intervention:

1 Are the objectives of the training intervention clear?
2 Is the intervention appropriate for the particular issues facing the team?
3 Is the intervention appropriately timed?
4 Does the intervention attempt to cover too many areas?
5 Are means for sustaining change built in to the intervention?
6 Are facilitators employed who have the knowledge and skills required to conduct team training interventions?
7 Will clear action plans emerge as a result of the team training intervention?
8 Will regular reviews be instituted as a result of the team training intervention?

Team training is undoubtedly very helpful for team performance when effectively conducted (see Salas *et al.*, 2006c for an excellent guide to designing such training). Moreover, the evidence suggests that training team members as a team in generic team-working skills is helpful. Recent evidence suggests that the use of CDs or other computer-assisted methods of delivery of team training is ineffective and that more team training needs to take account of organizational (not just team needs) and the organizational context, involving other teams and key departments rather than teams developing their skills in splendid isolation (Mathieu *et al.*, 2008).

This chapter has emphasized the need for teams to review their functioning on a regular basis. Where a team is low in task reflexivity it is necessary to address this failure of adaptability. Some fear that such questioning generates conflict and uncertainty about the team's direction. It is important to reassure team members that such reflexivity holds within it the seed of opportunity and greater effectiveness which can produce an enhanced sense of competence, confidence and greater aspirations amongst team members. Moreover, the research evidence on reflexivity has strongly suggested that teams which do reflect on strategies in this way are highly effective in long-term performance (West, 2000). Reflexivity should therefore not simply occur during team-building interventions; it should be part of the texture of the day-to-day life of the team.

Key Revision Points

- What are the stages of team development?
- What is the evidence for the effectiveness of team training?
- What is team training?
- Does team training work?
- What are the main types of team training interventions?
- When would you use them and why?
- How would you go about designing a team training intervention for a team you work in based on this chapter?

Further Reading

Guzzo, R.A. and Dickson, M.W. (1996) Teams in organizations: Recent research on performance and effectiveness. *Annual Review of Psychology*, 47, 307–338.

Salas, E., Wilson, K.A., Burke, C.S. and Wightman, D.C. (2006a) Does crew resource management training work? An update, an extension, and some critical needs. *Human Factors*, 48, 392–412.

Tannenbaum S.I., Salas, E. and Cannon-Bowers, J.A. (1996) Promoting team effectiveness, in *Handbook of Work Group Psychology* (ed. M.A. West), John Wiley & Sons, Ltd, Chichester, pp. 503–529.

West, B.J., Patera, J.L. and Carsten, M.K. (2009) Team level positivity: investigating psychological capacities and team level outcomes. *Journal of Organizational Behavior*, 30, 249–267.

Web Resources

http://www.teamtechnology.co.uk/tt/t-articl/tb-basic.htm (last accessed 9 August 2011).

An introduction to the basic concepts of team building – and how to tell whether you need to focus on individual skills, small team relationships, overcoming team islands, or changing organizational culture

http://www.teamtechnology.co.uk/team-building-activities.html (last accessed 9 August 2011).
This page provides you with a comprehensive overview of team-building activities. They will give you some ideas on what you can do in your team.

http://www.innovativeteambuilding.co.uk/pages/articles/basics.htm (last accessed 9 August 2011).
A summary article on team working and team building.

Part 3

Team Working

This section focuses on the core processes of working in teams, identifying the key elements of team working and providing guidance for ensuring that the team is functioning effectively. It explores the elements that make up the dance of teams and the positive and negative impact of different processes such as setting objectives and conflict. The priority task is to ensure that the team has a clear and appropriate direction – a team vision – an inspiring statement of its purpose which is then carefully translated into clear objectives. This is the subject of Chapter 6.

Chapter 7 explores what it means to be a team player, exploring the importance of interacting with other team members, sharing information and influencing decision making. Interaction is about frequent and useful contacts; leading to sharing of useful information; and finally to the development of effective team decision making that draws on the relevant knowledge, skills and abilities of all team members. This chapter also identifies some of the obstacles to good teamwork that are endemic in many human interactions, such as dominance, failure to listen, obsequiousness towards high-status others, and the rush to judgement. It offers practical and tested strategies for overcoming them.

Chapter 8 introduces the idea of a commitment to quality as an essential orientation for teams and explores how team members can work together to ensure that their teamwork produces high-quality and excellent outcomes. The chapter describes the strategies, tools and techniques that teams can employ to ensure they have a commitment not only in intent but also in practice to such high-quality outputs.

Effective Teamwork: Practical Lessons from Organizational Research, Third Edition.
By M. A. West. © 2012 John Wiley & Sons, Ltd. Published 2012 by John Wiley & Sons, Ltd.,
and the British Psychological Society.

Of course, working in teams has many challenges including complex problems to be solved, the emotional demands of working in high-demand situations as a team member, and the inevitable conflicts that characterize the work of teams, made up of diverse individuals with varied backgrounds and experiences. Chapter 9 describes a variety of methods for promoting creative thinking in teams and ensuring high levels of innovation, from the basics of brainstorming through to active exercises that encourage divergent and radical thinking which can challenge the status quo. The level of innovation is a highly accurate barometer of team functioning in many situations, since it indicates the extent to which team members are truly integrating their diverse perspectives to achieve high-quality and relevant outputs from their work.

Our well-being and effectiveness is profoundly affected by our emotional experiences, be they at work or outside of work. The emotional environment that teams create affects individual well-being and team performance. Positive teams work more effectively and are both more productive and more innovative. Chapter 10 emphasizes the need for team members to provide each other with social support which contributes to such positive environments, describing the different dimensions of emotional support, appraisal support and instrumental support. Practical ways to support fellow team members are described as well as some of the pitfalls of misjudging what is needed. Case examples bring the guidance to life and offer parallels that enable the reader to relate the provision of social support to their own experience.

When people with different backgrounds, experiences, attitudes, skills and motivations come together to achieve shared goals, they inevitably disagree. In general such disagreement is a healthy process in teams but when it spills over into conflict and sustained negative emotion it is damaging to individuals and to team effectiveness. Chapter 11 deals with this difficult issue of conflict in teams and recommends ways of minimizing destructive conflict and encouraging instead 'constructive controversy' that ensures that team members feel affirmed by their colleagues, even when there are disagreements. The chapter also describes how to manage 'difficult' colleagues in ways that do not involve 'scapegoating' even if individuals have to be managed out of a team.

This section therefore offers practical advice for team members and team leaders about the day-to-day problems and processes of working in teams, using knowledge gleaned from academic research and professional practice. It is a guide to ensuring that the dance of teamwork is elegant, coordinated, engaging and highly efficient. Following the prescriptions offered in these chapters will enable readers to work in dream teams, far more effective than the vast majority of teams in modern organizations.

6

Setting Team Direction

Whatever you can do, or dream you can, begin it. Boldness has genius, power and magic in it. Begin it now. (Goethe)

Key Learning Points

- Defining team objectives, vision, mission and action plans
- Why vision and objectives are central to team effectiveness
- The key dimensions and elements of team vision
- Developing a team vision
- Defining and developing a team strategy

Team Objectives

Teams are created to perform a task that individuals working alone or in parallel could not complete or could only complete with great difficulty. The task defines the team therefore rather than the reverse. Once the task is identified, the team can then define its objectives. In our research with many teams across many different organizations, sectors, and nations, we have found clarity of team objectives is the single most important predictor of team success. Yet many teams do not have clear objectives or members disagree about what those objectives are or they are stated in such an imprecise way that they are little more than feel-good statements with no practical

Effective Teamwork: Practical Lessons from Organizational Research, Third Edition.
By M. A. West. © 2012 John Wiley & Sons, Ltd. Published 2012 by John Wiley & Sons, Ltd., and the British Psychological Society.

value being added to the team's challenge to reach its goal. Teams should therefore always set clear objectives. Goal-setting theory (about the most axiomatic and well-supported idea in social science) makes it clear that objectives should be clear, challenging and, ideally, team members should be involved in setting the objectives (Locke and Latham, 1990, 2002). Teams should set no more than six or seven objectives. These should have measurable outcomes and they should have a time specification: 'We will increase sales volume by 15% by the financial year end'.

However, as the reader may infer, increasing sales volume by 15% may not be the most motivating objective for team members, especially if they fail to gain in any way from the improved performance. Team leaders therefore might want to think about something more inspiring for the team to aim at and the notion of 'vision' as a compelling direction to pursue is used in many teams and organizations for this purpose. We will come back to the issue of objective setting shortly but first it may be helpful to explain the myriad of terms around team direction – specifically vision, mission, objectives and goals.

- A *vision statement* outlines what a team wants to be, or how it wants its impact upon the world in which it operates. It focuses on the future and provides inspiration.

  To ensure our course is the most sought-after undergraduate marketing course in the United Kingdom.
  To be rated the best team for after-sales service in the company.
  To be a model of good practice for all the primary healthcare teams in the city.
  To be the most friendly and helpful retail team in the company.

- A team *mission statement* articulates the fundamental purpose of the team. It identifies who the customers are and the key processes involved in the team's work. It also specifies the desired level of team performance.

  We will provide a research-based, rigorous and challenging learning experience for students, which enables them to get graduate-entry jobs in marketing in leading corporations nationally and internationally.
  We will offer an after-sales service to our customers that ensures they are always delighted by the timeliness, helpfulness and appropriateness of our responses to their needs.
  We will deliver healthcare based on the needs of the community, the preferences of patients and their carers and a commitment to health promotion that ensures we have a positive impact on the health of the community overall.
  We will offer an outstanding retail service to customers based on ensuring the goods they require are made available when they need them; that

staff are friendly, helpful and engaging; that we minimize delay and confusion and maximize ease and enjoyment for our customers.

By taking the time to clearly define team vision, mission and, by extension, objectives, those who work within teams have a greater chance of being effective and creative in their work (Pritchard *et al.*, 1988; Tubbs, 1986). Visions should not be plucked from the sky. They should relate to the wider vision and mission of the organization, and to the values of team members. An example will illustrate. Consider the vision of the Springwood Primary Healthcare Team:

Springwood Primary Healthcare Team

Vision: *We will improve the quality of life for those we serve by ensuring their health care is leading edge and humane.*

Mission: *Our mission is to promote the health, growth and well-being of all of those in our community, including patients, relatives, community members and practice members by respecting the individual, encouraging cooperation and collaboration and emphasizing excellence in all we do.*

The team based their vision on the wider purpose of their organization, which was to provide high-quality and safe care for all in the community. They also based the vision on the values of team members:

- *respecting, valuing and supporting all the people we serve*
- *cooperation between professions to provide best-quality care*
- *freedom of choice for all individuals*
- *the importance of equal access to treatment for all*
- *the value of health promotion equally with illness treatment*

Team objectives: Springwood defined the following objectives as a result of articulating its vision statement:

1   *To put equivalent resources (people, time, money) into health promotion as into illness treatment – measured by resource allocation*
2   *Involve all team members in setting objectives and improve our functioning of a team continuously – measured by improvements in team functioning as measured by ARTP (Aston Real Team Profile+)*
3   *Promote the control and quality of life of those with chronic diseases (e.g., diabetes, asthma) – measured by their ratings of quality of care and control over symptoms*

4 *Improve health outcomes in the Springwood community by seeing decreases in heart disease, cancer, obesity, and drug and alcohol abuse*
5 *Improving the quality of relationships we have with other organizations and teams with which we must work (hospital, other primary healthcare teams, social services) – measured by annual ratings from them of our cooperativeness.*

These objectives are derived directly from the vision of the team and from its mission statement. They describe clearly the overall aims that team members have for the practice's work.

Some key points about the shaping of objectives are:

Objectives should be clear – everyone in the team has to understand the objectives and understand them to mean the same thing.

Objectives should be challenging – easy to achieve objectives are not motivating; challenging but achievable objectives are.

Objectives should be measurable – it should be possible to clearly demonstrate the extent to which the team has been successful in achieving its objectives by reference to data, whether in the form of increases in sales revenue, customer ratings of satisfaction, the ratings of other teams about the effectiveness of the team, or reduced team member absenteeism. Without measurement, the team has no clear idea of whether it has been successful.

Objectives should be shared and understood by all team members – thus if any member of the team is asked what the team objectives are, he or she should be able to produce the same list as those produced by other team members. Memorizing them is great but not necessary – having the list in a drawer or on computer is enough. But they should be sufficiently familiar to all team members for them to be able to recall most.

Team members should be involved in setting the objectives – involvement in goal setting massively increases people's commitment to those goals.

There should be no more than six or seven objectives – short-term memory restrictions mean people have difficulty holding more than seven items in their heads. Moreover, larger numbers of objectives indicate a failure of teams to prioritize what are their critical tasks for success resulting in ineffectiveness.

One of the objectives should focus on improving inter-team working – teams must work effectively with the other teams and departments in (or indeed outside) their organizations with which they have to work to deliver goods and services effectively. This is an essential requirement for any team.

Objectives should be time-based – usually teams set objectives for the year ahead and their performance is evaluated on the basis of whether they have achieved their objectives in that timescale. For shorter lived teams this would not make sense so shorter time scales would be required. However, having a clear timescale for the achievement of the objectives is required for obvious reasons.

From the vision therefore, grows a solid mission statement, from which, in turn, can be derived the team objectives. These guide the development of detailed action plans which prompt specific actions by team members. Articulating the vision provides the basis for all of the team's activities. Surprisingly few teams take the time out to work out their vision, mission statement, objectives and action plans. Yet considerable research reveals that such planning makes it much more likely that action will ensue (Gollwitzer and Bargh, 1996). Action planning leads to action. Failure to plan in teams often results in failure to act. We therefore take some space below to explore the dimensions of a vision and explain how the process of developing a team vision can be accomplished.

Vision is a shared idea of a valued outcome which provides the motivation for the team's work. In order to develop a statement of team vision, a number of dimensions must be considered. These should include its clarity, motivating value, attainability, the extent to which it is shared by team members, and its ongoing development. Each of these dimensions is described below.

Clarity. In order for a team to determine its objectives and actions it must have a clear vision and be clear about the overriding purpose of the organization of which it is a part. If team members are unsure of what the shared orientations, values and purposes of their colleagues are, it is difficult for them to articulate a clear statement which encapsulates these orientations and values. This requires that team members communicate about their work values and orientations. They must then find a form of words which expresses accurately and clearly these shared values, interests and motivations. Later in this chapter the steps in fashioning a clear statement of vision are described.

Motivating value. The values that we bring to our work influence the effort we put into it. Consequently for a team to work well together, team members must have some shared sense of the value of their work. For example, in healthcare settings people do work which accords with a basic value of helping others. To the extent that the vision reflects the underlying values of the team it is likely to motivate team loyalty, effort and commitment (Locke, 1990; Locke and Latham, 1990; Locke *et al.*, 1981).

In other settings it may not be so easy to engage people's values in the organizational objectives of the team. However, values about excellence in work, respect for individuals, and the growth and well-being of team members can be expressed within almost any context. For example, a team engaged in collecting financial debts may value treating all individuals with respect and consideration. It may also decide that team member skills should be enhanced and developed in order to encourage greater excellence both in team working and in relationships with others. Working in teams, where the vision or values are inconsistent with one's own can create difficulties. For example, within a team in a personnel department which is being directed to appoint people on contracts offering little job security, poor pay, and poor career development opportunities, team members may work less hard simply because the approach is inconsistent with their values. Many people experience working in situations where they feel that the work that they are required to do is in conflict with their core values. The consequence is that we work less hard or look for alternative jobs – we are less motivated and less committed.

Attainability

> That man is truly free who desires what he is able to perform, and does what he desires. (Rousseau)

When a team is set unattainable objectives it will be de-motivated. It may also lead to some of the problems described in the last chapter, such as free riding and social loafing. Consequently team members' commitment and motivation may be substantially reduced. This depends to some extent upon the nature of the task they are being asked to perform. A top management team at OXFAM may be less de-motivated by the difficulty of achieving food for all by the year 2010, simply because of the enormous motivating value of the vision of the team. There is, therefore, a trade-off between attainability and the motivating value of a team's vision.

Sharedness. The vision should also be shared and this is partly itself dependent upon the extent to which the vision is negotiated. Where team members feel they have made a real contribution to the determination of the vision and that, more importantly, it is in accord with their personal values, they will be more motivated and committed to its achievement (Latham and Yukl, 1975, 1976).

Ability to develop. A danger of team working is that decisions about vision made at one point in time, become cast in stone. Because teams are constantly evolving – the people within the teams are changing their views, developing new skills and changing values – it is important that the vision of the team evolves in the same way. Similarly, the environment within which the team operates goes through change; organizations change strategies and society changes its views. There is more emphasis now on flexible patterns of working and on environmental protection and equal opportunities. Teams which formerly might not have considered these issues may now need to give them careful consideration. Consequently a team's vision must be regularly reviewed in order to ensure that it is alive, evolving, up-to-date and representative of the changing values and orientations of team members. Otherwise, team vision can become a strait jacket within which the team is prevented from developing in new directions.

The Elements of Team Vision

There are eight major elements of team vision upon which a team's vision may focus:

1. Consistency with organizational objectives
The team vision should be aligned with and derive from the organization's overall purpose and strategy. Teams are sub-elements in a wider organization structure and their success will be judged on the extent to which they make valuable contributions to the overall purpose of the organization. In some circumstances a team may decide that it is important for its own values, purposes and orientations to act as a minority group which aims to bring about change in organizational objectives – an unusual circumstance we examine carefully in Chapter 12.

2. Customer/ service receiver needs
The team must focus on providing excellence in service to its customers, whether they be customers within or outside the organization. There is much evidence that teams which focus on customer needs and providing outstanding service to them are much more effective in general than those which do not. To what extent are service receivers seen as people who are to be merely satisfied, rather than people who are to receive the best quality of service available? For example, a teaching team in a university department might prefer to emphasize research excellence above the quality of teaching provided to students. Alternatively, they may strive to admit as many students as possible, putting pedagogical excellence second. A car maintenance team may emphasize satisfying the customer above ever-increasing profitability.

3. Quality of product, service or function
A major emphasis within organizations is the quality of services and functioning within organizational settings. Team members may also discuss the extent to which top quality will characterize their own working relationships. This may be reflected in the speed with which requests for information within the team are met, and also the quality of information which is eventually produced.

4. Value to wider society

It is unusual for some teams to take time out to consider the value of their work for the wider society. Consideration of this and ways in which it can be enhanced is an important way of encouraging both team cohesion and greater team effectiveness. Such consideration may promote conflict if team members perceive their work to be irrelevant to the wider society or if there are conflicts between team members about the potential value of the team's work. However, such conflict enables team members to achieve clear perception of the purposes of their work and therefore enhances team effectiveness and creativity.

5. Team-climate relationships

Team-climate relationships are often neglected when teams discuss their functioning. If team members have such difficult relationships that members are inclined to leave the team, long-term team viability is threatened. Teams therefore need to consider the type of team climate they wish to create. Team climate refers to aspects of teamwork such as warmth, humour, amount of conflict, mutual support, sharing, backbiting, emphasis of status, participation, information sharing, level of criticism of each other's work, and support for new ideas. Chapters 6 to 10 consider various ways in which the team climate can be enhanced.

6. Growth and well-being of team members

Another element of vision is support for the skill development and well-being of team members. Growth, skill development and challenge are central elements of work life and teams can be a major source of support. They may provide opportunities for skill sharing and support for new training. One issue is the extent to which team members will support skill development and training which may further someone's career, although this may not contribute immediately to team effectiveness.

Another area of concern for a team is the general well-being of its members. This is especially true for those working in conditions of high stress, such as caring professionals. The social support that team members provide can have a buffering effect, preventing stress-related illnesses.

7. Relationships with other teams and departments in the organization

Teams rarely operate in isolation. They interact with other teams and departments within the organization, for example, in cooperating in cross-functional teams or competing for scarce resources. Teams must be committed to working effectively and supporting other teams and departments within their organization.

Groups often compete as a result of 'group identification', where people tend to favour their own group and discriminate against other groups, leading to destructive working relationships (see Chapter 11).

8. Relationships with teams outside the organization

Similar issues arise in considering team relationships with other organizations. For example, BBC TV *Continuing Education* production teams are concerned with issues that affect the whole community. In producing programmes about how families can function most effectively, they may therefore want to work closely with the relevant voluntary and professional organizations. On the other hand, a team may decide to take a very critical orientation to the work of these organizations and may wish to distance itself in the making of a programme. In order for a team to have a clear shared vision about its work, it must make explicit (where relevant) the quality and nature of relationships it seeks with organizations and individuals.

A related concept to vision, mission and objectives is strategy and it is worth taking time to be clear about this concept and differentiating it from the topics we have considered thus far. Strategy is a metaphor derived from the domains of battles and wars. We go on to consider the concept of strategy in the context of teamwork.

Strategy for Teams

A way of designing strategy is to separate out the elements that together make up strategy. These are: domains, vehicles, differentiators, economic logic and sequencing and stages. Each of these is explained below with an example from a business consultancy team (Aston Organization Development, www.astonod.com), developed from the work of a university work psychology department.

Domains

Domains are the content of team's activities and the products or services they offer. In the case of Aston Organization Development (AOD), this includes consultancy to organizations that wish to introduce team-based working; products in the form of manuals, guides and test instruments that help with the introduction of team-based working; consultancy to organizations that wish to promote innovation and creativity; and products including test instruments to assess levels of creativity and innovation in organizations, as well as instruments to assess the supportiveness of the environment for innovation.

Vehicles

Vehicles include the means by which these products and services will be developed and delivered, including people, marketing, partnerships, and contacts. AOD identified the vehicles as the principal consultants in the business (mostly work psychologists), and associated consultants (skilled colleagues not employed by AOD but known to the principal consultants as competent practitioners who would welcome additional work). AOD also saw their extensive networks of contacts with senior managers and HR directors in organizations as important vehicles for their work, since these contacts potentially offered important business opportunities.

Differentiators

What differentiates the team's work and makes it unique and identifiable? This is an important question to answer since it relates to the commercial value of the team's work as well as to valued identity for team members. Why would people remember the team unless there were aspects of its work that differentiated it from others? AOD recognized that the academic reputation of its principal consultants and their research expertise and credentials made the team stand out from consultancies in general. This was a consultancy whose work was supported by a solid research base. Moreover, their focus on team-based working was unusual since very few, if any, consultancies offered a service designed to help with introducing organization-wide team-based working.

Economic logic

How will the team ensure that it is funded to do its work and that there are sufficient resources to implement the elements of the strategy? Any team has to ensure that the economic logic for its strategy is worked out and articulated. AOD identified earnings from consultancy during its early phases as a source of income that would allow it to slowly develop web- and CD-based instruments which could be sold commercially and which would potentially be a major income source. Public speaking by two of the best-known consultants would also ensure a steady income stream in the first year. Finally, the AOD team identified the value of developing booklets that managers could use for practical advice on developing creativity and innovation in organizations, on conducting research in organizations and for managing change. These would have mass market appeal for managers at all levels and would provide another income stream in the first years of the company's operation.

Sequences and stages

Strategies need to have time plans that are realistic and do not require team members to try to accomplish too many tasks all at the same time. In what order and with what duration will plans be put into effect? AOD decided that for the first two to three years the principal focus would be on delivering large-scale consultancy support to organizations requiring help to introduce team-based working and encourage creativity and innovation. An intermediate step (two to four years) would be the development of booklets and first examples of web-based questionnaire instruments which organizations could use to assess aspects of functioning. Licensing of users of instruments and high-profile marketing would be the final stage of the team's five-year strategy.

By thinking through these five elements of strategy, teams can articulate a strategy that enables them to chart their directions and activities for the future. The vision provides the destination; the strategy provides the means for getting to the destination.

This chapter began by emphasizing the fundamental importance of team vision for effective team working. This is because without a clear beacon to guide it the team can often be diverted from its course by organizational demands, the changing interests of team members, or other external pressures. With a clear sense of vision, rooted in the shared values of members, and a practical and thoroughly developed strategy, the team will maintain a good course towards its valued aims and objectives.

Key Revision Points

- What are the differences between team vision, mission and objectives?
- What key points should be considered when setting team objectives?
- What are the dimensions and elements of team vision?
- What are the elements of a team strategy?
- What is the difference between team vision and team strategy?

Further Reading

Gollwitzer, P.M. and Bargh, J.A. (eds) (1996) *The Psychology of Action: Linking Cognition and Motivation to Behavior,* Guilford Press, New York.

Locke, E. and Latham, G. (1990) *A Theory of Goal Setting and Task Motivation,* Prentice Hall, Englewood Cliffs, NJ.

Locke, E. and Latham, G. (2002) Building a practically useful theory of goal setting and task motivation, *American Psychologist, 57,* 705–717.

Pritchard, R.D., Jones, S.D., Roth, P.L. *et al.* (1988) Effects of group feedback goal setting, and incentives on organizational productivity. *Journal of Applied Psychology, 73,* 337–358.

Web Resources

http://www.leadership-and-motivation-training.com/developing-a-team-vision-statement.html (last accessed 9 August 2011).
This resource can help you develop a good team vision statement.

www.astonod.com (last accessed 3 August 2011)
Aston OD is a spin-out company from Aston Business School which develops team working within and across organizations in the United Kingdom and offers a wealth of practical resources for developing teams and team-based working.

7

Team Playing

Difference of opinion leads to enquiry and enquiry to truth. (Thomas Jefferson)

Key Learning Points

- Team interaction frequency and team performance
- Information sharing in teams
- Barriers to team decision making
- How to improve team decision making
- How to build a sense of safety in teams

Being a team player means having a clear focus on working as a team member to enable the team to achieve its objectives and working towards that. Being a team player means being positive and supportive to all other team members and creating an atmosphere of confidence, enjoyment and engagement in the team. Being a team player means continually working to ensure good relationships in the team and between the team and the rest of the organization. In essence, being a team player means participating fully in the team.

We create teams in order to utilize the skills, knowledge and abilities of people who make up the team in ways that ensure their collective efforts enable them to accomplish tasks they could not manage alone. Participation

Effective Teamwork: Practical Lessons from Organizational Research, Third Edition. By M. A. West. © 2012 John Wiley & Sons, Ltd. Published 2012 by John Wiley & Sons, Ltd., and the British Psychological Society.

involves encouraging team members to meet together, share information and ideas, and debate fully and intelligently the best way of accomplishing the task of providing products or services for customers and clients. Team participation involves team members taking individual and collective responsibility for team objectives, team strategies and team processes. While team work implies differentiation of roles and responsibilities and thereby that people will take leadership positions, this does not mean that the team leader is solely responsible for determining team objectives, strategies, processes and outcomes. On the contrary, in effective work teams, all team members are aware of and sensitive to team functioning and therefore take responsibility for ensuring success.

Team participation includes four key elements: interacting, information sharing, influencing and ensuring safety.

Interaction

In order for a group of individuals who share a common goal to be called a team they must have some ongoing interaction, otherwise their efforts are essentially uncoordinated and disaggregated. Teams interact during task performance and socially; both are equally important. Social interactions might include parties, lunches or informal chats in the corridors to discuss family matters or sporting events. These interactions strengthen the attachment, cohesion and familiarity which enable people to feel safe with one another. Interaction during task performance provides an exchange of information, communication, etc., which enables the team to coordinate individual member efforts to achieve their shared goals. Interaction also contributes to the development of shared mental models about the nature of the task and how it should be performed. In effect they learn to dance the dance of teamwork better, the more time they spend dancing together. Imagine the success of a football team that only met to play together once or twice a year, compared with a team that played together and discussed their performance every week.

Shared mental models can be defined as 'an organized understanding or mental representation of knowledge that is shared by team members' (Mathieu *et al.*, 2005, p. 38). Recent work suggests that it is not just the degree of 'sharedness' of such mental representations of the team task, the team's technology or the team's interactions, but also the accuracy or quality of the underlying model (Edwards *et al.*, 2006). One consequence of team interaction, information sharing and influencing (as we will see) is improved accuracy of such shared mental models.

Case Study

Team interaction

I was once asked to act as a facilitator for a team that provided consultancy services to a large organization. On the first day the team emphasized how effective they were as a team. But after an hour or two of interaction the team had split into two opposing groups in separate rooms, accompanied by strong expressions of anger and hostility. It emerged that the team had not met together for over 18 months and had assumed they shared similar orientations and objectives in their work. In fact, team members were working at cross purposes and, even after two days together, there was still some tension over their differing orientations to the work. This seemed to be due to the surprise of discovering these differences rather than to any intrinsic incompatibility in their work orientations. They assumed they had a shared mental model of their task, their interactions and the team as a whole but, in reality, this was far from the truth.

What this case study suggests is that interaction and meetings are vital for team functioning. Without regular meetings, both formal and informal, important information is withheld and assumptions and expectations may be built up which are not matched by reality. Indeed our research results reveal that even poor team meetings are better than no team meetings at all, since members get to exchange information in small informal dyads or groups before, after and even during meetings (Borrill *et al.*, 2000). Without frequent interaction, team members begin to diverge in their views about what is important for the team, and perceptions and expectations of other team members' actions become more and more inaccurate. Misapprehension and misunderstanding lead to poor coordination and to conflict. These in turn lead to team ineffectiveness. Poor relationships, negativity and suspicion are the product of insufficient interaction and fatally undermine team functioning.

How often should team members meet together? Some teams will need to meet more often than others and meetings between some team members will need to be more frequent than between other team members. The greater the complexity of the task and the time urgency the team faces, the more often teams should meet. Teams should meet *minimally* once a month, in order to update one another on developments and realign their team activities around the team's objectives. At least every six months, teams should take time out (a day or two days) to reflect upon and modify as necessary their objectives, their strategies for achieving those objectives and team processes such as communication and the participation in decision making. Such reflexivity predicts team innovation and effectiveness – far from this being a waste of time, teams that take such time out are more productive and innovative than other teams (Widmer, Schippers and West, 2009).

Poor meetings are better than no meetings at all, but well-conducted meetings create a sense of team potency (a belief that the team will be successful in its activities) and ensure that teams are working effectively together towards achieving objectives. How can we ensure effective interactions in team meetings? The key is how team meetings are chaired.

Chairing meetings

- Arrange meetings with a clear agenda and only include items on the agenda that are important – don't waste time talking about routine stuff that will happen anyway. The choice of items for the agenda is critical – ideally these would be the six or seven team objectives and nothing else. The more time spent thinking through what needs to be on the agenda and in what order the better. The fewer items on the agenda, the more in-depth and productive the meeting will be. Specify the start time and end time of the meeting in advance. Establish a norm of team members arriving on time. Hold the meeting in a location that is comfortable (has windows to see out of, for example), has appropriate equipment (such as flip charts, projector, web-conference facilities as necessary). Ensure there is someone to chair or coordinate the meeting. Rotating chairs is a nice democratic idea but team meetings should be chaired by those who have been effectively trained to chair them. Work out rough timings for topics beforehand, to give a sense of what needs to be covered in what time frames in order to get through the agenda. Stick to the agenda unless absolutely necessary.
- Encourage everyone who may have a view to share their views. Exploring ideas is helpful in decision making and the meeting will usually be more productive (and quicker) than if you suppress discussion. This may seem counter-intuitive but agreement is almost always quicker when everyone has had a chance to contribute. Ensure everyone is contributing during the meeting. Ask for the input of members who you know have expertise on the topic early rather than late to help shape the discussion. Use a variety of ways of encouraging discussion (have people discuss in pairs and small groups and report back). Summarize frequently. Ensure leaders or others do not dominate.
- Once views have been expressed and opinions discussed move efficiently towards a decision. Don't defer decisions unless it is really necessary (e.g., when crucial information is not available), avoid passing decisions

on to other meetings or committees (unless this makes sense in terms of knowledge, skills and positions of the people involved) and setting up sub-groups for more meetings. Avoid or use voting only as an absolutely last resort.

- Keep control of the meeting and maintain a positive climate by being optimistic, warm, polite, enthusiastic and committed to the work of the meeting. Acknowledge and thank people for their contributions. Take time out if things become heated.
- Review the usefulness of meetings at the end and discuss how they could be improved.

Why the emphasis on positivity in this section? Teams that interact in positive ways perform better than other teams. Losada and Heaphy (2004) analysed interactions among 60 business teams that varied in terms of performance. High-performance teams had a ratio of 5.6 positive interactions to each negative interaction in team meetings. For medium-performing teams the figure was 1.9 and for low-performing teams, it was 0.363. Moreover, in high-performing teams the balance of interactions involving advocacy of one's own position versus inquiry about another's position was about one to one (for every advocacy interaction there was one inquiry interaction). In moderately performing teams the figure was 0.7 (there were only 0.7 inquiry interactions for every advocacy interaction). For poorly performing teams the figure was 0.052. In these teams, members spent almost all their time advocating positions rather than seeking information about other's positions.

Box 11   Ground rules for team meetings

Everyone takes responsibility for:

- Keeping us on track if we get off
- Facilitating group input not just pushing your own position
- Raising questions about procedures (e.g., asking the group to clarify where it has got to in a discussion and offering summaries of the issues being discussed to make sure all have a shared understanding of them)
- Using good listening skills: either build on the ongoing discussion or clearly signal that you want to change the subject and ask if that is ok.

Information Sharing

Information in a team context is data which alters the understanding of the team as a whole and/or of individual team members. Managing information flows is therefore essential for team effectiveness, especially in teams engaged in complex task performance such as top management teams, nursing teams or research and development teams.

Information can be rich or poor to the extent that it alters understanding, that is, the more it alters understanding the richer it is. For example, in a changeover of teams in a chemical processing plant, information relating to potentially volatile reactions noted during the previous shift is rich information. It communicates to the team taking over the likelihood of risk. On the other hand, a computer print-out of the number of visits to children under five years of age made by a nurse during the course of one month, may communicate relatively little information to her supervisor, since it provides no indication of the difficulty of the visits or the quality of the work.

The medium of transfer of information is determined by its richness. The least rich information is transferred by paper or electronic mail messages. Slightly richer information is given in the form of telephone conversations or videoconferencing, but information is most richly transferred when people talk face-to-face. Voice inflexion, facial expression, body posture and gestures all add to the richness of information transfer. Moreover, in face-to-face meetings it is possible to ask questions and explore issues in depth. In general, use print and email to exchange information, communicate news and ask questions and always use face-to-face meetings to express concerns, complaints and find resolutions to conflicts. It is irresponsible to use email to attack, harangue or abuse others. Complex decision making is best done face to face – Chapter 13 on Virtual Team Working explores these issues in more depth.

Within teams therefore, the ideal medium is face to face. Of course, there is a temptation to avoid such direct communication since this may take up more time than the team can apparently afford. And many of us experience turgid meetings where little gets done that really makes a difference to organizational performance. However, when meetings are productive, teams still tend to err on the side of email messages and communicate too little face to face. Yet the whole basis of teamwork is communication, coordination, cooperation and transfer of information in the richest possible form. In our work in organizations with teams (www.astonod.com) we find that most teams need to improve information sharing and communication and to change the way they transfer information.

Increasingly, individuals find themselves working within dispersed teams, often with colleagues who live in different countries or in other situations

Case Study

Manufacturing success

Information flows vary enormously, depending upon the organizational settings. On a visit to an innovative manufacturing company in Scotland, I met the Personnel Director who had previously worked in the Civil Service. He told me that it took him a year of working in the manufacturing company to receive the number of written memoranda that he normally received in a week within the Civil Service. Another change was a much higher level of face-to-face communication in the manufacturing company, which led to a much richer understanding. The company was characterized by enormous flexibility, few rules and regulations and a high degree of innovativeness.

that provide little opportunity for informal or regular communication. Such teams need formal, regular communication and meetings where there are opportunities to chat informally or socialize to help increase cohesion and trust. An international computer company which has outlawed 'personal chat' via electronic mail may have saved a minimal amount on time and costs, but they have lost a great deal more through the reinforcement of already pervasive divisions within their international teams.

Virtual teams (e.g., of members distributed across several European countries), which rely on email, videoconferencing and telephone conferences are less effective and innovative than teams that are co-located (Agarwal, 2003). The richness of information transfer and the learning about teamwork are simply much greater among those working in co-located or face-to-face teams. Consequently virtual teams must work much harder to communicate effectively. At a minimum they should meet for some days prior to starting work together to agree team objectives, strategies, and decision-making and communication processes. Because we human beings are hard-wired to read information from faces, the loss of that information source in virtual teams inevitably means they are less effective than they would otherwise be. These issues are explored in greater depth in Chapter 12.

Influencing and Decision Making

A principle assumption behind the structuring of organizational functioning into work teams is that teams will make better decisions than individual team members working alone. A good deal of research has shown that teams

Exercise 5   Information sharing in the team

What information do you currently receive from each team member?

Name of team member	Content of information received	Current frequency (hourly, daily, weekly)	Preferred frequency
1.			
2.			
3.			
4.			
5.			
6.			
7.			
8.			

What information would you like from each team member?

Name of team member	Content of information desired	Desired medium	Desired frequency
1.			
2.			
3.			
4.			
5.			
6.			
7.			
8.			

are subject to social processes that undermine their decision-making effectiveness. While teams tend to make decisions that are better than the average of decisions made by individual members, they may consistently fall short of the quality of decisions made by the best individual member. The implications of this for the functioning of boards and senior executive teams are considerable. Organizational behaviourists and social psychologists have therefore devoted considerable effort to identifying the social processes that create deficiencies in team decision making:

1 Team members must take into account some of the hidden dangers of team decision making. One is the powerful tendency for team members to focus on information all team members share before the discussion starts and to ignore information that only one or two team members know about. Even when this information is introduced, team members are likely to unconsciously ignore it since it is not information they all share. Psychologists call this the **hidden profile** phenomenon and teams can avoid it by ensuring that members have clearly defined roles so that each is seen as a source of potentially unique and important information; that members listen carefully to colleagues' contributions in decision making; and that leaders alert the team to information that is uniquely held by only one or two members (Stasser and Stewart, 1992). It requires vigilance to overcome this phenomenon; even when participants are told about the problem in team meetings, they still fail to take account of uniquely held and important information offered by team members.

2 **Personality factors** can affect social behaviour in various ways. For example, shy team members who are hesitant to offer their opinions and knowledge assertively in team meetings, fail to contribute fully to the team's store of knowledge (Barrick *et al.*, 1998) resulting in poorer decision making.

3 Team members are subject to **social conformity** effects causing them to withhold opinions and information contrary to the majority view – especially an organizationally dominant view (Brown, 2000). Team members will often go along with what the majority think, even when they initially disagree with that position.

4 Team members may lack **communication skills** and so be unable to present their views and knowledge successfully. The person who has mastered impression management, smoothly presenting his or her position, may disproportionately influence team decisions even in the absence of expertise.

5 The team may be **dominated** by particular individuals who take up disproportionate 'air time' or argue so vigorously with the opinion of others that their own views prevail. It is noteworthy that 'air time' and expertise are correlated in high-performing teams and uncorrelated in teams that perform poorly; in high-performing teams experts on an issue tend to have their voices heard when that issue comes up for discussion.

6 Particular team members may be **egocentric** (such as senior organizational members whose egocentricity may have carried them to the top) and consequently unwilling to consider opinions or knowledge offered by team members contrary to their own.

7 **Status and hierarchy** effects can cause some members' contributions to be valued and attended to disproportionately. When a senior executive is present in a meeting, his or her views are likely to have an undue influence on the outcome.

8   'Group polarization' refers to the tendency of work teams to make more extreme decisions than the average of individual members' opinions or decisions. Team decisions tend to be either more risky or more conservative than the average of individuals members' opinions or decisions. Thus shifts in the extremity of decisions affecting the competitive strategy of an organization can occur simply as a result of team processes rather than for rational or well-judged reasons (Semin and Glendon, 1973; Walker and Main, 1973).

9   In his study of failures in policy decisions, social psychologist Irving Janis, identified the phenomenon of **'groupthink'**, whereby tightly knit groups may err in their decision making because they are more concerned with achieving agreement than with the quality of the decisions made. This can be especially threatening to organizational functioning where different departments see themselves as competing with one another, promoting 'in-group' favouritism and groupthink (see Chapter 8). This is especially likely where there is a dominant leader in the team.

10 The **social-loafing effect** is the tendency of individuals in teams to work less hard than they do when individual contributions can be identified and evaluated. Individuals may put less effort into achieving high-quality decisions in meetings, if they perceive that their contribution is hidden in overall team performance (Karau and Williams, 1993).

11 Diffusion of **responsibility** can inhibit individuals from taking responsibility for action when in the presence of others. People seem to assume that responsibility will be shouldered by others who are present in a situation requiring action. In organizational settings, individuals may fail to act in a crisis involving the functioning of expensive technology, assuming that others in their team are taking responsibility for making the necessary decisions. Consequently, the overall quality of team decisions is threatened (Latané and Darley, 1970).

12 The study of brainstorming groups shows that quantity and often quality of ideas produced by individuals working separately are consistently superior to those produced by a group working together. This is largely due to a **'production-blocking'** effect. Individuals are inhibited from both thinking of new ideas and offering them aloud to the group by the competing verbalizations of others (Diehl and Stroebe, 1987).

What role does the team leader play in decision making? There are many situations where teams need leaders. In moments of crisis there may not be time for the whole team to discuss the appropriate course of action in depth. One individual may be required to accept responsibility and take decisions for the good of the whole team. In most circumstances, however, teams can sanction individuals to take the decisions in specific areas of the team's activity. In order to achieve a balance between excessive democracy and authoritarianism, team reviews of decision-making processes should be conducted every six months to a year. The purpose of these reviews should be to determine which team members should take executive decisions on behalf of the team and in which areas.

The stepladder technique for decision making

In order to overcome the problems of team decision making described above, Rogelberg and colleagues (Rogelberg, Barnes-Farrell and Lowe, 1992) proposed a strategy called 'the stepladder technique'. This involves each member of the team presenting his or her views to the team without having heard the views of other team members first. The aim is to build a complete picture of the varied inputs of the team before they consider their collective problem interpretation or decision. This approach can be adapted for electronic use very efficiently given the widespread use of email and shareware. Each team member is given time to think through the particular problem or issue before sending a document to the team presenting his or her views. Each member emails his or her preliminary views about the appropriate course of action before viewing others' preliminary solutions. A final decision is delayed until all members of the team have had an opportunity to present their views and there has been a full and inclusive face-to-face discussion. This approach gives each member of the team time to reflect upon the particular problem in order to prepare his or her case, independent of other team members.

The approach leads to a greater number or range of ideas being presented since conformity processes are minimized. It also inhibits social-loafing effects since individual accountability is emphasized and there is no opportunity for individual members to hide behind others' contributions. Furthermore, because each member is required to present his or her views without the benefit of having heard all the other team members' views, divergent perspectives are more likely to be offered, leading to constructive debate. This improves quality of discussion and decision making. The team is exposed to the continual input of fresh ideas which have not been affected by team norms, and this prompts a more vigorous exploration and evaluation of contrasting ideas. Considerable evidence indicates that such exploration of divergent opinions within teams leads to better quality decision making (Tjosvold, 1998).

Another cause of poor decision making is the tendency to go with the first acceptable solution rather than to generate a range of solutions and then to select the best option (a phenomenon called 'satisficing'). By delaying decision making until every team member has had an opportunity to present his or her views, the number of possible solutions or options available to the team is maximized (Lam and Schaubroeck, 2000).

Exercise 6   A short form of the stepladder technique for decision making

1   Allow 10 minutes – all individuals within the team engage in analysing the problem and coming up with potential problem solutions.
2   Allow 10 minutes – team members work in pairs to present and discuss their respective solutions separate from other team members.
3   Allow 10 minutes – two pairs of individuals present their solutions to each other and discuss the solutions. This process continues until the whole team comes together.
4   The whole team considers solutions presented, final discussions take place and a decision is made. About 40–60 minutes should be allowed for creating the one best solution for the problem.

The stepladder technique is a method of decision making that can overcome some of the problems of team decision making. By enabling members to participate fully, commitment, intrinsic interest, creativity and the input of all members' abilities, knowledge and skills are increased.

In experimental studies, teams often fail to outperform their best individual member in quality of decision making. Because the stepladder technique increases the likelihood of each individual member being heard, opportunities for the best individual member to display his or her expertise are increased considerably. This is important because recent research has shown that unless the best individual member happens to be assertive and dominant, he or she is unlikely to influence team decisions sufficiently. Where expertise and 'air time' are correlated, teams tend to perform well. In poor performing teams 'air time' and expertise tend to be uncorrelated.

How effective is the stepladder technique? Research evidence indicates that there is no difference in the time taken for decision making between teams using the stepladder technique and more conventional techniques. However, the quality of team decision scores is generally significantly better than in conventional teams. Moreover, more than half the stepladder teams exceed their best members' scores, compared with only one tenth of conventional teams.

These statistical findings tell one story, but the impressions of those in stepladder groups reveal further important information. Stepladder group members report feeling much less pressured to conform; tend to agree on the final group decision, perceive themselves as working unusually well together, and perceive the group as more friendly. They also see themselves as having worked harder on the task than do conventional group members. Moreover, there tends to be more questioning of views and ideas in stepladder groups than in conventional groups.

In effect, stepladder groups continually re-make their decisions, and this has beneficial effects on team decision making. It is significant that the most productive members in stepladder groups report that they have more chance to say what they want (more so than any other group members), which suggests that the stepladder approach reveals knowledge and individual expertise to other group members. In other words, better ideas are not only more likely to be expressed, but are more likely to be attended to and recognized as better.

Creating Safety in Teams

It is a truism of human behaviour that commitment, exploration and involvement are most likely to occur when people feel safe. Just as children who have strong and secure bonding with their parents are more likely to explore their surroundings extensively (Ainsworth, 1982), so too are people in teams more likely to take risks in introducing new and improved ways of doing things if they feel they are unlikely to be attacked or denigrated by other team members. The child taken to the park by a parent will be more likely to leave the parent's side sooner and make longer forays into the park if they are securely bonded and attached to that parent. Where children have poor relationships with their parents, they are likely to hover anxiously close rather than explore their new surroundings. In therapy, clients are likely to explore threatening aspects of their own experience when they feel safe from attack and supported by their therapist. It is not for purely ideological reasons that Carl Rogers urged therapists to adopt an attitude of unconditional positive regard for patients. Such an orientation is likely to induce feelings of safety and thereby encourage greater exploration of difficult experiences. Similarly, where the climate in teams is positive, supportive and enabling, team members are more likely to explore and implement new and improved ways of doing their work, thereby promoting innovation and effectiveness. Clarity of goals, regular interaction, appreciation and recognition, humour, backing each other up and openness will all increase the sense of psychological safety in teams.

Where the team is perceived as unsafe, members behave cautiously and maintain a kind of anxious watchfulness in their work. I have seen several top management teams led by dominant managers whose impulse control was poor and who lost their tempers often, attacking other team members.

Box 12   Creating an atmosphere of trust, support
and safety

Team leaders can contribute to an atmosphere of trust, support and
safety in teams by encouraging members to feel engaged, energetic and
enthusiastic about the work. If members of a team start to be dis-
tressed, mistrustful and nervous, then the team climate will mirror
this. To create trust leaders must also encourage team members to take
risks and rely on each other. The best way they can do this is to model
trust themselves. Leaders should specify clearly for the team what they
are required to do and then trust them to find the best ways of achieving that (specify ends but not means). Leaders must provide team
members with support when they want it of course, but must show
clearly that they trust the team to do the job and do it well. Leaders
should encourage team members to take risks with each other too. We
trust when we find we can take risks. Leaders can emphasize that team
members share the same fate; they must trust each other if they are to
achieve the goal. By encouraging open, honest communication between
team members, leaders can help team members to see that they share
the same values in their work.

   Where the team is perceived as unsafe, members behave cautiously
and maintain a kind of anxious watchfulness in their work. For example, if a team member feels she is being criticized constantly by another
team member, she will be less likely to suggest new and improved
ways of doing things. Each team member has a responsibility to promote safety and this responsibility should be agreed early on.

   But safety is not the same as comfort; it encourages risk. You should
therefore build safety by encouraging support and discouraging
threats between team members. If one team member makes others feel
threatened, coach the person and deal with the problem effectively.
Chronic anxiety and anger in your team not only undermine team
safety, they also damage team members' health (Goleman, 1995). You
can build safety by encouraging team members to accept each other,
encouraging humour, warmth and support.

Team were consequently unlikely to suggest new ways of providing
customer services and offering ideas for improving team functioning. Each
team member has a responsibility to promote safety, though the team
leader plays a particularly influential role. This involves encouraging
others to offer their views and then supportively exploring those ideas.

Trust in teams is vital to team members' preparedness to cooperate (Korsgaard, Brodt and Sapienza, 2003).

In a revealing study on safety in teams, Edmondson (1996) found major differences between newly formed intensive care nursing teams in their management of medication errors. In some groups, members openly acknowledged and discussed their medication errors (giving too much or too little of a drug, or administering the wrong drug) and discussed ways to avoid their occurrence. In others, members kept information about errors to themselves. Learning about the causes of these errors, as a team, and devising innovations to prevent future errors were only possible in groups of the former type. In these groups there was a climate of safety developed partly by the leader. Edmondson gives an example of how, in one learning-oriented team, discussion of a recent error led to innovation in equipment. An intravenous medication pump was identified as a source of consistent errors and so was replaced by a different type of pump. She also gives the example of how failure to discuss errors and generate innovations led to costly failure in the Hubble telescope development project (http://ntrs.nasa.gov/archive/nasa/casi.ntrs.nasa.gov/19910003124_1991003124.pdf). Edmondson (1996, 1999) argues that learning and innovation will only take place where group members trust other members' intentions. Where this is the case, team members believe that well-intentioned action will not lead to punishment or rejection by the team. Edmondson argues that safety '… is meant to suggest a realistic, learning-oriented attitude about effort, error and change – not to imply a careless sense of permissiveness, nor an unrelentingly positive affect. Safety is not the same as comfort; in contrast, it is predicted to facilitate risk' (Edmondson, 1999, p. 14).

Safety is the affective context within which people are more likely to engage in effective team working based on trust, acceptance, humour, warmth and support. Together these lead to the involvement, commitment and creativity of team members in team functioning and, equally important, to a positive climate which enhances the mental health of people at work. The next chapter examines what can go wrong in a team even when there are clear visions and objectives, and high levels of participation.

Key Revision Points

- Why is team interaction so important?
- How often should teams meet?
- What are the main information media that teams use and which communicate information best?
- What are some of the main barriers to effective team decision making?
- How can they be overcome?
- How can we build a sense of psychological safety in teams?

Further Reading

Borman, W.C., Ilgen, D.R. and Klimoski, R.J. (eds) (2002) *Comprehensive Handbook of Psychology (Vol. 12): Industrial and Organizational Psychology*, John Wiley & Sons, Inc., Hoboken.

Gold, N. (ed.) (2005) *Teamwork: Multidisciplinary Perspectives*, Palgrave Macmillan, Basingstoke.

Guzzo, R. and Salas, E. (eds) (1995) *Team Effectiveness and Decision Making in Organizations,* Jossey-Bass, San Francisco.

Kozlowski, S.W.J. and Bell B.S. (2002) Work groups and teams in organizations, in *Comprehensive Handbook of Psychology (Vol. 12): Industrial and Organizational Psychology* (eds W.C. Borman, D.R. Ilgen and R.J. Klimoski), John Wiley & Sons, Inc., Hoboken.

March, J.G. (1994). *A Primer on Decision Making,* Free Press, New York.

Mathieu, J., Maynard, T.M., Rapp, T. and Gilson, L. (2008) Team effectiveness 1997–2007: A review of recent advancements and a glimpse into the future. *Journal of Management,* 34, 410–476.

Thompson, L. (2000) *Making the Team: A Guide for Managers,* Prentice Hall, London.

Web Resources

http://ntrs.nasa.gov/archive/nasa/casi.ntrs.nasa.gov/19910003124_1991003124.pdf (last accessed 8 August 2011).
A description of the Hubble Telescope problems.

http://www.foundationcoalition.org/publications/brochures/effective_decision_making.pdf (last accessed 8 August 2011).
A detailed article on effective decision making in teams.

www.astonod.com (last accessed 3 August 2011)
For many resources and guidance on developing team-based working and effective team working.

8

Team Quality Management

The hottest places in hell are reserved for those who, in time of great moral crisis, maintain their neutrality. (Dante)

Have you learned lessons only of those who admired you, and were tender with you and stood aside for you? Have you not learned great lessons from those who braced themselves against you, and disputed the passage with you? (Walt Whitman)

Key Learning Points

- Conformity processes in teams and the dangers of 'Groupthink'
- Team defence mechanisms and how to overcome them
- The value of constructive controversy
- Techniques for encouraging team task focus
- Minority views and dissent in teams

Teams exist to get a job done or achieve a set of objectives. Their principle commitment should therefore be to doing that. In well-functioning teams, inevitably, that means team members will have constructive debates about how best to do the task. Ensuring the team has a task focus and is concerned with ensuring high quality in their processes and outputs is the subject of this chapter.

Effective Teamwork: Practical Lessons from Organizational Research, Third Edition.
By M. A. West. © 2012 John Wiley & Sons, Ltd. Published 2012 by John Wiley & Sons, Ltd., and the British Psychological Society.

So far, we have considered the importance of a clear vision or set of objectives along with high levels of participation in a team. These two elements are necessary but insufficient to guarantee effective team working. There is evidence that these very factors in isolation can be the seeds of disastrous outcomes. Consider the following account as an illustration of how clear objectives and high levels of participation and cohesion may lead to quite the opposite in the effectiveness of teamwork. In 1961, an aura of optimism, enthusiasm and vigour surrounded the United States presidency. President Kennedy and his advisors were young, enthusiastic and had captured the optimism of many Americans with their commitment to civil rights and democracy. However, at the beginning of the presidency, this group characterized by high levels of vision, cohesiveness and participation was responsible for one of the major foreign policy fiascos of the decade. This was the support of the invasion of Cuba in the Bay of Pigs affair. Against much intelligence information that indicated the likely failure of such an adventure, Kennedy and his advisors authorized the CIA to support Cuban exiles in an invasion. The Cuban army easily repulsed the invasion, capturing or killing the exiles. Afterwards many commentators questioned how Kennedy and his advisors could have concluded that the adventure would have been successful (http://en.wikipedia.org/wiki/Bay_of_Pigs_Invasion).

Groupthink

In a revealing analysis of the affair, Irving Janis (1982) came to the conclusion that a dangerous pattern of group processes was responsible. Janis argued that Kennedy's Cabinet was prone to the detrimental effects of 'groupthink'. Groupthink arises where five conditions are present:

1   The team is a highly cohesive group of individuals who are more concerned with their own cohesiveness and unanimity than with quality of decision making.
2   The group typically insulates itself from information and opinions from outside and particularly those that go against the group view.
3   Members of the group rarely engage in any kind of systematic search through the available options for appropriate solutions, choosing instead to go with the first available option on which there is a consensus.
4   The group is under pressure to achieve a decision.
5   One individual dominates the group – this is a particularly important factor in the development of groupthink, especially if it is a dominant leader.

Each of the following is a symptom of groupthink:

- Where the conditions for groupthink exist, a cohesive group will exert strong pressures on dissenting individuals to conform to the view of the majority.
- The group has a shared illusion of unanimity and correctness. Dean Rusk, Kennedy's Secretary of State for Defense, described how there was a 'curious atmosphere of assumed consensus' within the group.
- Members ignore or dismiss cues that there may be dissent within the group. Indeed some members of the Kennedy Cabinet later described how they had felt inhibited from offering ideas or views opposing the Bay of Pigs plan, even when they felt privately that there were major problems with it.
- Group members block information from outside the group. Bobby Kennedy (US Attorney General at the time), described how he had become a self-appointed 'mind guard' to the group, threatening outsiders holding opposing opinions and accusing them of disloyalty to the President.
- Where strong groupthink pressures exist, outgroups are ridiculed as too stupid to be a threat or too untrustworthy to be negotiated with. *'The picture ... therefore, is of a tightly knit group, isolated from outside influences, converging rapidly on to a normatively "correct" point of view and thereafter being convinced of its own rectitude and the inferiority of all other competing opinions (or groups)'* (Brown, 2000, p. 213).

Groupthink consists of the following characteristics:

An illusion of vulnerability;
Excessive optimism and risk taking;
A tendency to rationalize and discount warnings;
Stereotyping of the opposition;
Self-censorship;
Failure to use expert opinion.

All lead to a failure to solve problems effectively because of a need for unanimity and cohesiveness.

Subsequent research has provided some support for Janis' ideas but by no means all. This more recent research suggests that cohesiveness is not an important factor for the emergence of groupthink but that the style of the leader is. Vinokur *et al.* (1985) studied decision making in six conferences of experts and consumers meeting to evaluate new medical technologies. The results suggested that decision making processes and outcomes were not affected detrimentally by group cohesiveness, but that processes and outcomes were poorer if the chair of the meetings did not use a facilitative style. The research evidence seems clear: directive leaders inhibit the expression and exploration of opposing opinions and reduce the quality of decision making by pushing their own points of view too hard. If the job is diagnosing and treating breast cancer, for example, the consequences for the team and those they serve can be disastrous. Peterson and Hunt (1997) added a further piece to the jigsaw of our understanding by showing that leaders who were directive about the decision outcome or ends (trying to achieve team buy-in to their viewpoint) inhibited good team decision making. Those who were directive about processes in meetings, encouraging inputs from shyer and controlling the inputs of the more dominant or unruly members enabled high-quality decision making. What does seem helpful is to discuss how decisions will be made at the start of the discussion, to review the dangers (not discussing unshared information – the hidden profile problem) and to agree some basic ground rules for meetings (see Chapter 7).

Team Pressures to Conform

The effects of group pressures on individuals to conform are well known. In Asch's research (Asch, 1956) participants were shown into a room to join others already there. Those in the room before the experimental participants were, unbeknown to the experimental participants, confederates of the researcher. A series of vertical lines was flashed on a screen and both participants and 'confederates' were asked to determine which of three lines was of the same size as a standard line. These were unambiguous stimuli. On most occasions, the confederates chose the line that equalled the length of the standard line but on a number of occasions they unanimously picked a wrong line. Fully three-quarters of the experimental participants went along with the majority on at least one occasion, even though subsequently they reported having been aware that this was the incorrect line. They indicated that this was due to a desire not to be different from the majority, especially where the majority was unanimous. A number of studies have revealed similar effects that majorities have a powerful influence on the behaviour of people in teams.

Encouragingly, there are individual differences in the extent to which people will go along with the majority. In Asch's experiments, some individuals (25% of those who participated) never went along with the majority, while others conformed to the majority opinion on all occasions. Moreover, the size of the group is important in influencing the majority influence. The results showed that when an individual was confronted with only one person who was responding in an inconsistent manner, he or she was unlikely to be influenced. Under pressure from a majority of three, conformity jumped to 32%, from only 14% with a majority of two (Bond and Smith, 1996). If there was another dissenting person in the group, participants answered incorrectly in only 9% of cases compared with 36% when they were in a minority of one. Moreover, there are cultural differences in the extent to which people will conform (Smith and Bond, 1993); people in collectivist cultures such as China, Japan and Brazil show a greater tendency to conform to the majority than those in individualistic cultures such as the United Kingdom and the United States.

Obedience to Authority

In hierarchical groups, members tend to be obedient to authority. Within teams with a dominant leader, people are likely to go along with the leader rather than assert their own opinions. In a chilling demonstration of this danger, Stanley Milgram examined the extent to which individuals would be obedient to the commands of an experimenter to give electric shocks to an individual learning word pairs (Milgram, 1963, 1965a,b). The person learning the word pairs was, in fact, a confederate of the experimenter who faked the electric shocks. Out of 40 people participating in the experiment, 26 obeyed the orders of the experimenter to the end and continued to give (apparent) electric shock punishment to the learners, up to and beyond the point where they were led to believe that the learners had been severely injured. This was despite the fact that in many instances the individuals administering the shocks were clearly suffering great tension and concern about what they were doing. One observer related:

> I observed a mature and initially poised executive enter the laboratory smiling and confident. Within 20 minutes, he was reduced to a twitching, stuttering wreck that was rapidly approaching a point of nervous collapse. He constantly pulled on his ear lobe, and twisted his hand. At one point, he pushed his fist into his forehead and muttered: "Oh God, let's stop it".

Yet he continued to listen to every word of the experimenter, and obeyed to the end. This research suggests that there are dangers in team settings that can result in conformity and obedience to authority in the face of clear rational evidence against a given course of action.

Team Defence Mechanisms

If we think of a team as somehow a 'living entity' in its own right, it would not be surprising for it to have developed mechanisms to survive in a changing environment. Just like an organism, a team develops an immune system to fight threats to its stability. Often this system is such an integral part of the norms and unwritten rules of the team that it is very difficult to detect. Such team defences are sometimes referred to as 'defensive routines' that are set into motion automatically and without deliberate intention on the part of any individual (Argyris, 1990).

One example of a defensive routine is team members continually blaming the organization or another team or department, senior managers or resources problems, for performance difficulties the team is experiencing. Therefore, regardless of what goes on within the team, such as a failure to deal with one member not doing their work effectively, team members tend to see problems as caused by circumstances outside the team. Team members maintain a superficial cohesion and collude together in not addressing their performance problems. If the job of the team is critical such as (to use the earlier example) to conduct diagnoses of women with breast cancer, the consequences can be disastrous. In one study, we observed an incompetent but dominant and aggressive surgeon make mistakes that he refused to allow the team to discuss. We intervened and persuaded the team and its members to report the problems to the hospital chief executive.

At their best, these defensive routines help protect the team from experiencing unnecessary turmoil. They are, however, designed to reduce pain and embarrassment, and in doing so can inhibit team functioning. Moreover, in trying to maintain the status quo, team members may employ defensive routines that prevent the team from dealing with the root causes of problems. The nature of team defensive routines is that they are undiscussable; and their undiscussability is also undiscussable! Exposing defensive routines is all the more difficult because they are so very hard to detect. People become immensely frustrated at the struggle involved in implementing a clearly sensible innovation, particularly when they are unable to understand why it is proving so difficult and why it arouses so much hostility. The barrier is often a defensive routine.

Defensive routines make the unreasonable seem reasonable, and are often employed in the name of caring and diplomacy. One example of a defensive routine is where team members continually blame the organization, senior managers and resources problems for difficulties that the team is experiencing. Consequently, they maintain a kind of cohesion by colluding together to avoid addressing their own performance problems.

Defensive routines are particularly likely to develop in teams within organizations that have 'blame cultures'. These are places where the reaction to failures, errors or near misses is to search for someone to blame; someone who can carry all the responsibility for the problem. This is not a good environment for learning. Team members should encourage learning by asking '*What* not *who* was the underlying cause of the problem and what

Box 13   Overcoming defensive routines

- Have arguments well thought out; reasons should be compelling, vigorous and publicly testable.
- Do not promise more than can be delivered; others can seize on unrealistic promises to reject what is essentially a good idea.
- Encourage team members to discuss mistakes and discourage blaming. Use mistakes as a means of learning (ask 'what can we learn from this?').
- Always try to look beneath the surface and encourage team members to do the same. Continually ask 'why?' of those who resist the change.
- Surface and bring into the open subjects that seem to be undiscussable, despite the potential hostility this may generate.
- Learn to be aware of when you are involved in or colluding with defensive routines.
- Try to see through the issues of efficiency (doing things right) to the more important questions of effectiveness (doing the right things). Unfortunately, it is probably when team members start asking questions at this level that they meet most resistance.
- Focus on doing the difficult, important tasks that will really make a difference to the team or organization.

can we learn from this about how we work?' Also, they can ask 'How can we change the way we work so that this problem does not occur again?'

Commitment to Quality

How can a team function in ways that minimize conformity, obedience to authority and the effects of defensive routines? By making outstanding performance of the task their first priority and by ensuring appropriate use of structures, strategies, techniques and norms that enable teams to resist these influences effectively. One method described earlier is the stepladder technique for decision making (see Chapter 7). Changing team structure by reducing the influence of hierarchies within the team is key. Below, we explore some of the techniques or orientations that can be adopted to ensure high-quality team performance and decision making.

Task Focus/Constructive Controversy

Task focus refers to team members' preparedness to examine their team performance critically. Dean Tjosvold has coined the term 'constructive controversy' to describe the conditions necessary for effective questioning within a team (Tjosvold, 1998).

Research evidence amassed by Tjosvold and others, suggests that when teams explore opposing opinions carefully and discuss them in a cooperative context, quality of decision making and team effectiveness is dramatically increased (see also West, Tjosvold and Smith, 2003).

> Controversy when discussed in a cooperative context promotes elaboration of views, the search for new information and ideas and the integration of apparently opposing positions. (Tjosvold, 1991, p. 49)

Tjosvold has shown convincingly over a quarter of a century of research endeavour that a lack of constructive controversy can lead to disastrous team decisions. The failure to adequately explore divergent views in a supportive context can lead to decisions such as the Bay of Pigs invasion and the Challenger space shuttle disaster. In the latter case, engineers suppressed controversy over the fact that opinions differed about the appropriateness of flying the shuttle in cold weather. Tjosvold argues that there are three elements to controversy:

- elaborating positions
- searching for understanding
- integrating perspectives.

Elaborating positions. First, team members should carefully describe their positions, explaining how they have come to their decisions in relation to any particular issue the team is discussing, whether it be to do with the team task, the technology, the team's interactions or with the team itself. They should also indicate to what extent they are confident or uncertain about the positions they have adopted.

Searching for understanding. Team members with opposing viewpoints should seek out more information about other's positions and attempt to restate them as clearly as possible. There should be attempts to explore areas of common ground in opposing positions along with an emphasis on personal regard for individuals whose positions oppose their own. This process will lead to greater creativity and outcomes that are more productive.

Integrating perspectives. Team members should encourage integration by working to resolve controversy based on the principle of achieving high-quality team performance in relation to the products, services or functions

Table 3 Constructive controversy.

- Constructive controversy is necessary for:
- Creativity
- Independent thinking
- Quality checking
- Professional development
- Team development.

- *Constructive controversy involves:*
- Exploration of opposing opinions
- Open-minded consideration and understanding
- Concern for integration of ideas
- Concern with high-quality solutions
- Tolerance of diversity.

- *Constructive controversy exists when there are:*
- Cooperative team climates
- Shared team goals
- Members who confirm each other's personal competence
- Mutual influence processes.

- *Constructive controversy does not exist when:*
- Competitive team climates dominate
- Team goals are not primary
- Team members question each other's personal competence
- There are processes of attempted dominance.

they provide. Team members should attempt to influence their colleagues towards a solution based on shared, rational understanding rather than attempted dominance. Finally, members should strive for consensus by combining team ideas wherever possible rather than using techniques to reduce controversy, such as majority voting. Strategies such as voting merely postpone controversy and invite poor decision making. Table 3 shows the conditions within which team constructive controversy can exist.

Encouraging Constructive Controversy in Teams

- Teams can encourage constructive controversy by coaching team members to play with and combine diverse ideas and to explore all team members' views in an open-minded way, so that creative ideas emerge.
- Independent thinking is encouraged by having the team consider all team members' views and suggestions since this discourages the tendency to conform to the majority view.

- Team members should consider all team members' views based on whether their proposals would improve the team's service or the products it provides for customers/clients. They base judgements then on quality, not (for example) on the status of the person proposing the idea.
- Team members should have vigorous and supportive discussions of alternatives since such comprehensive decision making encourages all team members to develop their critical thinking and to learn from each other in the course of teamwork.
- As the team practises these creative, rigorous and open-minded approaches to making decisions and constructively using disagreements, they learn, grow, become more confident in their individual abilities and more skilled in the team dance together. They learn to feel safe and to trust.
- Team leaders can encourage team members to explore opposing opinions by having them carefully describe their positions and explain how they have come to their decisions in relation to any particular issue. Advocates of a position should indicate their level of confidence or uncertainty about their positions.
- Team members with opposing viewpoints should seek out more information about other team members' positions and attempt to restate them as clearly as possible. Team members should search for ways of integrating opposing positions.
- Leaders should coach team members to strive for consensus by combining team ideas wherever possible rather than using techniques to reduce controversy, such as majority voting.
- Team leaders can encourage team members not to focus on winning in the process of making decisions. They should be primarily concerned with making excellent decisions that lead to the best-quality products or services for their clients.
- Constructive controversy does not exist when there are competitive team climates. Team members can alert each other if they seem more interested in winning arguments than finding the best solutions.
- Team goals should be primary – shared objectives should steer the work of the team.
- If team members publicly question their colleagues' competence, destructive arguments about team decisions erupt and quality of decision making suffers. Team leaders should discourage such discussions and, if they feel there is a problem of competence, deal with these issues privately.
- Team members should build cooperative team climates, characterized by trust, supportiveness, safety and a professional approach to work. Leaders can emphasize the team's shared goals because, when team members are aware of their shared goals, they work towards the same

end. This unites them and enables them to use disagreement as a means to better quality decision making.

- Leaders should also encourage team members to communicate their respect for each other's competence and commitment. In this way, they will feel that disagreements do not represent attacks on each other's ability and this will be clear to all.

The team's dance will reflect the extent to which all team members engage, contribute and shape each other's views. All are open to others' reactions to their positions and to having their views shaped or changed by others within the team, regardless (for example) of their status in the team. The team is an arena in which all play, strive and contribute to shaping the team's direction in the interests of their shared vision. In a good sports team, team members talk to each other to encourage better team performance throughout the game.

Devil's advocacy

In order to cope with the potential flaws in his Cabinet's decision-making strategies President Kennedy introduced a number of initiatives. First, he brought alternative and often extreme viewpoints into Cabinet discussions to promote diversity of opinion and more creative decision making. Secondly, he promoted the idea of delaying decisions until they were necessary rather than rushing to first solutions. Thirdly, he appointed someone within the team to challenge quickly and vigorously any decisions considered by the team. Bobby Kennedy, the then Attorney General, was appointed to this position of devil's advocate. He later described how during the Cuban Missile Crisis in 1963, his role was to criticize opinions offered within the team in order to ensure that arguments were carefully examined for strengths and weaknesses. This led, he argued, to better quality decision making and possibly saved the world from an all-out nuclear war between the Soviet Union and the West. The Devil's advocate is the individual within the team whose responsibility it is to challenge arguments and ideas and seek out weaknesses within them. However, research (Nemeth, Rogers and Brown, 2001) suggests that this is worse than having no Devil's advocate. We are impressed and encouraged to think independently only by the courage of a genuine dissenter in a team. When we observe a colleague arguing against the minority view, it encourages us to think independently also. Appointing someone who all know is pretending to disagree with the team's view, can mislead team members into thinking they are genuinely debating issues in a thorough and vigorous way. In fact, such sops to dissent undermine independent thinking and challenging debate. It is the courage of genuine dissent that inspires us to think both more deeply, more divergently and more independently.

Negative brainstorming

Negative brainstorming is a particularly useful technique for promoting task focus and critical thinking in teams. It is useful for testing a new proposal, or for evaluating an existing strategy, practice or objective. The technique has three steps:

Step 1. Once a promising idea has been proposed (or in the case of an existing practice, the practice or strategy has been clearly identified), the team brainstorms around all possible negative aspects or consequences of the idea. This brainstorming should be as uninhibited as positive brainstorming in the classical approach (see Chapter 1). The intention is to generate a list of all the possible negative aspects of the idea or strategy no matter how wild or fanciful these possibilities might appear.

Step 2. Team members choose four or five of the most salient criticisms and examine these in more detail.

Step 3. The team then considers how the idea or existing practice could be modified to deal with each of the criticisms in turn. This third stage of the process is, therefore, essentially constructive in that the team is seeking to build on a new or existing practice in order to counter the major criticisms of it.

It may be that some fundamental weakness or difficulty is identified, which the team sees no way of overcoming. In this case, the idea or the existing practice may be abandoned. However, this is a benefit rather than a disadvantage of the process since it enables teams to identify at an early stage, any idea or approach that is likely to be unsuccessful.

This exercise is useful when an idea has reached the adoption and implementation phase of decision making. In addition to drawing out the weak points of an idea before implementation, it also encourages constructive criticism. People are often afraid of causing offence so they inhibit their criticisms. This approach makes it clear that team members are criticizing ideas and practices rather than people. When it is practised frequently, team members come to accept 'criticizing ideas as a way of improving on them' as good practice.

Stakeholder analysis

This is a useful method for exploring an issue in more depth and improving upon existing and proposed solutions. People in organizations often resist change because they anticipate the change will prevent them from doing their jobs as well as they would like – not because they are opposed to change per se. Teams therefore must put careful and creative thought into considering how any changes they plan might affect others in the organization – or how others in the organization might imagine the changes will affect them. The technique involves the team acting as if they were each stakeholder group in turn, and considering all the advantages and disadvantages arising from team objectives, strategies, processes or proposed changes. Stakeholders are all those interested individuals and teams, both internal and external to the team, who affect or who are affected by the team's objectives and practices. Team members then list all possible advantages and disadvantages in relation to the stakeholder group (see the example on page 00). Then team members modify the proposed objective or change in order to minimize the disadvantages to the stakeholder group and/or maximize the advantages. They do this for every major stakeholder in turn.

By carefully considering the effects upon the various stakeholders, team members can make the final objectives or proposed change more resilient. The technique may also alert the team to conflicts, which they can deal with using appropriate conflict-handling techniques (see Chapter 11).

Box 14   Stakeholder analysis in practice

1   **Proposed change**
    A large healthcare team which has always been run along tradi-tional lines has proposed that it will become an independent prac-tice, more like a self-governing team responsible for its own finances and administration. This proposal constitutes a major shift in team practice and philosophy. Who are the major stakeholders?

2   **Identify stakeholders**
    Patients, patients' relatives and carers, practice nurses, doctors, other staff, the community, professional associations, practice administrators and managers.

3   **Advantages and disadvantages of the change**

    Patients
    Possible advantages: improved speed of service; improved quality of care; improved administration.
    Possible disadvantages: the practice has more concern with money than with patients; competition may lead to poorer quality care.

    Doctors
    Possible advantages: better facilities; quicker decision making; more control over resources.
    Possible disadvantages: loss of medical emphasis; administrators will be more concerned with money than with patient care; special-ist areas and equipment will be neglected in the interests of satisfy-ing large-scale demand.

Practice managers
Possible advantages: more power; better quality decision making; clearer managerial responsibilities.
Possible disadvantages: greater accountability; need to generate income; conflict with hospitals or other independent practices.

4   **Adapting the change**
Having identified potential advantages and disadvantages from the point of view of each stakeholder group, the team then considers how the change can be modified to meet the various concerns, or how the process of change could be managed appropriately to reduce resistance.

Minority group influence in teams

Many people in large organizations believe that they cannot bring about changes that they see as necessary and valuable. The organization is too big and senior figures oppose the change they wish for. Research on minority group influence suggests otherwise. Minority group influence is the process whereby a minority (in terms of number or power) within a team or society brings about enduring change in the attitudes and behaviour of the majority. Exposure to minority group influence appears to cause changes in attitudes in the direction of the 'deviant view', but it also produces more creative thinking about issues, as a result of the cognitive or social conflict generated by the minority. Social psychological research on minority influence therefore has exciting implications for understanding organizational behaviour.

Traditionally researchers have believed that only majorities in teams and organizations can achieve control, usually through conformity processes. Serge Moscovici and Charlan Nemeth, however, have shown how minorities also influence the thinking and behaviour of those with whom they interact (Moscovici, Mugny and van Avermaet, 1985; Nemeth and Owens, 1996). Moscovici argues that minority group influence accounts for the influence on public attitudes of the environmental and feminist movements in the 1970s and 1980s. Repeated exposure to a consistent minority view leads to marked and internalized changes in attitudes and behaviours. When people conform to a majority opinion, they generally comply publicly without necessarily changing their private beliefs, as we saw earlier. Minorities, in contrast, appear to produce a shift in private views rather than mere public compliance. Moreover, some evidence suggests that even if they do not cause the majority to adopt their viewpoints, minorities encourage greater creativity in thinking about the specific issues they raise. They cause us to think more comprehensively and critically about the issues (Martin, Hewstone and Martin, 2007; Nemeth *et al.*, 2001).

Case Study

The manufacturing management team

Loxley Engineering Ltd designs, builds and supplies engineering solutions for a large number of industries. In just over 15 years Loxley Engineering has grown from a start-up company to an employer of more than 300 people with an impressive order book for deliveries in the next few years.

The Loxley Engineering Ltd management team consists of a Chief Executive, Head of Production, HR Director, R&D Director, Finance Director, Sales Director and Director of Quality. It is a well-established, cohesive and supportive team. When data from a questionnaire study which they had commissioned was fed back to them they were pleased with the results, but noticed that, in the commentary, their team was described as having few disagreements, little concern with high standards of performance, low levels of critical appraisal and only intermittent monitoring of colleagues' performance. The team had also voiced anxiety to the facilitator who administered the questionnaire about resistance they were meeting in the company when trying to implement changes.

The management team agreed to look at how they managed criticism and disagreement within the team (team quality management) and resistance outside the team. The facilitator working with them urged them also to consider how they shared information and the ways they monitored their decision making and performance. Team members were surprised at the requests since the questionnaire results had generally shown they worked well as a team. It became clear during the feedback meeting that members' commitment to team loyalty and cohesiveness sometimes overrode finding the best solution to problems. This also accounted for the negative reactions from employees that they encountered when implementing management decisions that had not been thought through carefully enough. Team members agreed to ensure they became more visible on the 'shop floor' and to use feedback from staff to appraise decisions made within the team. They also agreed to debate more thoroughly issues within the team when they had misgivings rather than agree for the sake of cohesion. Team members went on to use stakeholder analysis to step out of their roles as team members and to think more creatively about problems. The method also enabled the team to anticipate and therefore reduce resistance from other staff groups.

In one early study of minority influence, participants were shown blue and green slides and asked to categorize them accordingly. Those in the experimental group were exposed to a minority of people who consistently categorized some blue slides as green. This procedure had no impact on the majority's correct categorizing of the blue slides. However, when members of the majority were subsequently asked to rate some ambiguous 'blue-green' slides, over half identified the slides in a direction consistent with the minority view. A control group which was not exposed to a minority showed no such effects.

Charlan Nemeth suggests that minority influence leads to both creative and independent thinking (Nemeth and Nemeth-Brown, 2003). In one study, researchers exposed participants to a minority of people who consistently judged blue stimuli as green. Subsequently, the same group were placed in a situation where a *majority* incorrectly rated red stimuli as orange (the conformity paradigm described in the section on pressures to conform above). But the experimental group showed almost complete independence and did not differ significantly from control subjects, who made their judgements of the red stimuli alone. Those not exposed to minority dissent beforehand agreed with the majority's incorrect judgement of orange in over 70% of trials. Minorities therefore appear to encourage independence of thinking in those around them (see Nemeth and Owens, 1996 for a review).

In a further study (examining effects on originality), individuals exposed to a minority who consistently rated blue slides as green were asked to respond seven times in a word-association exercise to the words 'blue' or 'green'. Those exposed to a minority judgement gave significantly more word associations and with a higher degree of originality than those exposed to a majority view. Nemeth concludes that:

> This work argues for the importance of minority dissent, even dissent that is wrong. Further, we assume that its import lies not in the truth of its position or even in the likelihood that it will prevail. Rather it appears to stimulate divergent thoughts. Issues and problems are considered from more perspectives, and on balance, people detect new solutions and find more correct answers. (Nemeth, 1989, p. 9)

This positive, optimistic message suggests that where a minority within the team is powerfully committed to a particular change, through persistence, it can achieve greater creativity in team thinking around the issue, albeit at the price of some conflict. In a study of newly formed postal workers' teams in the Netherlands, Carsten De Dreu and I found that minority dissent in teams that were characterized by a high level of participation, were highly innovative (De Dreu and West, 2001).

Conclusion

The exploration of opposing opinions and a concern with excellence are essential elements in team effectiveness without which teams may flounder in mediocrity. Teams that generate such an orientation to their work are more likely to develop a belief in their ability as a team to cope with specific challenges they face – known as team efficacy. Moreover, as a result of continually learning how to work together effectively and achieve outstanding outcomes, they develop a generalized confidence in the ability of the team to cope with whatever challenges are thrown at them – what researchers call team potency. Team efficacy and team potency both predict team performance over time; teams that believe in their ability to get the job done well and that believe in the team's ability to rise to whatever challenges are much more effective, productive and innovative over time. But these are not empty attitudes borne of puffed-up pride. They develop in response to team members collectively wrestling with challenges and finding solutions that provide high-quality outcomes for those the team serves (Gully *et al.*, 2002; Kowlowski and Ilgen, 2006).

With a commitment to quality and excellence in their work, team members can combine their knowledge and skills to create teams that are sparkling fountains of creativity. The next chapter explores these themes by describing the factors that promote creativity and innovation.

Box 15   Bringing about change: a minority influence strategy

1   The minority needs a clear and well-developed vision of the purpose and outcome of the change. This should be a single statement. An attractive, appealing, compelling vision statement will, by repetition, cause others in the team who were initially opposed to the new proposals to think more creatively and openly about the issue.

2   A majority is more likely to accept a minority viewpoint if it is argued coherently and consistently. Therefore, the minority should develop carefully, and repeatedly rehearse, the content of the vision, supporting arguments and plans for implementation of the vision in practice. Moreover, individuals should ensure that they have at least one ally in the team who will also argue the case. Minorities of two are effective. A minority of one will invariably be

ineffective. The greater the degree of unanimity and commitment to the change among the minority members, the more likely is it to be successful.

3   It requires stamina to maintain the change process in the face of frequent setbacks and stiff opposition.

4   In order to manage resistance the minority in the team need to consider carefully all possible objections to the change and build into their arguments ways of responding positively and convincingly. This may mean modifying plans accordingly beforehand (see the section on stakeholder analysis above). Team members should develop convincing and well-rehearsed counter arguments. At the same time, it is important to listen actively to other members of the team and to be seen to listen to their concerns using some of the techniques described earlier in relation to constructive controversy.

5   Information dissemination is also important in the change process since misunderstanding generates much resistance. The minority in a team should ensure they present coherent and convincing arguments to all other team members. They must **prepare, rehearse, present, present** *and* **present** again.

6   If possible the team leader should be committed to and thoroughly rehearsed in the arguments for the change. However, in the absence of support from those hierarchically superior, consistency of argument and repeated presentation is likely to lead to everyone in the team thinking more creatively around the issues over time, though at the price of some conflict in the team.

7   Participation in the change process is the single most effective way of reducing resistance. This may be accomplished by team meetings and sharing of information. It should also be a real attempt to get the views of others in the team about how to accomplish the changes most effectively and what the major obstacles are likely to be.

Key Revision Points

- Why is a focus on high-quality task performance in teams important?
- What are group conformity processes and how do they undermine team performance?
- What is 'groupthink' and under what circumstances is it most likely to arise?
- What are team defence mechanisms and how can teams overcome them?
- What is constructive controversy, why is it necessary in teams, and what conditions in teams support it?

- What techniques can teams use to encourage high-quality task focus and excellence in decision making?
- What is minority group influence in teams and under what conditions will it affect the majority's thinking?
- How could you use minority influence theory to plan a change strategy for your team?

Further Reading

Argyris C. (1990) *Overcoming Organizational Defences: Facilitating Organizational Learning*, Allyn and Bacon, Boston, MA.

Cannon-Bowers, J.A. and Salas, E. (eds) (1998) *Making Decisions Under Stress: Implications for Individual and Team Training*, American Psychological Association, Washington, DC.

Gully, S.M., Incalaterra, K.A., Joshi, A. and Beaubien, J.M. (2002) A meta-analysis of team-efficacy, potency, and performance: Interdependence and level of analysis as moderators of observed relationships. *Journal of Applied Psychology*, 87, 819–832.

Guzzo, R.A., Salas, E. and Associates (eds) (1995) *Team Effectiveness and Decision Making in Organizations*, Jossey-Bass, San Franciso.

Kozwlosksi, S.W.J. and Ilgen, D.R. (2006) Enhancing the effectiveness of work groups and teams. *Psychological Science in the Public Interest, 7*, 77–124.

Martin, R. and Hewstone, M. (eds) (2010) *Minority Influence and Innovation: Antecedents, Processes and Consequences*, Psychology Press, London.

Martin, R., Martin, P.Y., Smith, J.R. and Hewstone, M. (2007) Majority versus minority influence and prediction of behavioral intentions and behavior. *Journal of Experimental Social Psychology*, 43, 763–771.

Moscovici, S., Mugny, G. and van Avermaet, E. (eds) (1985) *Perspectives on Minority Influence*, Cambridge University Press, Cambridge.

Nemeth, C.J., Rogers, J.D. and Brown, K.S. (2001) Devil's advocate versus authentic dissent: Stimulating quantity and quality. *European Journal of Social Psychology*, 31, 707–720.

Nemeth, C.J. and Nemeth-Brown, B. (2003) Better than individuals? The potential benefits of dissent and diversity for group creativity, in *Group Creativity* (eds P. Paulus and B. Nijstad), Oxford University Press, Oxford, pp. 63–84.

West, M.A., Tjosvold, D. and Smith, K.G. (eds) (2005) *The Essentials of Teamworking: International Perspectives*, John Wiley & Sons, Ltd, Chichester.

Web Resources

Bay of Pigs invasion: http://en.wikipedia.org/wiki/Bay_of_Pigs_Invasion (last accessed 10 August 2011).

Challenger space shuttle disaster: http://en.wikipedia.org/wiki/Space_Shuttle_Challenger_disaster; http://ethics.tamu.edu/ethics/shuttle/shuttle1.htm (last accessed 10 August 2011).

Cuban Missile Crisis: http://library.thinkquest.org/11046/days/index.html; http://en.wikipedia.org/wiki/Cuban_Missile_Crisis (last accessed 10 August 2011).

http://www.abacon.com/commstudies/groups/groupthink.html (last accessed 10 August 2011).
Symptoms and solutions to the issue of groupthink in teams.

www.astonod.com (last accessed 3 August 2011)
For many resources and guidance on developing team-based working and effective team working.

9

Creative Team Problem Solving

The most incomprehensible thing about the world is that it is comprehensible. (Albert Einstein)

Key Learning Points

- The difference between team creativity and innovation
- The four climate factors that influence innovation in teams
- The stages of creative problem solving
- Techniques for developing creative ideas in teams

It has become a cliché to speak of rapid change in society. Organizations change with bewildering frequency, as they are privatized, acquired, rationalized, restructured, reorganized or liquidated. One major cause of this rapid change is the external socio-economic environment within which organizations find themselves. Competition has become a global rather than a national phenomenon. Organizations have become international rather than national. Information technology has made our worlds infinitely richer in opportunities and demands. Moreover, the demands of consumers are shifting constantly, as people require new and different commodities and services to meet their needs; populations age and we face the global challenge of protecting our planet from the damage we are doing to it.

Effective Teamwork: Practical Lessons from Organizational Research, Third Edition.
By M. A. West. © 2012 John Wiley & Sons, Ltd. Published 2012 by John Wiley & Sons, Ltd.,
and the British Psychological Society.

Global financial crises have created huge challenges for organizations, nations and economic blocs such as the European Union.

If we lived in a climate where the weather changed constantly from hour to hour, sometimes hot, sometimes wet, sometimes cold, sometimes snowing, we would have to prepare for every eventuality and adapt quickly. We would have raincoats, cool clothes, umbrellas, warm clothes and even the occasional shelter as we made our way around. Similarly, in their rapidly changing environment, organizations need to be highly adaptable. Just as human beings have adapted to their environments by finding new and improved ways of organizing societies and work, so organizations too must be innovative in order to survive.

In response to increasing complexity and change many organizations have made the team the functional unit otf the organization. Instead of individuals being responsible for separate pieces of work, groups of individuals come together to combine their efforts, knowledge and skills to achieve shared goals. Consequently, for organizations to be innovative, teams also must be innovative, adaptable and essentially creative in their response to problems both within their organizations and in the wider environment (Ford and Gioia, 1995; Henry, 2001; Runco and Pritzker, 1999a,b). But how?

Team Innovation

Team innovation is the introduction of new and improved ways of doing things by a team. Creativity and innovation are distinguished in the following ways: creativity refers to new ideas; and innovation (which includes creativity) also requires that creative ideas are put into action, within a team, organization or society. Creativity is the development of ideas; innovation implementation is making them happen in practice. Innovation includes both creativity and implementation therefore.

Figure 1 shows a model of team innovation, which emphasizes the importance of some principal factors examined in earlier chapters (West and Anderson, 1996). The model demonstrates how shared vision, task focus (a commitment to excellence), participative safety and support for innovation, all determine the level of a team's innovativeness. In research in a wide variety of organizations, my colleagues and I have shown how these four factors are powerful predictors of team innovation (West 2002).

Vision/shared objectives

In Chapter 6 we noted that vision partly determines the effectiveness of teams at work. But there is also strong evidence that a clearly stated mission is important in predicting success in innovation. In a major research study

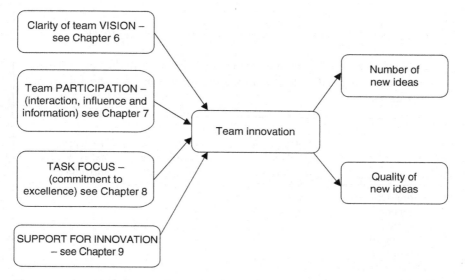

Figure 1   A model of team innovation.

of 418 project teams Pinto and Prescott (1987) found that a clearly stated mission predicted success at each stage of the innovation process, that is, at conception, planning, execution and termination.

Participative safety

High levels of participation mean low resistance to change and high levels of innovation in teams. The more people participate in team decision making through having influence, interacting with those involved in change processes, and sharing information, the more likely they are to invest in the outcomes of those decisions and to offer ideas for new and improved ways of working (Amabile, 1997; Heller *et al.*, 1998). The level of safety in the team is also important, since work team members are more likely to take the risk of proposing new ways of working in a climate that they see as non-threatening and supportive (Edmondson, 1999; Sternberg and Lubart, 1996). There is certainly evidence that amongst teams of scientists, innovation is high when the atmosphere within the team is warm, supportive, but intellectually demanding (Andrews, 1979; Mumford and Gustafson, 1988). Evidence from studies of individuals clearly indicates that positivity (levels of positive emotions) are related to divergent thinking and creativity (Isen, 1993, 1999).

Exercise 7   How innovative is your team at work?

Compared with other similar teams, how innovative do you consider your team to be? Circle the appropriate response for the following task areas:

	Highly stable: few changes introduced		*Moderately innovative: some changes introduced*	*Highly innovative: many changes introduced*
Setting work targets or objectives	1	2	3 4	5
Deciding the methods used to achieve objectives/ targets	1	2	3 4	5
Initiating new procedures or information systems	1	2	3 4	5
Developing innovative ways of accomplishing targets/objectives	1	2	3 4	5
Initiating changes in the job contents and work methods of your staff	1	2	3 4	5
Total score			☐	

Administer this questionnaire to all members of your team and calculate the average level of innovation. If the team scores above an average of 4, team members see the team as innovative. Scores of 3 or below should be considered an indication that the team should be more creative and adaptive. This is also dependent upon the context of the team's work. For example, in a nuclear power plant, highly creative teams would not be a good idea where standard operating procedures should always be followed. Therefore, when analysing the questionnaire it is important to bear in mind the context within which the team is working. In general, however, the level of innovativeness of teams is a very good barometer of their functioning – the better they function as a team, the more innovative they will be.

Task focus or commitment to excellence

In the last chapter, we saw how 'groupthink' and 'process losses' reduce the effectiveness of team performance and team decision making. Similarly, highly cohesive teams may inhibit attempts at innovation if they treat them as threatening deviations from team norms and practices rather than contributions to improving customer or client service. High levels of participative safety alone might lead to reluctance to challenge poor or even potentially dangerous plans for innovation, on the basis that such challenges would represent a threat to the team's warm, interpersonal climate. Indeed, the evidence from research in this area is that minority group influence leads to higher levels of debate but is a major cause of innovation in teams (Nemeth and Owens, 1996). We need to avoid situations in which those who want to introduce innovations in teams see the risk of conflict and so avoid innovation in order to maintain team harmony. That can be accomplished by building a sense of trust and psychological safety.

Task focus or commitment to excellence mean that team members have a shared concern with quality of performance and therefore have systems for evaluation, modification, control and critical appraisal. Improved task focus and commitment to high quality will produce innovation by encouraging diversity and creativity, whilst at the same time ensuring high quality of innovation via the careful examination of ideas proposed (Tjosvold, 1998).

Support for innovation

Levels of team innovation are high when team members expect, approve and practically support attempts to introduce new and improved ways of doing things. Team members may reject or ignore ideas or they may offer both verbal and practical support. What is more difficult to recognize is the underlying lack of support in teams whose members are positive about new ideas but do nothing to help implement them or whose members passively resist their implementation.

Many teams in organizations, as part of their overall objectives, express support for the development of new and improved ways of working, but they do not provide the practical support to enable the ideas to be put into practice. Teams have *espoused theories* (the way that they say they work) and *theories in use* (the way that they actually work) (Argyris, 1978) and where these do not coincide, innovation is less likely.

High levels of both verbal and practical support will lead to more attempts to introduce innovations in teams. Verbal support is most helpful when team members initially propose ideas. Practical support can take the form of cooperation in the development of ideas as well as the provision of time and resources by team members to apply them.

Box 16   The 'yes, and ...' method

People often look for faults in a new idea when it is first raised. This can have the effect of reducing enthusiasm and the preparedness of people to offer new ideas. The 'yes, and ...' method is a way of avoiding the 'no', and 'yes, but ...' traps which are often the end of a new idea. Try saying 'yes', and then building on the idea in a meeting before deciding that it will not work. Try to build on the positive or add your own positive idea to the suggestion. This is a simple but very powerful technique, which, if applied as a rule in departmental meetings, can change the climate substantially. It also enables team members to identify quickly the person who finds it hardest not to slip back into 'yes, but ...' ways.

Some teams have difficulty providing even verbal support for innovation, however. But, if people seem inherently resistant to new ideas then teams are likely to propose only those ideas they feel sure will win support – this usually implies ideas that offer little challenge to the status quo. Minimizing risk by not giving verbal support often means minimizing innovation. A simple technique a team can use to promote support and openness to new ideas in meetings is the 'yes, and ...' method (see above).

Creative Problem Solving in Teams

We tend to think of problem solving as being a single activity, but a good deal of research indicates that there are a number of distinct and important stages. Each requires different kinds of skills and activities. It is therefore useful to distinguish between the different stages, and to use appropriate skills for each. Four well-established stages are problem exploration, developing alternative ideas, selecting an option, and implementing the preferred option:

Stage 1 – Exploration
↓
Stage 2 – Ideation
↓
Stage 3 – Selection
↓
Stage 4 – Implementation

Stage 1 – Exploration

The most important stage of team problem solving is clarifying and exploring the problem. Team members usually begin to try to develop solutions to problems before clarifying and exploring and, if necessary, re-defining the problem itself. But the more time spent in exploring and clarifying a problem before attempting to seek solutions, the better the quality of the ultimate solution. Moreover, the time saved by careful exploration of problems, outweighs the time expended on this task. Problem exploration can take the form of goal orientation or stakeholder analysis (see Chapters 6 and 8). In one company I visited, the team made the fascias for the dashboards of cars, depicting petrol gauges etc. There were repeated imperfections in the fascias and they focused on the suppliers of the photographic materials that went into the fascias for many weeks. Only when a team member began to think creatively did they discover there were imperfections in the water supply they were using to wash the materials, and were able to find a cheap and quick solution (in the form of a water filter) to the right problem. Prior to this they had busy trying to find expensive solutions to the wrong problem.

Stage 2 – Ideation

Having suspended attempts at solution development during Stage 1, the next step is to develop a range of alternative solutions to the problem as defined. When making decisions, teams generally seek for 'one way out'. One idea is proposed and the team goes with that idea, making appropriate modifications as are perceived necessary. Research on team problem solving suggests that it is most effective to begin by generating a range of possible solutions. This is the stage when having a safe climate with verbal support for innovation and using 'yes, and …' responses is particularly important to promote a sense of confidence. Teams can use techniques such as brainstorming (techniques which are described later in this chapter) and it should be a stage which is both playful and challenging, when all ideas are welcomed and encouraged. Yet, despite understanding the ground rules, teams rarely ringfence creative ideation time free from critical evaluation.

Stage 3 – Selection

Next, the aim is to encourage constructive controversy about appropriate ways forward. It is necessary and desirable to be critical and judgemental, but this needs to be done in a way that is constructive and personally supportive. If Stage 2 has generated many solutions, it may be necessary to select the three or four solutions that appear most promising, but it is important to avoid selecting only those which fit the current way of doing things. It can be helpful if at least one potential solution is a completely new way of dealing with the issue. In relation to each idea, a stakeholder analysis and/or a negative brainstorming session can be conducted. These techniques enable people to anticipate the likely reactions of others to proposed solutions. Negative brainstorming also helps to seek out, in a constructive way, all possible defects in the solution suggested, and to remedy these by building on new ideas. Teams should not select a solution simply because it is a solution rather than because it is the *best* solution. In their eagerness to achieve 'closure' and avoid further uncertainty or ambiguity, team members are sometimes too prepared to overlook problems inherent in solutions they have adopted.

Stage 4 – Implementation

Teams that conduct the first three stages carefully, will find that implementation is the least difficult and most rewarding stage of the problem-solving process. During this stage teams should be open to possible teething problems that arise and be prepared to modify the implementation process appropriately. At the same time, they should also manage the implementation stage in a way that ensures that the original idea is implemented rather than weakly watered down when the realities of implementation are faced. Losing the courage of our convictions and going for a compromise is unlikely to satisfy anyone in the team. At the implementation stage, the innovator should gain support in the form of resources, time and cooperation, from others outside the team who may have influence on the effectiveness of the implementation process. Key to this stage is persistence in implementing change completely and successfully. For example, a Human Resources Management team that implemented an appraisal system reported their success in ensuring that more than 90% of staff had appraisals in the previous year. However, when I and colleagues gathered data on the appraisal process from employees, only 30% of them reported having an appraisal meeting that was of any help to them. Ensuring implementation is carried through effectively and achieves the aims of the original initiative is vital. This takes courage for the team to be persistent.

These then are four distinct stages of problem solving. Next we explore techniques which teams can use at each of these stages of creative problem solving (see VanGundy, 1988; West, 1996).

Techniques for Promoting Creativity within a Team

Creativity and innovation techniques

These techniques are simply aids and are not themselves magical sources of solutions. Creativity is 95% hard work and 5% serendipitous discovery. Therefore, when teams use these techniques, members should put in a good deal of effort to see how the ideas they generate can help practically in dealing with the challenges the team faces. What will not work is a passive approach that assumes the right answers will just appear as a result of using the techniques.

These creativity techniques provide new and different ways of looking at the issues that teams face, and wild, 'off-the-wall' alternatives to existing methods of dealing with challenges.

Technique 1 – classical brainstorming
In classical brainstorming (sometimes called 'idea showers'), group members produce as many ideas as possible, even Utopian or fantastic ideas. The aim is to produce a large quantity of ideas, not necessarily to worry about quality. Judgements are suspended and participants accept all ideas offered. Group members try to use each other's ideas to stimulate more ideas that are new (called 'piggy-backing'). So the essential guidelines are:

- quantity of ideas
- judgements suspended
- piggy-backing.

The best way to conduct brainstorming is to give team members an opportunity to generate ideas alone or silently before sharing them with the rest of the team. At this point piggy-backing can occur. The advantage of everyone sharing their ideas is that it produces fruitful social interaction, and gives team members the ownership of participation and involvement in the generation of new ideas for change. It is also valuable to encourage new wild, different ideas in the brainstorming process, rather than brainstorming simply within the current paradigm of the team. Above all, there should be an element of fun in brainstorming. It is sometimes the wildest, craziest ideas, which contain within them the seed of a very different and productive new approach to the task or issue that the team is facing. The person who threw in the idea of a texting facility to the mobile phone concept had no idea that it would prove to be such a huge success in terms of usage.

Technique 2 – brainwriting pool
This technique is a variant of classical brainstorming which builds on the superior performance of individuals over groups in brainstorms (see Chapter 1) and has the effect of generating very large numbers of ideas, within a short space of time. Team members, seated around a table, have blank sheets of paper with space to record ideas. After generating five or ten ideas, team members place the sheets in the middle of the table. Each member then continues writing more ideas on the sheets filled in by other team members. They are urged particularly to piggy-back upon the ideas that others have already developed. A session of 20 minutes can produce literally hundreds of ideas from within

a team. There is little redundancy because all participants can see the ideas produced by others. Furthermore, team members, while receiving stimulation from the ideas of other members of the team, can proceed at their own pace.

This is a system that teams can use when members find it difficult to get together at the same time. Ideas sheets can be circulated over shareware or email and added to over a period of days. 'Brain-netting' involves setting up a file in a network system to which all team members have access. The problem or issue is headlined at the top of the file and then team members simply add their ideas or suggestions to those of their colleagues within the file. Team members do not need to be together to conduct the brainstorm of course and they all have a record of the outcomes of the process.

Technique 3 – negative brainstorming
This technique has been described fully in Chapter 6 and can be used very effectively to improve creatively on existing or proposed objectives, strategies, work methods or processes.

Technique 4 – goal orientation
The goal orientation technique is useful at the problem exploration and clarification stage and involves critically examining and challenging targets and goals. It can also be used for re-examining the ways in which problems and ideas are defined. This is invaluable in encouraging team members to identify and challenge basic assumptions that are often taken for granted. The approach leads to the framing of new targets and goals, and there are usually many more than were originally identified by the team. The formula of preceding goals with the words 'how to …' 'I wish …' is helpful for clarifying goals. Try to list as many 'how to …' and 'I wish …' as possible. Then the team should decide which are the most desirable, important, necessary, creative, visionary, practical, attainable, etc. and begin to develop practical action plans to try to achieve them.

Example. How to deal with traffic jams:
   How to reduce the number of cars on the road.
   How to get bigger roads.
   I wish we could get rid of traffic altogether.
   How to get instant teleporting.
   How to stop travel.
   I wish we could shrink cars.
   How to control traffic flow.
   How to get lots of people in each vehicle.
   I wish we could coordinate travelling plans.
   How to always go by plane.
   I wish I could hitchhike safely everywhere.

Table 4   Table of elements: A novel social event.

People	Place	Activities	Time	Purpose
Team members	Restaurant	Raise money for charity	Weekend	Learning to swim
Team members and partners	Park	Get to know each other	Friday evening	
Children only	Boat	Have a good time		
Team members and customers	Paris	As a reward		
Handicapped children	Bahamas	Treasure hunt		
Partners only	Motorway	Learn new language		
Team members' pets	Beach	Play golf		
	Swimming pool Hotel Theatre	Play tennis		

Technique 5 – table of elements
The table of elements is a technique for breaking a problem or issue down into a set of elements or components, brainstorming within each, and then choosing from among the various components, those ideas that seem most promising or creative in taking the team forward. It generates an enormous number of potential solutions to a problem in a very short space of time. It is only suitable for problems or issues that can be broken down into components and elements.

Example. The team has to come up with an idea for a novel social event that will bring people together for a good time outside work. The elements of this problem could be identified as: the people who will come to the event; where the event will be held; what activities will take place; when the event will be held; what the purpose of the event will be. The team then brainstorms ideas under each of these elements, or headings (see Table 4). The next stage involves choosing potentially wild or promising ideas from among the many combinations of possibilities generated by the table of elements. In this exercise, it is worth throwing in quite different ideas within each part of the brainstorm in order to enable team members to break out of existing ways of thinking. Participants can also choose an array of items from within the elements purely at random (i.e., stick a pin in each column to produce a novel combination). Inevitably, such strategies generate solutions that may appear outlandish or nonsensical at first sight. The purpose of these exercises is, however, to stimulate new ways of looking at problems and this provides 5% of the creativity. The other 95% comes from the team in seeking to make the wild idea into a workable option.

For example, if the following items are selected:

– *children only*
– *Bahamas*
– *treasure hunt*
– *weekend*
– *learning to swim*

it is possible to combine them into the following more practical solution:
At the social event at a swimming pool, an activity especially designed for the children of team members could be arranged (children only). It could involve a game of pirates (learning to swim), looking for gold tokens (treasure hunt) on a treasure island (Bahamas).

The process of using the table of elements takes only 10 or 15 minutes to complete, but can generate literally tens of thousands of ideas within that time.

Technique 6 – stakeholder analysis
This is described in Chapter 8 and is a way of thinking through change proposals or team objectives from the perspectives of those principally affected by the team's work. It can provide valuable direction for teams in modifying change proposals or objectives appropriately.

Using Creativity Techniques in Team Meetings

It takes courage to use these creativity techniques in team meetings. As in response to any new idea some team members may respond with only half-hearted support, others will ridicule, and still others with outright resistance. All creativity and innovation involves taking risks and, if the team is persistent and confident in introducing the techniques, they will work. It is rather like jumping off a high diving board: you have to have a go at it and take the plunge. In teams, you have to keep trying in order to develop skill and confidence in using new techniques. Using these techniques makes team meetings much more productive and far more engaging than the typical round of what are pejoratively referred to in organizations as 'meetings, bloody meetings'.

It is helpful also to string together a number of these creative techniques. How this is done is itself an opportunity to be creative. Remember the importance of the four steps of problem solving mentioned above when putting a team session together, that is, exploration, ideation, selection, and implementation.

Think carefully about how to use time in team meetings and which creativity techniques to try. You should allocate sufficient time for each technique so that the team is neither too rushed nor too bored during their application. Make sure the team has a facilitator (you or someone else) who understands the use of the techniques and does the job of a facilitator rather than dictates or controls. There should also be appropriate and sufficient materials for recording ideas, such as flip charts and overhead projectors.

In recording people's ideas in a team, the facilitator should write exactly what the individual has said (whenever possible). It is appropriate occasionally to paraphrase a particularly long contribution, but only with the agreement of the individual who has made the proposal. Check the wording with them and see that they are happy with what you have produced. Try to note every contribution, especially those that are humorous or throw-away comments, since they can be a good source of creative ideas. To help create the right sort of climate in a team for creativity agree some ground rules before getting started. You can write these on a flip chart to act as a reminder throughout the session.

Ground rules will vary according to the particular aims of the team. A typical set of ground rules for a creative session might well include:

- be concise
- show interest and support
- jot down all stray thoughts
- suspend judgement
- say 'yes, and ...', rather than 'yes, but ...'
- take risks – include the unusual and strange.

If the flow of ideas is drying up, try taking a creative break from the problem. There are numerous ways of doing this, such as word-association games, going out for walks, story telling, etc.

Other Influences on Team Innovation

Teams do not exist in isolation and multiple factors determine the creativity and innovativeness of teams. Extensive research indicates that the climate of the team – vision, participative safety, task focus and support for innovation – principally determines the level of team innovation (West, 2002). But other factors are also important. Box 17 describes how, taking account of relevant research into these other influences, you can facilitate creativity and innovation in your team.

Box 17   Fostering team creativity and innovation

There are a number of simple steps you can take to encourage creativity and innovation in your team. The first is to **decide together to be a creative team.** The decision to be creative and support creativity in the team is a major step. Then **recognize that creativity and innovation are not easy** and encourage team members to be aware of this. People resist change very often in organizations so conflict is a common characteristic of innovation. Questioning the person who comes up with an idea too closely, joking about the proposal (even in a light way), or simply ignoring the proposal may well lead to the person feeling defensive, which tends to reduce their creativity and that of everyone else in the group. To ensure your team is creative **select diverse people with diverse experience and knowledge.** Innovation requires diversity of knowledge bases, professional orientations and disciplinary backgrounds. Their diverse perspectives can lead to radical innovations. This also requires a high level of integration. The members of your team have to be clear about and committed to their shared objectives. And they need to participate in decision making effectively. It is important that you **build a supportive team.** We think creatively when we feel free from pressure, and when we feel safe and positive. Experimental manipulations of stress levels have shown that higher levels of stress lead to greater reliance on our usual solutions and much less creative thinking (Claxton, 1998 a,b). When we feel positive emotions we are both more creative and more cooperative. So create a positive emotional environment. Paradoxically, you must also **challenge the team.** Teams innovate (i.e., they implement their creative ideas in practice) when they are under pressure (West, 2002). The assertion that 'necessity is the mother of invention' is based on sound understanding of human behaviour. So make sure the team task is truly challenging and stretching and constantly encourage team members to feel the team can accomplish the task. **Emphasize team creativity not just productivity.** That way people will learn that you really do value creativity. But also **make team members stop work** in order to be creative. Your team needs to stop work from time to time (at least every six months) in order to remind themselves or discover what it is they are really trying to achieve, and to review the ways the team is going about the task. Then they can reaffirm or change direction, improve ways of working and generate more ideas for new and improved services for clients. Reflexivity is a powerful process for promoting creativity and innovation.

Exercise 8 How innovative are you at work?

The following questionnaire explores your feelings about innovation
and change at work. How far do you agree or disagree with the
following statements (indicate the appropriate number)?

	Strongly disagree 1	Disagree 2	Not sure 3	Agree 4	Strongly agree 5
I try to introduce improved methods of doing things at work.	[ ]	[ ]	[ ]	[ ]	[ ]
I have ideas which significantly improve the way the job is done.	[ ]	[ ]	[ ]	[ ]	[ ]
I suggest new working methods to the people I work with.	[ ]	[ ]	[ ]	[ ]	[ ]
I contribute to changes in the way my team works.	[ ]	[ ]	[ ]	[ ]	[ ]
I am receptive to new ideas which I can use to improve things at work.	[ ]	[ ]	[ ]	[ ]	[ ]

The average score for 250 employed males and females on this
scale was 19.0. If you score 20 or over you have a high propensity
to innovate. Take the average score for your team to determine
whether your team has a high or low propensity to innovate. If the
average score is high, it is more likely the team will produce creative
ideas.

This chapter has examined ways in which teams can promote innovation
and creativity in order to remain adaptable and effective within their organizations. In one study of over 2000 male and female British managers, we
found that the vast majority had introduced new and improved ways of
doing things when they changed jobs (Nicholson and West, 1988). They

changed the objectives of their jobs, the methods, scheduling, practices and procedures, and even the people they dealt with and how they dealt with them. It is significant that in the job-changing process, people moving into existing jobs are highly innovative – moulding and improving the jobs to fit their way of doing things. Moreover, people who have the opportunity to be innovative at work, introducing new and improved ways of doing things, are far more satisfied with their jobs than those who do not have such opportunities. It was a remarkable finding in the study that, among those who took a job move leading to reduced opportunities for innovation, the negative effects upon their mental health were greater even than amongst those managers and professionals who had become unemployed.

The opportunity to be creative and innovative at work is central to our well-being (Marmot *et al.*, 1999). Having our need to be creative and innovative met is a major source of satisfaction for us at work. Teams have an overwhelming influence on the extent to which people are able to be creative in their workplace; a team climate supportive of innovation is crucial (Oldham and Cummings, 1996). It is through attention to creating a climate in which people are clear about their objectives, have a sense of safety with their fellow team members, experience high levels of participation, and emphasize quality in the work, that the individual desire to innovate is translated into practical team outcomes, which promote both team effectiveness and team member well-being.

Key Revision Points

- What are creativity and innovation?
- Which four climate factors most influence team innovation?
- What are the four stages of creative problem solving and which should demand most attention?
- What techniques can a team use to develop creative ideas?
- How could you use these in practice in a team meeting?
- What should a team leader do to encourage team creativity and innovation?

Further Reading

Amabile, T.M. (1997) Motivating creativity in organizations: On doing what you love and loving what you do. *California Management Review,* 40, 39–58.
Claxton, G. (1998) *Hare Brain Tortoise Mind – Why Intelligence Increases When You Think Less,* Fourth Estate Ltd, London.

Claxton, G. and Lucas, B. (2004). *Be Creative: Essential Steps to Revitalize Your Work and Life,* BBC Books, London.

Ford, C.M. and Gioia, D.A. (eds) (1995) *Creative Action in Organizations: Ivory Tower Visions and Real World Voices,* Sage, London.

Paulus, P.B. and Nijstad, B.A. (2003) *Group Creativity: Innovation Through Collaboration,* Oxford University Press, Oxford.

Runco, M.A. and Pritzker, S.R. (1999a) *Encyclopaedia of Creativity, Vol. 1, A–H,* Academic Press, London.

Runco, M.A. and Pritzker, S.R. (1999b) *Encyclopaedia of Creativity, Vol. 2, I–Z,* Academic Press, London.

Thompson, L. and Choi, H.S. (eds) (2006) *Creativity and Innovation in Organizational Teams,* Lawrence Erlbaum, Mahwah, NJ.

Web Resources

Developing Innovation in Teams, at
http://rapidbi.com/management/team_innovation/ (last accessed 11 August 2011).

www.astonod.com (last accessed 3 August 2011)
For many resources and guidance on developing team-based working and effective team working.

10

Team Support

False friendship, like the ivy, decays and ruins the walls it embraces; but true friendship gives new life and animation to the object it supports. (Richard Burton)

Key Learning Points

- The importance of emotions in understanding teams
- The four social dimensions of team working
- The four types of social support and how they affect team members
- How teams can support members' growth and development
- How to build a positive social climate

The fundamental human drive and pervasive motivation to form and maintain lasting, positive and significant relationships helps us to understand the functioning of teams at work, and in particular the emotions manifested in work groups. Satisfying this need to belong, according to Baumeister and Leary (1995), requires that all our important relationships (including those in our primary work teams) are characterized by:

- frequent interaction
- a sense of stability and continuity

Effective Teamwork: Practical Lessons from Organizational Research, Third Edition.
By M. A. West. © 2012 John Wiley & Sons, Ltd. Published 2012 by John Wiley & Sons, Ltd., and the British Psychological Society.

- mutual support and concern
- freedom from chronic conflict.

Most current research and theories about the functioning of teams fail to take account of the solid evolutionary basis of our tendency to form strong attachments and by extension to live and work in groups. Human beings work and live in groups because groups enable survival and reproduction. By living and working in groups early humans could share food, easily find mates, and care for infants. They could hunt more effectively and defend themselves against their enemies. Individuals who did not readily join groups would be disadvantaged in comparison with group members as a consequence. The need to belong, which is at the root of our tendency to live and work in groups, is manifested most profoundly in the behaviour of children and infants. Children who stuck close to adults were more likely to survive and to be able to reproduce, because they would be protected from danger, cared for and provided with food. And we see across all societies that when there is danger, illness or the darkness of night, people have a desire to be with others. This is a clear indication of the evolutionary protection offered by group membership. Adults who formed attachments would be more likely to reproduce and adults who formed long-term relationships would stand a greater chance of producing infants who would grow to reproductive age.

> Over the course of evolution, the small group became the basic survival strategy developed by the human species. (Barchas, 1986, p. 212)

This fundamental human motivation to belong therefore shapes much human behaviour and for our purposes helps to explain emotional reactions in teams. The absence of one or more of the characteristics of belongingness (frequent interaction, continuity and stability, mutual support and concern, and freedom from chronic conflict and negative feeling) will lead to at best weakly cohesive teams and at worst conflict and disintegration. Our tendency to concentrate on task characteristics and organizational contexts often blinds us to these fundamental socio-emotional requirements of team-based working. For the benefits of team working are both improved task performance and emotional well-being for team members (Carter and West, 1999). Indeed, a recent review of all published studies on team working and attitudes, including satisfaction, commitment and cohesion, suggests a consistent pattern of positive associations between teamwork and psychological variables (Rasmussen and Jeppesen, 2006). Moreover, the greater the interdependence between team members and the wider the autonomy of the team to do its work in its own way, the more positive are the psychological consequences.

By recognizing the influence of the need to belong upon the behaviour of individuals in teams we can come to understand something of the range and underlying causes of emotions in teams. Being accepted, included and welcomed in the team will lead to feelings of happiness, elation, contentment and calm. Being rejected, excluded or ignored will lead to feelings of anxiety, depression, jealousy or loneliness. Team members' emotional reactions are stimulated by real, potential or imagined changes in their belongingness within their work team. Real, potential or imagined increases in belongingness will lead to an increase in positive individual and team-level affect. Decreases in belongingness will be associated with threats to the individual and a sense of deprivation that will lead to negative emotions.

Teams play important roles in enabling people to cope with everyday work challenges and in providing the social and emotional support that contribute to the quality of our lives, both at work and more generally. In our research, we have found that people working in teams are less stressed than those working alone, or in looser groupings (e.g., departments) (Carter and West, 1999). There are important differences too in the job-related mental health of those who undertake demanding and monotonous tasks between those who do and do not have opportunities for social contact with work colleagues through the day. Those who can chat to and joke with other workers suffer fewer problems of job-related mental health than those who, because of noise or the design of their jobs, are unable to enjoy conversation with those around them (Cohen and Wills, 1985; Ganster, Fusilier and Mayes, 1986; Manning, Jackson and Fusilier, 1996). Team support is therefore an important element in conceptions of team effectiveness. Moreover, the better the functioning of the team (in relation to the four climate factors we described in the previous chapter), the less stressed are team members.

The Emotional Life of Teams

When a new work team is formed, team members experience positive emotions and it is a cause for celebration. When new members join teams too there can be positive emotion and warm expressions of welcome. Team members can encourage this by ensuring there are rituals to welcome new members. Encouraging two-way relationships in teams is helpful since satisfaction in relationships is a consequence of both the costs as well as the rewards of team membership. One-way relationships in which we only give or only receive are uncomfortable for us; we are happier in teams in which all members both give and receive support (Baumeister, Wotman and Stillwell, 1993).

What about negative emotions? Our basic anxiety results from a millennia-old feeling of being isolated and helpless in a potentially hostile world. Not surprisingly then, we get anxious at the prospect of losing our relationships or at threats of social exclusion. Frequent member changes and threatened dissolution of the team cause anxiety. High levels of conflict also produce anxiety since team members are likely to develop a tense watchfulness in anticipation of conflict. Team leaders can minimize anxiety by ensuring stability of team membership and by resolving conflicts early. If the team has to disband, they can prepare team members in advance and mark the ending with a celebration of the team's success.

Team members feel jealous when they feel excluded by, or are less in the favour of, a particularly powerful or attractive team member – especially if it is the team leader. Team leaders should give attention and support to all team members and not just those they feel personally compatible with or who they feel are most competent (see Box 18 on Team Leader–Member Exchange). Loneliness in contrast is not simply a result of lack of contact with others. There are no differences in levels of social contact between those who are lonely and those who are not (Williams and Solano, 1983). The crucial factor is spending time with the people you are close to. Team

---

Box 18   Team leader–member exchange

This approach describes the different kinds of relationships that may develop between a team leader and followers and what the leader and the follower give to and receive back from the relationship. The model proposes that leaders have different reactions to different followers (Graen and Cashman, 1975). When the leader has team members with whom they get on well or who are similar to them (personal compatibility) or team members who they perceive to be competent, they both trust and spend more time with them than they do with other team members. The reverse applies to those who are perceived as less compatible or competent. Not only do leaders spend less time with them, they also have more formal relationships with them. Team members know very well which group they are in – the 'in-group' or the 'out-group'. The attributions of leaders to members of these different groups are systematically different. The successes of in-group members are attributed to their ability or hard work while their failures are attributed to situational or environmental factors. The reverse is true for out-group members. In-group members are trusted with the more interesting assignments and desirable tasks, are given more information and are taken into the leader's confidence much more. How can a team leader therefore correct performance deficiencies apparent amongst team members in ways other than adopting favourites (summarized by Yukl, 2010, pp. 243–246):

- Gather information about performance problems rather than jumping to conclusions about employees' motivation or competence;
- Try to avoid attributional biases that assume the problem lies with the person rather than the situation;
- Provide corrective feedback as soon as possible after the performance problem becomes apparent;
- Describe the problem briefly to the person;
- Explain the consequences (for the team, customer, organization) of the performance problem;
- Be calm and professional rather than angry, resentful or embarrassed;
- Work together with the employee to try to identify the reasons for the problems in performance;
- Invite suggestions for ways of correcting the performance problem;
- Express confidence in and support for the employee;
- Show a sincere commitment to helping the person;
- Agree on the steps forward to correct problems;
- Summarize and agree the content of the discussion.

(Adapted from Woods and West, 2010)

members who work in multiple teams or short-lived project teams will have many social contacts, but may feel lonely because they cannot develop close ties. They should be encouraged to have a 'home team' where they spend more time, get more social support and discuss their learning needs.

Team members can best manage emotions in teams by providing each other with strong social and emotional support. Below we examine the three principal social dimensions of team working: social support, support for growth and development and social climate. Each of these dimensions contributes to team member well-being and long-term team viability, as indicated in Figure 2.

Social Support

There are four main types of social support: emotional, instrumental, informational and appraisal, and we need to distinguish between verbal and enacted support.

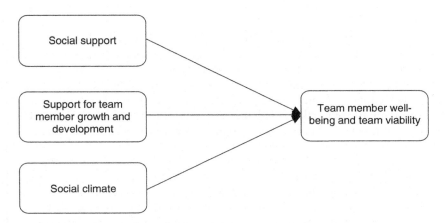

Figure 2 The social dimensions of team working. All these factors contribute to team viability and team member mental health.

Emotional support

This is the kind of social support that we most readily identify. It is the notion of a shoulder to cry on, an encouraging word and sympathetic understanding of another's emotional pain:

Case Example

Louise, a nurse, had been visiting one particular family on an intensive basis. The family had a baby, Jonathan, who was at some risk of cot death (sudden infant death syndrome). On Tuesday morning, she arrived in her office to discover that baby Jonathan had been rushed to the Accident and Emergency Department in the early hours of the morning, only to be pronounced dead on arrival. The child had all the classic signs of sudden infant death syndrome.

Louise was shocked and upset and immediately called her manager to inform her of the tragic event. Her manager listened briefly to what Louise had to say, then carefully informed her of the steps that she must take to inform the local Health Authority and advised her of the importance of writing up her notes very quickly. The manager told Louise that they would get a chance to talk again in a couple of weeks when she next visited Louise's locality. Louise put down the phone and felt a mixture of grief and frustration. Her grief and emotional burdens were unchanged. On the contrary, they were heavier and complicated by a frustration with her manager demanding immediate bureaucratic action in response to the event.

One of Louise's colleagues then arrived in the office and knowing how frequently Louise had been visiting Jonathan and his family, said she sympathized, acknowledging how terribly upset Louise must feel about the event. Louise then began to cry and her colleague put an arm around her in comfort.

Later in the day they met to talk again and the colleague, by listening and being supportive, enabled Louise to talk about her own feelings of guilt that she had not done enough to prevent the cot death. Louise felt guilty at not being more assertive in insisting that the baby was admitted for observation and nutritional support. By expressing the guilt and discussing the feelings with her colleague over the ensuing weeks, Louise was able to work through these feelings and cope.

Here is an example of a colleague providing emotional support both immediately when the support was most urgently needed, and on a continuing basis. Emotional support involves being an active, open listener. It does not involve giving advice or direction, rather it is simply providing the space within which people can express their emotions. It also involves a sense of caring towards the person receiving the support. Louise's colleague understood the grief she must feel and enabled her to express that by acknowledging it openly, placing her arms around her and giving her permission to cry. Finally, the colleague offered the opportunity for continued emotional support rather than withdrawing too swiftly.

To what extent should team members provide emotional support for non-work-related difficulties such as marital difficulties, death in the family, illness, or financial problems? If a colleague is experiencing emotional difficulties related to their lives outside work, it is often desirable and necessary that team colleagues should provide support. But a line has to be drawn between team members offering appropriate and valuable emotional support to colleagues and delving inappropriately into one another's private lives without invitation in ways which might undermine work relationships. There is no simple rule since it depends very much on relationships between team members and the particular circumstances in which people find themselves. Involvement in a team member's personal life should only happen where there is a clear invitation or request from that team member. Sometimes colleagues at work can appear somewhat predatory in their desire to involve themselves in the emotional lives of those around them. This can be destructive for individuals as well as potentially damaging to working relationships. Remember, the primary purpose of the team at work is to complete a task, do a job, achieve its objectives. When building relationships becomes the primary focus, the team is likely to fail its clients and customers, and may well end in interpersonal conflict.

There are some emotional difficulties that require professional help. Where a team member is frequently or deeply depressed; where problems of drug abuse or alcoholism are evident; or where an individual appears suicidal, team members should recommend to such colleagues that they seek professional advice and help. It is important that team members know the limitations of their competence in providing emotional support rather than attempting to provide professional counselling. Many organizations now employ the services of a counsellor or a counselling agency, however, and these should usually be a first rather than a last resort.

Informational support

Social support is not only about being warm, empathic and caring. It is also about doing practical things to aid team members:

Case Example

Sarah, the nurse in a healthcare team, is responsible for regularly checking up on David, a 12-year-old anorexic boy. But as she was becoming increasingly anxious about David's weight loss and depression, she went to speak with Kate, one of the doctors. Kate was sympathetic and listened attentively to Sarah's anxieties. At the same time, she advised Sarah to contact the Atkinson Morley Hospital in London, which specialized in the treatment of eating disorders. Kate suggested that Sarah talk with the head of the relevant department at the Hospital to see whether the child should be admitted. Sarah was able to use Kate's information about the name of the hospital, the specialist and their telephone number in order to make contact and get expert advice. As a consequence, Sarah's anxiety was somewhat relieved and she was given practical means for aiding David in his illness.

In this case, informational social support has valuable consequences. The extent to which team members provide each other with informational support of this kind is an important element in the overall social supportiveness of the team.

Instrumental support

Instrumental support refers to the practical, 'doing' support that team members offer to one another.

These are all examples of instrumental support where one team member provides practical action to aid another in achieving the goals that they were aiming for. This may occur in a situation of crisis or simply as part of routine work. Social support in whatever form and at whatever time has an important impact upon the social climate, the well-being of team members and the viability of a team.

Case Examples

- Jenny, a teacher, had received a call from her childminder to say that her daughter was unwell. She wanted to go home quickly, but had another lesson before the end of school which she was reluctant to cancel because of important work that the children were due to do. Her colleague, overhearing the conversation, offered to take the final class for her, enabling Jenny to go home.
- A receptionist in an advertising agency was overloaded with paperwork as she tried to put together the notes of clients due to see the advertising executives that morning. Her colleague, seeing her overloaded, then took half of the pile in order to relieve her of some of the work.
- A researcher needed to find an organization within which she could try out a questionnaire she was developing which looked at team effectiveness in organizations. Her colleague telephoned three or four different people he knew in different organizations who he thought might be willing to provide access for her to conduct her questionnaire study. He negotiated with each and, finding one who was willing, then provided the name and address to the researcher.

Appraisal support

Team members can provide useful social support by helping their colleagues in the process of making sense of or interpreting a problem situation. This need not involve offering solutions, but would involve helping the individual examine a range of alternative appraisals of any given problem situations.

Here is an example of an individual whose colleagues provided appraisal support which enabled him to deal with his predicament in a constructive and positive way. The way colleagues within teams help us to appraise situations can therefore be an important contributor to the overall social climate of the team.

The more that team members support each other, the more cohesive the team becomes. This leads to better mental health of team members since we know there is a strong and positive relationship between social support at work and job-related mental health (Ganster *et al.*, 1986; Manning *et al.*, 1996).

Case Example

Many individuals face job insecurity and Chris was one of them. He had worked in the same financial services organization for 15 years but suddenly found that the future of the organization was in jeopardy following the 2008–2009 financial crash. He then talked with two of his team colleagues about his own future as they discussed possible options. They suggested that there were two or three career possibilities within the parent organization for him, but also that there might be better opportunities outside. They offered appraisals of the situation which ranged from the most threatening, that is, unemployment, through to seeing the situation as one which was full of potential and promise for Chris (since it might give him the opportunity to specialize in areas which previously he had been denied because of the demands of the organization). Chris began to see that there were important positive opportunities in the situation that was not as threatening as he had first thought. He decided to explore with much more vigour the various alternatives open to him and succeeded in landing a job that offered more opportunities for growth and development than the one he had previously occupied.

Support for Team Member Growth and Development

Opportunities for learning, growth and development are of enormous importance to people's job satisfaction. Those who find themselves in mundane, monotonous, repetitive jobs are usually much less happy at work than those whose jobs are challenging and provide opportunities for new learning and development (Hackman and Oldham, 1976). The latter tend to be more committed to their jobs, their teams and their organizations and are consequently more productive.

The process of growth and development planning enables people to assess themselves realistically, and then determine their skill, training and development needs. Team members can work together in planning ways of meeting their needs for growth and development and in providing feedback about skills and strengths. Such team-based growth and development planning also improves communication and understanding between team members, leading to shared understanding about needs, goals, values and strengths.

Skill development

One way of beginning this process is for team members to list their own and others' strengths, skills and principal weaknesses. This enables the team both to ask and to answer important questions: What skills would team members like to develop further? Do team members have the opportunity to develop these skills in their current jobs? What professional or technical skills do team members want to develop further? How can the team get the training or support to enable its members to develop these skills? What support can the team offer to ensure individual team members get the training and development opportunities they want?

Job enrichment

It is useful for the team to consider how team members' roles can be enriched or enlarged to make them more fulfilling and satisfying (Hackman and Oldham, 1976). In particular, how could jobs within the team be changed to enable team members to achieve more of their goals, to align their jobs more appropriately with their values, interests and skills, and to provide opportunities for development, challenge and change? The characteristics of work roles influence team-member learning, well-being and their creativity and innovation (Hackman and Oldham, 1976; Oldham and Cummings, 1996). There are five core *job characteristics* that can be enriched: *skill variety, task identity, task significance, autonomy*, and *task feedback*. Skill variety refers to the degree to which a job requires different activities in order for the

Exercise 9   A team exercise to promote job enrichment

Enrich jobs by asking team members to help each other find answers to the following questions:

1   What would you add to or take out from your work objectives in order to enrich or enlarge your job?

'I would add the chance to liaise directly with patients over their problems and requirements from the practice. The current method of feedback through comments sheets placed in the reception area creates too much formality and is an obstacle to direct communication.'

2   How would you change the methods that you use to achieve work objectives in order to enrich the job?

'There would be much more communication within the team about the health of whole families, rather than just individuals within families in relation to treatment and care.'

3   How would you change the scheduling of the work that you do, that is, the order in which different parts of the job are done in order to make the job more satisfying to you?

'I would deal with medical records for just one hour in the morning and then write reports and do telephoning after that. I would keep the afternoons free for meetings with other members of the team rather than do all these things jumbled up.'

4   Which individuals, teams or organizations would you work with more (or less) in order to enrich the job and make it more satisfying for you?

'I would work more directly with the GPs and the counsellor in considering the needs of particular families or patients.'

5   In what ways would you liaise differently with the people with whom you work to make the job more satisfying for you?

'I would like team members to take more initiative and share responsibility for team objectives so that I have less of a directive role as a GP.'

6   In what areas of the job would you like the freedom and resources to introduce new and improved ways of doing things?

'I would like to work in a smaller sub-team within the practice working solely on identifying new and improved ways of providing services for clients.'

Working with other team members to examine these issues from your particular standpoint makes job enrichment more possible than doing the exercise in isolation. Team members can then provide a socially supportive role in helping the individual find the time to get additional training in order to facilitate job enrichment.

work to be carried out and the degree to which the range of skills and talents of the person working within the role is used. Thus a nurse working with the elderly in their homes may need to use her professional skills of dressing wounds, listening, counselling, being empathic, and appraising the supports and dangers in the person's home. Task identity is the degree to which the job represents a whole piece of work. It is not simply adding a rubber band to the packaging of a product, but being involved in the manufacture of the product throughout the process, or at least in a meaningful part of the process. Significance of the task in terms of its impact upon other people within the organization, or in the world at large, has an influence on creativity. Monitoring the effectiveness of an organization's debt collection is less significant than addressing the well-being of elderly people in rural settings, and may therefore evoke less creativity. Autonomy refers to the freedom, independence, and discretion for the people performing tasks, in determining how to do their work and when to do it. When people receive feedback on their performance they are more likely to become aware of the 'performance gaps'. Consequently they are more attuned to the need to initiate new ways of working in order to fill the gaps. Of course this also implies they have clear job objectives. Team members can discuss how their roles could be enriched on each of these core job dimensions.

Balance between Home and Work Life

One of the mistakes we make is to separate our work lives out from the rest of our lives and to treat work as though it were somehow the only important part of life. We all have to find ways of integrating the demands of work life with the demands and needs that we have in our non-work lives. An intrinsic part of growth and development planning is considering our personal goals and finding ways of integrating our work-related goals with them. The team can help in enabling or supporting the individual in finding a balance between home and work life. Indeed, those who do achieve such a balance are likely to bring the richness of their non-work lives to the team and to their work. Those who fail to find a balance are less likely to work effectively within the team (Shore and Barksdale, 1998).

Social Climate

The general social climate of a team is a product both of team task processes described in previous chapters as well as the social processes described earlier in this chapter. There are some additional simple rules of intra-team conduct that can help the quality of overall relationships within the team

Case Example

Debbie was a new lecturer in a university who had lived apart from her partner while they both undertook training. In her new role, it seemed clear that she would again be unable to see much of her partner while he finished his training in another city. Her team discussed how they could help. They agreed that she should do all her lecturing in the first two of the three terms so that she could spend more time in the third term writing chapters and books based on her research, and living with her partner. They also agreed that she should share the courses she taught with another team member so that she could have five-day weekends every other week in order to spend time with her partner. This creative way of managing the team's work enabled Debbie to spend much more time than she had planned with her partner. It was a temporary arrangement for two years until her partner finished his training but it was hugely important to her. She felt immensely committed to the team as a consequence, was highly productive in her research because she had substantial blocks of time for writing, and made an extra effort with her teaching to ensure it was an outstanding success in the unusual circumstances. Finding creative ways of helping team members to keep a good work and home life balance is seen as part of their responsibility by members of well-functioning teams.

such as the politeness of team members taking the time to greet each other in the morning; enquiring after the success of non-work events in colleagues' lives such as birthdays, weddings, holidays, etc. Taking the time to show interest and concern about the lives of others in the team is a simple and symbolic way of affirming relationships and caring – a kind of 'social grooming'. Other symbols of warmth and regard, commonly used in teams, are giving of birthday cards and celebrating the successes of individual team members. I have seen the corrosive effects on team social climate of the failure of managers to observe basic rules of politeness and to nurture warmth in the team by not saying (among other sorry examples) 'good morning' to junior staff as they arrive for work each morning. Warm, positive, enthusiastic optimism encourages a sense of belonging and community within the workplace.

Another positive element in team social climate is *humour*. Non-aggressive humour is a rich source of positive feeling within the team, encouraging both closer team relationships and creativity. By developing a relaxed, enjoyable atmosphere, team members are likely to be committed to the team and to enjoy their jobs. Humour is also a form of creative play that fosters an ethos of innovation within a team (Barsade and Gibson, 1998). Research on humour at work reveals that jokes can stimulate creativity and encourage the development of trust in teams (Clouse and Spurgeon, 1995). Moreover, successful leaders tend to use humour many times more often than others (Goleman, Boyatzis and McKee, 2002).

More formal approaches to promoting a positive team climate are also useful such as parties at team members' homes, shared activities such as fitness routines, jogging, football games (which involve both genders); and other sporting activities such as badminton, swimming, etc. Non-work-related interactions can promote relationships in the team that contribute to the overall social climate but are not essential. Research on cohesion and team performance, suggests it is a bi-directional relationship.

Group cohesion is conceptualized as having three elements: interpersonal cohesiveness (people like each other as people); task cohesiveness (there is a sense of unity around the team in its task performance); and group pride (the team's pride in its performance and reputation as a performing unit). All three elements predict team outcomes (like effectiveness) but predict even more strongly the team's performance behaviours such as task focus and conscientiousness (Beal *et al.*, 2003). Moreover, good performance in turn predicts cohesion (Mullen and Copper, 1994).

Conclusions

The message of this chapter is that the three social dimensions of team functioning (social support, support for growth and development, and general social climate) influence the team's longer-term viability, but also impact upon the mental health and job satisfaction of individual team members. In short, teams are communities and we should nurture them. Psychologists may sometimes over-complicate what are relatively simple aspects of human behaviour and perhaps the most unguarded message of this chapter is that team members can help each other and themselves by being positive and supportive to each other at work. The message of all the major world religions is the same: our purpose in any sphere of activity should be to care for those around us. The Dalai Lama expresses this simple principle in his repeated clear prescription: 'be kind to one another'. No less should this apply in the world of work.

Key Revision Points

- Why are emotions in teams important to consider?
- What are the four dimensions of belonging?
- What are the four forms of social support in teams?
- What are the three elements involved in supporting the growth and development of team members?
- How can teams build a positive social climate?

Further Reading

Beal, D., Cohen, R.R., Burke, M.J. and McLendon, C.L. (2003) Cohesion and performance in groups: a meta-analytic clarification of construct relations. *Journal of Applied Psychology,* 88, 989–1004.

Cameron, K., Dutton, J.E. and Quinn, R.E. (eds) (2003) *Positive Organizational Scholarship: Foundations of a New Discipline,* Berrett-Koehler, San Francisco.

Goleman, D., Boyatzis, R. and McKee, A. (2002) *The New Leaders: Transforming the Art of Leadership into the Science of Results,* Little, Brown, London.

Linley, A., Willars, J. and Biswas-Diener, R. (2010) *The Strengths Book,* CAPP Press, Warwick, England.

Linley, P.A., Harrington, S. and Garcea, N. (eds) (2010) *Oxford Handbook of Positive Psychology and Work,* Oxford University Press, Oxford.

Rasmussen, T.H. and Jeppesen, H.J. (2006) Teamwork and associated psychological factors: A review. *Work & Stress,* 20, 105–128.

Seligman, M.E.P. (1998) *Learned Optimism: How to Change your Mind and Your Life,* Pocket Books, London.

The Mind Gym (2009) *Relationships,* Sphere, London.

Web Resources

http://www.lcsc.edu/mcollins/groupandteamdynamics.htm (last accessed 11 August 2011).
A summary on group and team dynamics.

11

Conflict in Teams

Washing one's hands of the conflict between the powerful and the powerless means to side with the powerful, not to be neutral. (Paulo Freire)

Difficulties are meant to rouse, not discourage. The human spirit is to grow strong by conflict. (William Ellery Channing)

Key Learning Points

- The organizational causes of team conflicts
- Types of conflict in teams
- How to resolve team conflicts
- Interpersonal conflicts in teams and how to manage them
- How to manage difficult team members

Team Conflicts

Conflict is not only endemic but, if it is constructive, desirable in teams (Deutsch, 1973). Constructive team conflict can be a source of excellence, quality and creativity. At the same time we know that conflict in teams can be interpersonally destructive and lead to poor team performance or the break up of the team altogether (De Dreu and van de Vliert, 1997). This occurs

Effective Teamwork: Practical Lessons from Organizational Research, Third Edition. By M. A. West. © 2012 John Wiley & Sons, Ltd. Published 2012 by John Wiley & Sons, Ltd., and the British Psychological Society.

especially where the conflict takes on a personal quality which results in team members attacking one another, or denigrating each other's skills, abilities or functioning in some way. This is unhealthy for both the individuals concerned and for the team as a whole. Although job insecurity or work overload can be major causes of stress, it is often the conflicts with colleagues that keep us awake at night (Romanov *et al.*, 1996). Why do these occur and what can we do to prevent or overcome them?

Types of Team Conflict

A systematic review of all the research on team conflict suggested that high levels of any type of conflict damage team functioning (De Dreu and Weingart, 2003). These effects were more pronounced when team members were more interdependent and the researchers concluded that task conflict in general does not have positive effects on team performance.

There are three types of conflict in teams. Conflict about the task (e.g., 'which new product should we launch'); conflict about team processes (e.g., 'It's your job to do that not mine'); and interpersonal conflict (e.g., 'I think you are a rude and irritating person!') (De Dreu and Van Vianen, 2001; Jehn, 1997). Team diversity and differences of opinion about how best to meet customers' needs should be a source of excellence, quality and creativity, especially when the team's task is complex and challenging. But too much conflict (whether it is about the task or not) or conflict experienced as threatening and unpleasant by team members damages relationships and undermines the effectiveness of teams. What may be a comfortable level of debate for you, can be intensely uncomfortable for your colleagues.

Process conflict ('that's your job not mine'; 'I have a much heavier work-load than she does') and interpersonal conflict undermine team effectiveness and the well-being of team members whatever the level (De Dreu and Van Vianen, 2001). All team members should take responsibility for discouraging interpersonal conflict and ensuring that roles and responsibilities are sufficiently clear and fair in order that process conflict is rare.

Resolving Team Conflicts

How do we resolve conflicts? We can *avoid* the conflict. Neither side gets its needs met and the conflict is likely to arise in the future. We can give the other person what they want and *accommodate* them. The consequences are that they get what they want and I don't. I feel resentful and they expect me to accommodate them every time. We can *compete* to win against them at all costs and, if we do, their needs are not met and they are likely to harbour resentment that may manifest in the next conflict. *Compromise* sounds good but it means that neither of us get our needs fully met – still, it is a better solution than the other three. Or, we can *collaborate* to find a creative solution that meets both our needs. This is what is called a 'win–win' solution. It is the ideal since both parties are happy and their relationship is stronger because of the successful conflict negotiation.

Fisher, Ury and Patton, in their classic book on negotiating, *Getting to Yes* (1999), describe four steps involved in principled or ethical negotiation to resolve conflicts. First, separate the people from the problem. We should not make the mistake of attributing the problem to the people. Human beings usually explain people's behaviour by attributing it to their personalities rather than to the situations they find themselves in. If you see a parent shouting angrily at their child in the street, you interpret this as an indication of their aggressive personality. It could be that the child has narrowly missed being knocked down, having run into the street and the parent is angrily shouting at them as a reaction to the scare they have just had. He or she may normally never raise their voice to the child. This error in how we interpret behaviour is so deeply ingrained we are unaware of it. Psychologists call it the 'fundamental attribution error'. It also explains why problems in teams are often, and usually wrongly, attributed to 'personality clashes'. Focus on the problem that is causing the conflict, be tough on the problem and soft on the people.

Second, focus on interests not on positions. My daughters, Ellie and Rosa were fighting over the last orange in the fruit bowl, and I 'solved' the problem by cutting it in half. Rosa then squeezed her half out to make a juice drink and threw the residue away. Ellie scraped the peel to make zest for a cake she was making, and again, threw the rest in the bin. My 'solution' meant that both only got half of what they could have had if I had taken the time to find out what their underlying interests were rather than their stated positions ('I want the orange'; 'No, I want it'). Similarly, in team conflicts we should work out what the underlying interests or needs of the parties are rather than focusing on the stated positions.

Third, invent options for mutual gain. When you are in a conflict, your ability to negotiate and resolve the conflict will be infinitely better if you try to find solutions that meet both parties' interests. This is the opportunity to use your creativity and think of solutions that meet or even exceed what both parties to the conflict are after.

- Determine what are the underlying needs of the parties to the conflict (as opposed to their expressed positions), because conflicts occur when one person's attempts to reach a goal are blocked by another.
- Work with them to find creative solutions that meet or even exceed both parties' needs. Do not fall easily back into compromise and remember

that team votes are a way of avoiding/delaying conflict rather than dealing directly and satisfactorily with the conflict.

Finally, insist upon objective criteria to ensure the negotiation reaches a fair conclusion, rather than deciding the outcome by force of will. If team members are in conflict over workload, try to find a way of evaluating the solution to show it is fair. For example, if two members of a teaching team are in conflict over how much teaching each should do (a debate about number of contact hours with students and size of classes), work out a standard taking into account both parameters and ensure that both have workloads which are more or less equal using this agreed measure.

Organizational Causes of Conflict

Work role or organization factors are the cause of most interpersonal conflicts in teams. These include:

- lack of clarity or lack of mutual understanding of roles. This leads to debates about who should do what, suspicions about whether the distribution of workloads is fair, and irritations caused by apparent 'interference';
- the absence of clear, shared vision and explicit goals. When it is not clear what the task of the team is, there are likely to be conflicts occasioned by competing objectives of team members. One person may want to focus on keeping good records while another may want to innovate, but if the task is not clear, then the conflict is unlikely to be resolved;
- inadequacy of resources. Trying to provide pensions advice for callers to a help centre when the computer system keeps crashing is likely to produce high levels of frustration among team members which may easily boil over into interpersonal conflict;
- differences in functional orientation in the team responsible for providing products for customers in one geographical area. The team member responsible for sales focuses on keeping the price of products down and getting the orders filled quickly. The team member responsible for producing the products will be more concerned with producing the product to a high quality and taking the time to do it properly rather than rushing the job and making mistakes. Inevitably they will come into conflict;
- status inconsistencies (finance assistant in the team dealing with a senior manager's expenses claims);
- overlapping authority (it's not clear who is in charge of an aspect of the task);

- task interdependence (where team members have to rely on one another to complete their part of the task successfully). In the construction of a product in cell assembly in manufacturing one team member may be dependent on another to get their part of the production right in order for the next team member to be able to complete their part of the task successfully. Frustrations arise when reliability of a team member is seen to be lower than acceptable (regardless of the cause);
- incompatible evaluation systems (quality of product versus speed of delivery versus cost of product).

In this case, personalities were not at the root of the problem. Rather it was due to a lack of clarity and mutual understanding of roles. There is often conflict between medical and social workers in the community. This is usually because they have not spent time exploring and clarifying each other's roles. The social worker may be unaware of the broader role of the medical worker taking responsibility for all aspects of a family's health and well-being, including the social and emotional aspects. Health workers, on the other hand, often fail to be sufficiently aware of the statutory responsibilities of social workers who ultimately may be accountable in law if a tragic event occurs.

Team members can overcome such conflicts, not by reference to the particular case, but by a full exploration of each other's roles and some negotiation around how the roles can effectively complement rather than compete with one another. Therefore, whenever there is conflict in a team,

Case Study

Gwen, a nurse in a primary healthcare team, was experiencing repeated conflict with the social worker attached to her team. They tended to disagree over cases of suspected non-accidental injury to children where Gwen felt that the social worker was too ready to involve the courts and the police and too dismissive of Gwen's knowledge of the families involved. The conflict had escalated to the extent that the two had had a heated disagreement in Gwen's office that was overheard by other members of staff. Gwen accused the social worker of being unfeeling and too autocratic. The social worker responded by telling Gwen that it was not her job to be doing social work and that she should be looking after the physical health of the family. He called her argumentative, interfering and non-communicative and accused her of not being able to work effectively in a team.

one of the first things to assess is the extent to which people are clearly aware of each other's roles and the objectives of those roles (Pondy (1967) offers a useful analysis of conflict processes). (See also an exercise in role negotiation and clarification described in Chapter 5).

Interpersonal Conflicts

Personality does play an important part in team functioning, as we saw in Chapter 3. This is the idea that groups of people have 'team personalities'. Some individuals may be dominant and leader-oriented while others may be more creative. Where there are two dominant leaders in a team there may be friction, especially if they hold opposing views about the team's direction. The conscientious or risk-avoidant person who is keen to ensure that a decision taken by the team is always right and has been thought through carefully will be unmoved by the enthusiasm and certainty of the creative person in the team. The creative individual may feel irritation at the sceptical questioning and lack of enthusiasm of the other when a new and potentially exciting proposal is discussed. Some of the differences between team members can be due to characteristic styles of working which, while valuable, may cause or friction. Recognition of the value of the variability of styles within teams helps to overcome such difficulties.

Managing interpersonal conflicts

There is no doubt, however, that sometimes conflicts between individuals within teams cannot be dismissed as due to role, organizational, or team personality-type factors. Irritations do arise and difficulties do have to be worked through. For the most part people will get on with others with whom they have to work. This is *the psychology of inevitability* – if a child is told that he or she will definitely be sitting next to another child in class over the course of the next year (whom he or she has not liked previously), the child's attitude tends to change. Similarly if we know in the future we have to work with certain individuals who we may have found difficult in the past, we may work harder to find strategies to work more effectively and cooperatively with them.

There are four ways of reacting to a difficulty that has occurred with another team member. The first is to be *passive,* which means doing nothing and pretending the problem does not exist, but as indicated above this may have long-term detrimental effects such as simmering frustrations which overflow inappropriately. The second strategy is to be *passively aggressive,* which is perhaps the most destructive strategy of all. This is where Geoff avoids Laurence, the other team member, doesn't talk to him, deliberately disagrees with every suggestion he makes, denigrates him to colleagues, or even sabotages his work secretly. Such passive-aggressive strategies allow team members no opportunity of reconciling the conflicts or difficulties since they do not involve owning up to the existence of conflict. Passive-aggressive strategies undermine the climate of the whole team and are very destructive to team functioning. The third approach is to be *aggressive*, attacking the other team member verbally face-to-face with the intention of hurting. Such a strategy is marginally more positive than passive-aggressive or passive approaches since it enables the individual team member to express his feelings. It tends to leave a thick residue of bitterness, resentment and coldness, which harms both team members and the deeper social climate of the team. The fourth strategy has been called *assertiveness,* which involves telling the other individual about one's own feelings and asking for changes in behaviour which may prevent a reoccurrence of the conflict. Here are illustrations of the difference between aggressive and assertive statements:

'You're incompetent and you've wasted a whole week's work for me.' (aggressive statement)

'I feel really upset because I relied on you to make sure this information was posted on time. And I feel upset because all my hard work of the week seems wasted.' (assertive statement)

Assertiveness therefore involves the clear expression of feelings and the use of 'I' rather than 'you' statements. It involves being clear about one's own feelings and wants from the situation, whereas aggressive statements simply involve the intention to hurt. Assertive discussions therefore demand that both sides try to use 'I' statements in talking about their feelings and in identifying behaviour and the consequences of behaviour. At the same time, there must be a mutual commitment to identify desired changes in behaviour which will prevent the reoccurrence of the problem.

But when conflicts between team members do arise and cannot be managed in ways so far described, how should team members proceed? Pretending major problems do not exist in a working relationship can be an effective strategy in the short term but the danger is that frustrations build and will erupt in a single destructive incident. Team members should try to work through interpersonal difficulties when they arise, in a constructive, open way. This means being clear with the other team member about difficulties and conflicts and setting aside time to talk through them. Avoiding or denying problems is unlikely to make a long-term contribution to team viability. It is clearly best if individual team members can resolve differences with colleagues on a one-to-one basis in an open and constructive way when difficulties first arise. This will be easier in a climate of perceived safety within the team where the development of sub-groups is positively discouraged.

Team members may have genuine differences (strong political differences for example), but if team members are committed to a shared team vision, and have emotional maturity they will not allow these differences to interfere with team success. We do not need to vote for the same political party in order to work together successfully in providing excellent customer support. Moreover, there is some evidence that when team leaders intervene to try to resolve interpersonal difficulties between team members, the situation is often made worse (De Dreu and Van Vianen, 2001). There is nothing wrong with agreeing to differ as long as it does not interfere with the effectiveness of the team. Professionalism means doing the best possible job and working effectively with other team members to do that. It does not mean building lasting friendships at work at all costs and avoiding working with people who hold different political views, have irritating habits or laugh too loudly.

Where team members are unable to resolve their differences and these are interfering with the team's work, it may be necessary to involve the team leader (or, where the team leader is one of the two protagonists, the team leader's superior). The strategy here should be for the team leader to give each person the opportunity to state his or her feelings about the issue. Once both sides have expressed their feelings, the facts of the case can be addressed. It is important to try to separate out feelings from facts since the two can become muddled in a discussion that can then lead to further hostility and misunderstanding. By carefully talking through the facts and feelings, the 'mediator' can enable both sides to present their cases fully and to explore, perhaps without agreeing on an interpretation of previous events, how future difficulties might be avoided. Mediation, therefore, involves four stages:

- explore the feelings of both team members
- explore the facts as perceived by both team members
- agree goals for avoiding a reoccurrence of the conflict
- agree action plans.

A final note of caution: there is sometimes a tendency for team members to wish to hold inquests over every small conflict that takes place within the team. This can have the effect of magnifying those inevitable but small differences that occur between team members on a day-to-day basis. Engaging in such focused, repeated and concentrated analyses can magnify conflicts and can be as detrimental to team functioning and individual mental health as avoiding discussion of conflicts altogether.

Difficult Team Members

What do you do if there is a particularly difficult member in the team who you feel disrupts the team's work? Your first task is to think carefully about the ways in which this person is difficult and why this person is difficult.

Case Example

The retail coordination team

Elaine was the young team leader in a new retail coordination team of a major oil company. Geoffrey, her oldest and most experienced team member, had been with the company for many years. Elaine discovered that, unknown to her, Geoffrey had been conducting work with a number of retail outlets in a nearby town using the team's resources, at the same time as conducting the major project for which he was employed. When Elaine expressed anger to Geoffrey, communication broke down.

A meeting was arranged with Petra, the Departmental Manager, where the initial feelings of both sides were explored and each was given an opportunity to express their frustrations. Elaine was angry since she felt Geoffrey had betrayed her trust by not giving her enough information; she felt she had been misled. Geoffrey expressed his frustration at Elaine not allowing him to proceed with the other projects when he initially suggested them and felt annoyed that he had to take Elaine's direction over his work.

Petra then encouraged some exploration of the facts of the case, over which there was some disagreement. Geoffrey insisted that he had at one point mentioned the projects to Elaine, while Elaine denied this and said that despite weekly meetings with Geoffrey she had never received any information about the fact that he was pursuing the other projects.

Petra then explored some goals for the future. Both sides agreed on a need to communicate more about all aspects of work, particularly because Geoffrey felt that he did not know enough about what Elaine was doing on a day-to-day basis and felt it was important for him to know as a team member. Both agreed to better communication about all aspects of their work. They set an action plan which involved both Geoffrey and Elaine meeting weekly to talk about the progress of the work and to update each other on activities. Geoffrey agreed not to engage in future activities without clear permission from Elaine.

Sometimes, when teams are in difficulty, team members can 'scapegoat' particular individuals, heaping all the blame for the team's failures on that person, and then trying to drive them away. In this way, they unconsciously try to rid themselves of the problems but are failing to address the real causes (Hackman, 2002).

We often label and treat as difficult people who are different in some way from other team members. The newcomer to a long-standing team, the woman who joins an all-male team, the computer wizard in a team of technophobes, or the Malaysian in a team of Australians are all examples of people who may be stuck with the label 'difficult' rather than valuably different. Yet the difference in perspective they offer may save the team from its own homogeneity. Difference can produce creativity, but team members have to value that difference.

Those who disagree with the majority are often labelled 'difficult' yet teams with high levels of participation and tolerance of dissent are much more creative and innovative than those that do not tolerate dissent. Think about whether those who are being labelled as 'difficult' are simply dissenting and, if so, encourage other team members to explore, value and be stimulated by their dissenting views. They could well be the most important members of the team. We may also think of team members as 'difficult' when we do not understand their role or how they contribute to the team's success. Role clarification and negotiation exercises help solve the problem.

Having considered these possibilities you may conclude that the difficult people are genuinely so. They may be dominating, poor at communicating, aggressive, sarcastic or gruff. The way to deal with these behavioural problems is to coach, not exclude the team member. Use coaching skills to help them set targets to improve their interpersonal skills and give feedback on their performance. If possible, encourage the whole team to take responsibility for helping the person to learn to work more effectively as a team member. Encourage, appreciate, shape and support the team member.

And if you have considered all these options and what you are left with is the recognition that there is someone in the team who does not share the team's core values, then perhaps they should be encouraged to leave the team and find a more suitable place to belong. If the team is committed to helping customers and communicating their respect for clients, yet the team member rigidly sticks to their view that the customers should be deceived or treated with contempt privately, then you should consider how to move them within or out of the organization. Your Human Resources Department can help. Teams are there to do a task (be it catching antelope, delivering products, supporting customers or diagnosing and treating women with breast cancer) and, in the end, should not tolerate stubborn behaviour that interferes with their effective performance of the task. But, remember that the final example is an unusual situation. It is much more likely your 'difficult' team members are perceived as such because of one or other of the explanations outlined above.

Key Revision Points

- What are the three types of team conflict, and which influence team performance positively or negatively?
- How do you resolve conflicts between team members?
- What are the usual organizational causes of team conflicts?
- How should we manage interpersonal conflicts between members?
- Why are some team members labelled as 'difficult' and what are the usual causes of this labelling?
- How should you manage 'difficult' team members?

Further Reading

De Dreu, C.K.W. and van de Vliert, E. (eds) (1997) *Using Conflict in Organizations*, Sage, London.

De Dreu, C.K.W. and Weingart, L.R. (2003) Task versus relationship conflict and team effectiveness: A meta-analysis. *Journal of Applied Psychology*, 88, 741–749.

Deutsch, M. (1973). *The Resolution of Conflict: Constructive and Destructive Processes*, Yale University Press, New Haven.

Jehn, K. (1997) A qualitative analysis of conflict types and dimensions in organizational groups. *Administrative Science Quarterly*, 42, 530–557.

Tjosvold, D. (1998). Cooperative and competitive goal approaches to conflict: Accomplishments and challenges. *Applied Psychology: An International Review*, 47, 285–342.

West, M.A., Tjosvold, D. and Smith, K.G. (eds) (2003) *The International Handbook of Organizational Teamwork and Cooperation*, John Wiley & Sons, Ltd, Chichester.

Web Resources

http://www.mindtools.com/pages/article/newTMM_79.htm   (last   accessed   11 August 2011).
An interesting article on resolving conflict in teams and building stronger teams by facing your differences.

http://www.icra-edu.org/objects/anglolearn/Conflict-Key_Concepts1.pdf (last accessed 11 August 2011).
A complete work by the ICRA Learning Resources on teams and conflict.

http://www.mediationatwork.co.uk/ (last accessed 11 August 2011).
A useful website on the use of mediation in conflict resolution.

Part 4

Teams in Organizations

Teams do not exist in modern organizations as separate entities drifting in vast oceans. They are tightly interconnected with many nodes in immensely complex networks that often extend well beyond the organization itself. How they manage those networks has a profound influence on their effectiveness since they are required to work effectively with other teams, departments and organizations, sometimes spanning country boundaries and integrating their efforts to ensure organizational objectives are met. And teams vary in function and life course in a wide variety of ways. Understanding the context within which teams work is the aim of the final section of the book.

Chapter 12 explains how organizations can support or impede the teams that make up the organization. Research suggests that organizational supports, climate, structure and culture play a crucial role in determining team effectiveness but that most organizations fail to provide the supportive context necessary for teams to perform to their best. This chapter systematically describes how organizations can support team working and how teams can support and, if necessary, challenge the organizations of which they are a part. It considers the role of HR practices, company climate, alignment of goals throughout the organization, reward systems and feedback processes that should nurture the functioning and effectiveness of teams right through the organization.

Chapter 13 draws on current research and practice to identify the challenges we all face in the modern world of working virtually via email, teleconference and telephone without the luxury of the day-to-day contact with fellow team members that our forbears enjoyed. An understanding of

Effective Teamwork: Practical Lessons from Organizational Research, Third Edition.
By M. A. West. © 2012 John Wiley & Sons, Ltd. Published 2012 by John Wiley & Sons, Ltd., and the British Psychological Society.

the particular challenges technology and dispersion present is beginning to emerge and practical ways of dealing with these challenges are described. Drowning in emails, getting locked into destructive email conflicts and trying to build shared understanding without meeting fellow team members face to face are typical challenges. This chapter offers guidance and advice on how to ensure the advantages of virtual working are captured and the pitfalls avoided.

Finally, Chapter 14 explores the structure, functioning and purpose of a key team in any organization – the top management team. How it functions has a huge influence on teams throughout the organization. Its purpose is therefore particularly important but all too often such teams are unclear about their objectives and display many of the faults of team working identified in earlier chapters. The top management team faces particular challenges that other teams do not face and, in addition, they have to manage the many process difficulties faced by all other teams. How they function often offers a model to the rest of the organization; if they are at loggerheads, this conflict will stream through the rest of the organization, undermining the effectiveness of all teams and departments. This chapter explains how to develop effective top management team functioning so that they are exemplary in their performance in order that the rest of the organization can benefit from their effectiveness.

12

Teams in Organizations

An empowered organization is one in which individuals have the knowledge, skill, desire, and opportunity to personally succeed in a way that leads to collective organizational success. (Stephen R. Covey)

Key Learning Points

- The six stages of introducing team-based working in organizations
- Types of team communication styles in organizations and their effectiveness
- What supports organizations should provide for teams
- The role of the Human Resource Management department
- Reward systems for teams
- What role teams should play in organizations
- A strategy for a team to change the organization
- Inter-team relationships and how to improve them

In this chapter, we focus on how to build organizations that are structured around teams and can accommodate this diversity and creativity to ensure team and organizational effectiveness. We have worked in teams throughout most of our evolutionary history and are therefore well equipped to continue to do so effectively. However, in the last 200 or so years, the large work organization has become the norm and we have had to learn how to work in

Effective Teamwork: Practical Lessons from Organizational Research, Third Edition.
By M. A. West. © 2012 John Wiley & Sons, Ltd. Published 2012 by John Wiley & Sons, Ltd., and the British Psychological Society.

groups larger than 5, 6, 7 or 8 people – the norm for most of modern history. Now we are charged with working in teams in a larger organizational context, not just focused on the team's work but also on its interrelationships with the larger organization. This is a major challenge because teamwork can be diluted to become a meaningless term applied to any structural grouping within the organization (such as a department) or the team concept can be adhered to but with a failure to ensure teams work effectively together with other teams in the organization. How the organization is structured and managed to ensure effective team working is therefore of very great importance for both team and organizational effectiveness. Mathieu *et al.* (2001) proposed we could understand teams in organizations by conceiving of the organizations as multi-team systems (MTS) whereby teams of teams work collaboratively to achieve organizational goals. Where there is effective coordination of these MTS teams benefit in terms of processes and performance (Mathieu *et al.*, 2006). This chapter therefore deals with a question of fundamental importance, neglected by researchers, consultants and managers: *How can we build organizations that ensure the effectiveness of teams as a way of working?*

Introducing Team-based Working (TBW)

The premise of this question is that there is huge unrealized potential of teams and that this is locked away by the failures of organizational leaders to recognize that teams will work only to the extent that the organization is structured around and values team working in practice. When teams struggle to function in tall, hierarchical organizations with rigid boundaries between departments, they generally fail (Harris and Beyerlein, 2003; Mohrman, Cohen and Mohrman, 1995). We must plant the seeds of teamwork in seed beds prepared to nurture and sustain them. In Figure 3 we describe the six stages involved in developing an organization so that it is structured around teams and ensures their effectiveness (for a detailed account of how to introduce TBW, along with guides, questionnaires and practical techniques, see West and Markiewicz, 2003).

Stage 1   Deciding on team-based working (TBW)

The first stage of introducing TBW requires that senior figures understand the value and benefits of TBW and also that there is a good understanding of the existing structure, culture and extent of team working in the organization. Senior managers have to be committed to the idea of organizing around teams, and those involved in the change process must review what needs to change in the structure and culture of the organization to enable

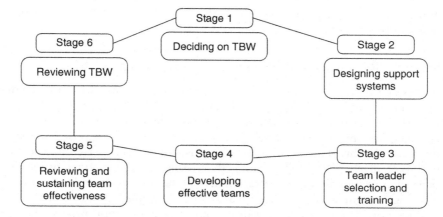

Figure 3 The six-stage process of introducing team-based working (TBW).

TBW. The change leaders must then develop a plan for implementing TBW and have a senior team in place to drive the change forward.

Stage 2 Developing support systems

This stage requires an examination of support systems relevant to team-based working such as Human Resource Management (HRM) systems, rewards, communication, training for managers and team members, and recruitment and selection practices, and making plans to adapt or develop them for TBW. Change leaders will determine what supports need to be in place so that team working can be nourished and spread within the organization. These include the following.

Stage 3 Team leader and team member selection

Establish criteria for team leader and team member selection (all employees can help with this), and then select them. Team leaders require training in the necessary knowledge, skills and attitudes as leading teams is very different from other kinds of leadership. Groups of team leaders can meet regularly to learn together how to be effective in their team leadership, by encouraging them to share problems, successes and surprises. Outstanding training for team leaders is available from www.astonod.com

Stage 4 Developing effective teams

This stage requires understanding and enabling the team development process, which includes clarifying objectives, roles, communication processes, and decision-making processes. The earlier chapters of this book described much of this material.

Stage 5   Reviewing and sustaining team effectiveness

In this stage, teams are coached to set criteria for the evaluation of team performance and to identify required changes to improve performance. Team leaders must examine performance, innovation, team members' satisfaction and their learning and skill development since all are vital areas of team performance. In this stage it is important to use an evidence-based diagnostic tool to regularly review the ongoing effectiveness of individual teams within their organizational context. Regular use of such tools provides an 'early warning' system which prevents teams from becoming dysfunctional and enables individual teams to focus development activities appropriately. There are a number of such tools on the market such as: The Aston Real Team Profile Plus – a quick and easily administered snapshot of how well the team's structure and processes are working to enable potential high-quality performance. More detailed is the Aston Team Performance Inventory – the most comprehensive team diagnostic tool available. The ATPI measures the input, team process, leadership process and output dimensions which predict long-term success for the team and, when administered to a representative number of teams within an organization, the potential success of the whole organization. See www.astonod.com for more details.

Stage 6   Reviewing team-based working

The final stage involves evaluating the contribution of TBW to the organization's effectiveness and making any necessary changes to ensure the continued and optimal contribution of TBW to the organization.

These then are the six main stages of introducing TBW but what does the organization look like when the process is complete? Introducing TBW involves dramatic, deep and wide-ranging change to the organization's structure and culture. In traditional organizations, there are command structures with status levels representing points in the hierarchy – supervisors, managers, senior managers, assistant chief executives and so on. In team-based organizations, the structures are collective. Teams orbit around the top management team and other senior teams (which themselves model the good teamwork described in the previous chapter), influencing and being influenced, rather than being directed or directive. The gravitational or inspirational force of different teams affects the performance of the teams around them.

The traditional organization has a chart with lines of reporting and layers of hierarchy but the team-based organization looks more like a solar system with planets revolving around each other and affected by the central force of the major planet (the top management team). The role of team leaders is to ensure that their teams work as powerful and effective parts of that solar system and that they think about how the system as a whole works, not just their particular planets. To do this they must continually emphasize integration and cooperation between teams. I suggest that team leaders keep asking leaders of those other teams they most work with 'How can we help each other more?', 'What are we doing that gets in the way of your effectiveness?' and 'Can we work together to come up with a radical new way of improving our services for customers?'

In traditional organizations, managers manage and control; whereas the role of the team leader in team-based organizations is to encourage teams in their organizations to be largely self-managing and take responsibility for monitoring the effectiveness of their strategies and processes. In one company I worked in, a production team videoed their performance in the production process and invited members of other teams to view the video and suggest ways in which they could dramatically improve their working methods. This led to radical improvements in productivity, quality and time taken for goods to reach the customers.

Organizational objectives, customer service, innovation and team working are the leadership mantras in team-based organizations.

The Relationship between Teams and their Organizations

Deborah Ancona and David Caldwell (Ancona and Caldwell, 1992) explored how teams 'bridge the boundaries', that is, how teams interact with their organizations as a whole. By studying teams interacting with their organizations, Ancona and Caldwell identified three main strategies that teams use in managing their organizational environments:

(a) **Ambassadorial activities**
    These involve communicating with and influencing senior management in order to promote the team's profile and to give senior management a picture of the team as effective, committed and innovative. The aim of ambassadorial activities is also to secure organizational resources and protect the team from excessive interference.

(b) **Task coordinator activities**
    These aim at improving communication with other teams and departments. Rather than being characterized by vertical communication (as is the case with ambassadorial activity), task coordinator activities focus on coordination, negotiation and feedback horizontally, that is, with departments and teams at the same organizational level. The aim

is to manage workflow activities in a coordinated way through negotiation and via feedback with other departments and teams, in order to achieve effective performance.

In the case of, say, an oil company training team this would mean engaging in high levels of communication with functional departments in order to gain information about training needs. The training team would also negotiate with those other departments in order to specify training course prices, priorities and frequencies. By seeking constant feedback on the adequacy of the training they would also be in a better position to coordinate and negotiate in the future.

(c) **Scouting activities**
These aim to provide the group with up-to-date information on market needs and requirements and on new technical developments. The aim of scouting activities is to be aware of changes occurring in the external environment of the team. One example comes from a research team established to examine the factors that contributed to the performance of manufacturing firms. One team member contacted other researchers on a regular basis to find out about new developments in the area, studied relevant journals to glean information about new methodologies, and consulted with academic contacts about related research. Such scouting activities provide a means of ensuring that a team is up-to-date with technical developments. This same team member also consulted with senior managers in other similar organizations to discover their principal questions about company performance in order to identify correctly market needs for the research.

Not all teams have a single dominant strategy for external activity within the organization. Some employ all three types of activities, while others focus on only one. Still others are isolationist, employing none of the strategies in any consistent way. Ancona and Caldwell found that team performance was not dependent upon the *level* of organizational communication that teams maintained. Far more important was the *type* of activities they engaged in. They found that teams that engaged predominantly in scouting activities had poorer performance than other teams. Moreover, internal processes within the team tended to be unsatisfactory. Task and team cohesiveness were both lowest in teams that adopted predominantly scouting activity strategies. In contrast, teams that adopted a 'comprehensive strategy' of a mix of ambassadorial, task coordinator, and scouting activities tended to have the highest performance, task process and team cohesiveness scores.

In the short term, ambassadorial activities were associated with the best team performance, good task processes and high cohesiveness. But, over the long term, a combination of ambassadorial and task coordinator external activities appears best. Comprehensive strategy teams were the most effective overall, though they seemed to pay a price of low team cohesiveness compared with the pure ambassadorial strategy teams.

Isolationist teams tended to do badly, though unlike the scouting teams, they did have higher scores on internal task processes and cohesiveness. It may be that these teams concentrated so much on internal processes that they neglected important organizational cues and so performed less well. Teams that engaged predominantly in scouting seemed to make their work so complex that they were unable to perform effectively. By constantly seeking new approaches, they were unable to adopt a single team plan that took them forward over any period. They could not make clear decisions about work plans or processes and could not implement a plan. Continual exploration brought conflicting information, requiring complex internal interaction. As the difficulty of decision making became greater, relationships within the teams suffered.

This research shows that, contrary to popular belief, it is not the amount of external communication that a team engages in which predicts successful team performance. Rather it is the *type* of external communication.

What do Teams need from their Organizations?

Hackman and his colleagues (Hackman, 1990) have concluded that there are six principal areas within which teams need organizational support: targets, resources, information, education, feedback and technical/process assistance in functioning. Examining the extent to which organizations provide team support in these areas can help in discovering the underlying causes of team difficulties.

Targets

Teams need support from an organization in determining targets or objectives. Surprisingly few teams receive clear targets from their organizations, often because organizational targets and aims are not sufficiently clear. It is striking, when team members try to outline their objectives and team targets, how few have clear notions of what is required of them. The implication is that teams should derive their targets and objectives by scrutinizing organizational objectives or mission statements. These are often such vague good intentions or abstract sentiments, however, that it is almost impossible for a team to derive clear targets. Where, through a process of negotiation, teams are able to determine their targets in consultation and collaboration with those hierarchically above them, there is usually a better level of performance.

Resources

The organization is required to provide adequate resources to enable the team to achieve its targets or objectives. Resources include having the right number and skill mix of people; adequate financial resources to enable effective functioning; secretarial or administrative support; adequate accommodation; adequate technical assistance and support (such as computers, blood pressure testing equipment, or whatever technologies are required for the team to be successful).

Information

Teams need information from the organization that will enable them to achieve their targets and objectives. If teams are not told about changes in strategy or policy they will not function effectively. Ensuring that relevant information reaches a team to enable it to perform effectively is an essential component of an organization's management. For example, an oil company that decides to develop large numbers of international teams with team members based in different countries has to communicate these plans to its training department in order that they can implement training for cross-cultural teams.

Education

Part of an organization's responsibilities for effective team functioning is to provide the appropriate levels and content of education for staff within teams. The purpose of such training and education is to enable team members to contribute most effectively to team functioning and to develop as individuals. This includes on-the-job training, coaching via supervisor, training courses, residential training courses or distance learning courses. There should be adequate access to training that is relevant to the team's work and of a sufficient quality and quantity to enable them to perform to maximum effectiveness (see www.astonod.com).

Feedback

Teams require timely and appropriate organizational feedback on their performance if they are to function effectively. Timely feedback means that it occurs as soon as possible after the team has performed its task, or occurs sufficiently regularly to enable the team to correct inappropriate practices or procedures. Appropriate feedback means that it is accurate and gives a clear picture of team performance.

For some teams it is difficult to gain accurate feedback. For a football team, feedback is immediate and is not dependent upon an organization, that is, match results are evident on a weekly basis. For a team responsible for providing training in one division of a major oil company, organizational feedback might take the form of senior managers' satisfaction with improved performance. This could include measuring the results from technical training courses in customer service in retail outlets (i.e., filling stations). Such information could come from surveys of customer satisfaction with retail operators' services. Organizations should aim to improve continuously in the extent to which they provide useful, accurate and timely feedback.

Technical and process assistance

Teams need their organizations to provide the specialized knowledge and support that will enable them to perform their work effectively. A primary healthcare team engaged in developing its practice objectives, by identifying the health needs of the practice population, might need the health authority to deploy a community medical officer to advise the team on patterns in local health and ill-health. For a training team in an oil company, technical assistance might take the form of specialist computing experts and marketing strategists, advising the company on how to communicate most effectively to managers throughout Europe, in order to market their training courses to managers in different functions.

Process assistance refers to the organizational help available when the team encounters team interaction or process problems. When there are unresolvable difficulties in the team, such as continual dissatisfaction with the effectiveness of team meeting, teams need to be able to turn to someone in the organization (or an external consultant) who can assist them. All team leaders should see this as a normal activity; as one team member said, 'it's like visiting the doctor when you have an illness; teams too need expert help from time to time'.

The Role of Human Resource Management (HRM)

In order to provide the supports that are necessary for team effectiveness, the HRM department of organizations must play a powerful role. They need to develop support systems to ensure the success of TBW by taking the following steps. HR managers must develop their knowledge about all aspects of team working, including team composition, team development, team processes, team performance management and particularly, inter-team conflict and how to manage it. They should visit five or six outstanding examples of team-based organizations to learn about good practice and to share their learning with everyone in the organization. The teams need clear, constructive feedback and they should help teams set goals and give feedback on the team's performance in relation to four areas:

- *The team's performance* – be it producing parts, treating patients, or providing customer service – likely to be best defined and evaluated by the 'customers' of the teams;
- *Team member growth and well-being* – the learning, development and satisfaction of team members;
- *Team innovation* – innovation is an outstanding barometer of team functioning. Teams should be fountains of creativity;
- *Inter-team relations* – cooperation with other teams and departments within the organization.

The HR department must make sure the reward systems reward teamwork as well as individual performance. Most important is for them to check annually whether team members see the reward system as transparent, just and motivating (see below for more detailed advice on reward systems).

When selecting new staff, the HR department should help team members take account of previous experience of applicants in working in teams, team-working competencies and the motivation to work in teams. Where team members manage their own selection, HR and an external participant can ensure probity and an alternative view so that team members do not simply select clones of themselves. The HR department should provide training for team members in working in teams (not just team-building events), training for team managers and for internal consultants working with teams (see Chapter 3). Both new and experienced team managers will also benefit from the support of a mentor. This may be a manager from another level of the organization or a team manager from another team who has experience of working with teams.

The HR department should use extensive communication devices to ensure everyone in the teams is clear about the purpose of the organization, its performance and the importance of teamwork. They can use regular emails, newsletters, conversations, rewards and even press releases to newspapers to communicate about successes. Moreover, they and managers should give quick, public and positive recognition to accomplishments of the teams and their members whenever possible.

Putting these systems in place means that teamwork is nourished and supported in the organization rather than hanging by threads. Team members will be motivated, the organization will become healthier, and the roles of team leaders will be challenging, interesting and rewarding, since they will not always be dealing with the problems created by lack of support for teamwork.

Box 19   Developing team reward systems

Reward processes make it possible to appraise and reward people on the basis both of the results they achieve and the extent to which their work promotes innovation, quality, team working and continual improvement. Reward processes demonstrate the organization's commitment to those values. Reward systems must therefore be open and clearly understood by all involved (Parker, McAdams and Zielinski, 2000). The focus of reward systems can include:

The individual team member

Here individual performance is appraised and rewarded. This can include individual rewards for contribution to team working where this is a specific target set for the individual. Performance-related pay can reflect individual contributions to the team's performance as rated by other team members.

The team

Here reward is related to the achievement of predetermined team goals. Reward may be distributed equally to each member of the team or it may be apportioned by senior management, by the team leader or in a manner determined by the team itself. It is important to note that where rewards are given equally to team members by an external party, this can lead to considerable resentment. Team members who do not pull their weight are seen as 'free riders' and their failures lead to resentment and demotivation amongst other team members. This will be exacerbated if the distribution of team rewards is achieved in ways that do not mirror the effort or contribution made by individual team members. It is important therefore that the reward system for the team is seen as fair by team members and this may involve some process by which team members themselves determine the distribution of the team rewards.

The organization

The performance of either the total organization or the business unit is reflected in rewards allocated to individuals or teams. Incorporating all elements (individual, team and organizational) provides a well-rounded reward system. In team-based organizations there must be a strong emphasis on team performance and as much delegation of decisions regarding team reward distribution as possible.

The keys to successful reward systems are:

- clear, achievable but challenging targets which team members understand, agree and ideally are involved in setting;
- clear and fair means of measuring team outcomes;
- team members working interdependently to achieve team goals;
- allowing the team a considerable degree of autonomy in the way in which it manages its work;
- giving the team access to the necessary materials, skills and knowledge to achieve the task;
- defining a reward valuable enough to be worth having, and delivered soon after the achievement of the outcome.

How can organizations go about designing systems for rewarding teams while still rewarding individuals? Reward schemes should emphasize the core value of teamwork and this needs driving home repeatedly. Many managers make the mistake of assuming that employees understand the organization's core values. They need to be repeatedly affirmed and spelled out. Managers should also strive to tell employees how they are performing continually (by providing mostly positive feedback) and to reinforce the messages about how the rewards link to the core values of the organization.

It also makes sense to create a smorgasbord of reward plans. Merck (a US company), for example, has an organizational level incentive that pays rewards to employees for the achievement of annual organizational targets. This is augmented by a system whereby team members nominate each other for outstanding team performance, which earns non-monetary rewards. For high-performing teams there is a quarterly stock option reward plan. Another company (ASCAP) allows all account services teams that meet their targets to receive an award that represents a percentage of the individual's base pay. In addition, there is a 'sales team of the year' ceremony to which all teams that exceed their annual targets are invited. Although only one team wins the big award, all the other teams receive a plaque and merchandise in recognition of their achievement.

Of course, all this means that senior managers have to budget for recognition activities in advance and to make sure there is sufficient resource to ensure the systems really have an impact. That also means planning to collect, process and feedback performance data. Those data must be of high quality and perceived to be reliable and valid by employees. The rewards must also be sufficiently substantial to matter to the employees since the value of payoffs are in the eye of the beholder. Some organizations offer a variety of rewards from which employees can choose: travel passes, money, a case of wine, time off with pay, flexitime working, etc. Employees can then choose rewards that are most valuable to them.

What do Organizations require from Teams?

Organizations need teams *to set and then achieve objectives* that enable the organization to achieve its own targets and goals. A financial services organization, for example, will require their teams to maximize profit, a charity to meet the needs of the people they serve and the training team in an oil company may be required to identify carefully training needs and respond to them strategically in order that the organization can achieve its overall objectives via the improved individual performance of employees.

Cooperation between teams is required by organizations, even when they are competing for office space, resources or staff. Competing teams may deliberately deceive one another or try to hamper one another's performance. When teams cooperate within organizations, not only is the organization more likely to achieve its objectives, but individual team performance is also improved. Competition between teams within organizations generally results in poor organizational performance (West *et al.*, 2003).

An increasingly common phenomenon within organizations is the use of *cross-functional teams*. These are combinations of people from different teams who come together to improve communication and decision making. For example, in a company that manufactures springs for the automotive industry, cross-functional groups may draw individuals from production, marketing, sales and customer liaison in order to identify and overcome quality and performance problems. Such cross-functional groups can address quality problems and ensure cross-team communication, coordination and cooperation. Cross-team collaboration and communication fosters high levels of creativity and innovation within organizations.

Organizations also need teams to be *agents of innovation, change and even revolution*. So far we have considered teams as though their objectives and those of the organization are consistently aligned rather than occasionally in conflict. A computing services team might feel that the managerial emphasis on cost cutting and reduction of waiting times for dealing with complaints jeopardizes the quality of support for customers. The oil company training team might oppose senior management's strategy of 'macho' management which emphasizes increasing employee insecurity, while imposing compulsory redundancies and new contracts. The training team, in conjunction with the HR department, might wish to oppose this policy and bring about organizational change. How is this to be done?

In Chapter 8, the literature on 'minority influence' was examined and this showed how minorities, by being persistent and consistent in the face of opposition, can bring about a subtle conversion of attitudes amongst majorities. This research has demonstrated convincingly how a well-organized minority may alter the thinking of a majority. The research also helps to partly explain how groups that start out as minorities, such as feminist or ecological movements, subsequently may bring about shifts in thinking, behaviour and even national policies. Serge Moscovici who pioneered research and theory in this area, has argued that innovation can only come about through the conflict created by minority influence (Moscovici *et al.*, 1985; see also Martin and Hewstone, 2010). How can a team draw on this understanding in order to change organizational objectives and strategy?

(a) *The team must have a clear vision of what it wishes to achieve*
For example, a personnel department may have developed a major commitment to the implementation of equal opportunities on a real rather than cosmetic organizational basis. Opposition from senior management may exist but as long as the team has a shared vision of equal opportunities for women, ethnic minority groups, and people with disabilities, they have a chance of success. In order to be effective and to sustain minority influence, the vision must be one that motivates and inspires team members – a future they really feel is worth fighting for.

(b) *The vision must be clearly articulated and coherently expressed*
In order to be effective, minorities must put across a clear, consistent message backed up by convincing underlying arguments. A team in which the minority vision is unanimously held and consistently argued for is many times more effective than an individual working alone – indeed it is exponentially more effective. Team members must present the same vision and the same arguments in favour of the vision. Where disagreement exists amongst members of a minority group they are not so effective in influencing the views of the majority and bringing about real change.

(c) *They must be flexible in responding to the views of others*
Minorities which are perceived to be radical and inflexible tend to be rejected by the majority as too extreme to bargain with. It is important for a minority to appear willing to listen to the views of others and make modifications to their proposals, while not fundamentally distorting their vision. The personnel department has to be prepared to listen to senior managers who argue that, say, introducing large numbers of untrained people very quickly into the organization may have a detrimental effect upon performance, or that any equal opportunities strategy should be managed in stages. Failure to respond to apparently

reasonable arguments can cause the minority to be dismissed. This should not involve a team compromising its fundamental objectives.

(d) *Persistence is essential*

For a team to bring about organizational change it must be persistent. Minority movements such as the feminists and ecological campaigns had influence partly because of the repeated presentation of the same coherent message and the same arguments. Minority influence occurs because of persistent communication. Where a team is defeated in a committee or in some managerial decision-making process, it should not give up but should maintain its stance and either go back to the same decision-making bodies or find alternative routes to influence the organization. Presenting the same message persistently across the organization is likely to have the effect of water dripping on a stone: eventually the stone will wear away. In short, the message is, *prepare, rehearse, present, and present again*. In other words, the vision and arguments for the team's position should be prepared and rehearsed in private and then the team should repeatedly present its approach to people throughout the organization.

(e) *Participation*

The single best way of reducing resistance to change is by involving people in the change process (Heller *et al.*, 1998). By seeking the views of people throughout the organization and encouraging others to be involved in contributing ideas to the proposals, the team can reduce the resistance of people in the organization to the proposed change.

(f) *The bad news*

An inevitable consequence of acting as an agent for revolutionary change is that the team increases organizational conflict. Repeatedly challenging organizational objectives or practices inevitably provokes conflict, often with people in higher status positions who have greater power. This is very threatening and deters many teams from engaging in revolutionary change processes. If a vision is worth fighting for, however, then team members will be prepared for the conflict that ensues. Such revolutionary approaches to organizational change also bring with them unpopularity. The majority in organizations tend to conform because it makes for a more peaceful life. Those who introduce conflict are likely to become unpopular since they raise anxiety. Again, if the vision is important to a team – for example, in the case of a hospital nursing team, improving the quality of health of those in their care – team members may be prepared to tolerate unpopularity or even job insecurity as the price they pay to achieve their vision of a better world. *Individuals should not try to implement this strategy for change alone since the research evidence suggests they are likely to fail and possibly to suffer. It is a group strategy for change.*

Such revolutionary teams may seem a threat to organizations. There is good reason for supposing that organizations that have no revolutionary teams are stagnant, however, since conformity processes have dampened down the fiery forces for change and innovation. Organizations need revolutionary teams just as they need people with vision. Heat is often produced through the friction created by sharply differing views within organizations and this heat can then fire creative and innovative processes.

Teams within organizations are required to meet objectives that further organizational aims. In order to do this they need organizational support and resources such as information, training, accommodation, equipment and managerial support. But organizations are political entities characterized by conflicting interests, goals and agendas, and teams must manage this environment effectively in order to survive. They must develop strategies which raise the team's profile with senior management and win resources, which coordinate their efforts with those of other teams and departments, and which monitor the environment to ensure they are up to date with 'market needs' and new technical developments.

To ensure long-term effectiveness, all teams should develop and sustain an evolutionary approach to their work, especially in changeable, uncertain environments. This involves regular reflection on the team's work and purpose, along with appropriate modification of activities and aims. Ultimately, team success and effectiveness is constrained or enhanced by the team's collective intelligence and integrity in its dealings with the wider organization.

Bridging across Teams

The strengths of team working in organizations are the involvement of all in contributing their skills and knowledge, in good collective decision making and innovation. The fundamental weakness is the tendency of team-based organizations to be torn and damaged by competition, hostility and rivalry between teams.

Early research in social psychology, such as the famous Robber's Cave study, showed how psychological group identification occurs almost immediately when people are randomly assigned to groups, with dramatic behavioural consequences of strong group loyalty and in-group favouritism (Sherif *et al.*, 1961). People develop group identification with the most minimal social cues (Billig and Tajfel, 1973; Tajfel, 1970; Tajfel and Billig, 1974). The tendency of people to discriminate in favour of their own group and to discriminate against members of out-groups is pervasive (Brewer, 2001; Turner, 1985). Moreover this in-group favouritism occurs spontaneously and without obvious value to the individual. Research indicates that there is no need for material advantage to the self or inferred similarity to other group members for group identification to occur. There is evidence that external threats lead to the creation of firmer bonds within groups (Stein, 1976) while at the same time increasing the threat of rejection to deviants

(Lauderdale *et al.*, 1984). Groups clearly seek solidarity when confronted by external threat.

The tendency of people to discriminate in favour of their own group is what we all do and is at the root of many of the most horrific conflicts in our world (Demoulin, Leyens and Dovidio, 2009). It does not matter whether it is football teams, gender, race, function (sales, production), or the other work team. The role of team leaders is to understand and recognize this tendency and take action to prevent, reduce or overcome it.

Box 20   The Robber's Cave studies

Sherif and his colleagues carried out three large studies of boys in typical American summer camps (Sherif *et al.*, 1961). The design involved three stages of group formation, inter-group conflict and conflict reduction. Initially, boys from well-to-do backgrounds, aged around 12 years, were assigned to one of two groups, each around 10 or 11 children in size. They had little contact with the other group, playing or working in different locations. The groups developed their own cultures, norms, nicknames and symbols.

In the second stage, a series of inter-group competitions was announced, with the winning group to receive a set of gleaming pen-knives and the other group nothing. Whereas in the first phase, the groups had coexisted quite happily they now developed intense dis-like, hostility and, on some occasions, even attacked each other physically. There was considerable 'in-group' bias and 'out-group' prejudice, with the boys exaggerating the effectiveness and success of their own group, and developing discriminatory and derogatory attitudes to the other group. Their leadership changed hands to a more aggressive individual. In some of the studies, the boys' existing best friends had initially been assigned to the other groups, but during this conflict stage 90% of them chose boys from within their own groups.

In the third and final phase, the experimenters tried to reduce inter-group conflict by creating 'superordinate goals'. For example, they arranged for the camp truck to break down several miles from camp, requiring both groups to pull the truck using a tug-of-war rope to get it 'jump started' and back to camp for lunch. Similar manipulations, which introduced superordinate goals (the groups shared an overall goal that eclipsed their immediate within-group goals), led to a reduction in inter-group conflict and hostility. Similar results have emerged from many studies of inter-group behaviour regardless of the age or gender of participants. They point to the fundamental nature of human inter-group conflict and the need to develop methods for avoiding it (see Brown, 2000).

These biases against other teams include attitudes in the form of prejudice ('when an order is not completed properly it's always the result of the sales people not getting us the accurate information in the first place, not our problems in production'); thoughts in the form of stereotyping ('the sales department are all greedy individualists'); and behaviour (refusing to give information to the sales department about the likely date of completion of an order). Threats (or perceived threats) between teams are at the root of much anxiety and anger within organizations which must not be allowed to persist. The hierarchy of threat ranges from threats to the team's social identity (male managers being threatened by the increase in numbers of female managers in a top management team); through threats to their goals and values (teachers feeling that managerial directives about what and how to teach threaten their commitment to inspiring students to learn); position in the hierarchy (managers perceiving the HR department as threatening their authority); to the group's very existence (doctors seeing nurse practitioners as a threat to their own existence). Such threats can be realistic as in the battle between departments for scarce resources or symbolic when values or norms are threatened (Hewstone, Rubin and Willis, 2002).

Leaders should deal with these problems between teams by directly addressing the issue. First, they should explain to team members that this hostility across team boundaries is a natural human tendency and that it can be overcome. Second, they should encourage team members to recognize that they have to learn to cooperate with and support other teams – that is in their best interests, the organization's, and their customers'. If there are legitimate grievances between the teams, these must be dealt with in a way that both sides see as just. Team leaders can hold meetings between themselves or between the teams to find solutions that both teams see as fair.

Leaders have to be alert to team members speaking negatively about particular departments ('the finance people are incompetent' or 'the HR department are meddlers') and should not buy into the conversation. They have to assert that it is inappropriate for them to talk about the other team in this way and suggest ways of addressing and solving the problems which cause them to be negative in their comments. That is one of the lonely parts of the team leader's role.

Within the business school I work in, academics and administrators are working together to provide a more complete and positive student experience. As a result, they are learning to work together and avoid overlaps and contradictory advice in providing for students' needs. Conflicts are being resolved creatively rather than smouldering and the result is a much better service and support for students. Team leaders encourage this by getting team members to identify the valuable contributions both academics and support staff can provide. As the groups cooperate, it has become clear to both that they should maintain their separate roles but work together.

Both sides bring complementary and much-needed skills to the task and need to work together and support each other.

Other practical techniques to use include:

(i)   *Team-member exchanges* – Team members can work for a period in other teams or visit as observers in order to increase mutual understanding and provide opportunities for individual development.

(ii) *Publicizing team news* – Internal organization newsletters are a forum for providing information about both the successes of good inter-team working, cooperation and support.

(iii) *Benchmarking* – When teams discovers new ways of working, or solutions to old problems, they should communicate them to all other teams so they can take advantage of the breakthrough. When team leaders use their positions to encourage this, they build an expectation that it is proper to share best practice and reduce unhealthy competition to be the best team.

Moreover, an open climate within the organization has a major impact in encouraging team empowerment and effective team processes (Mathieu *et al.*, 2006).

Conclusions

Teams do not exist in isolation within their organizations. They derive their purposes from those of the organizations they are part of, ideally contributing to that purpose by achieving their objectives and working effectively with other teams within the organization to enable them to succeed. Thoughtfully putting in place support structures and systems that enable teams to thrive is necessary for ensuring teams achieve their potential. There is a very large gap between the current reality and the desirable ideal in the majority of organizations. Taking some of the simple steps outlined in this chapter to provide an appropriate context and suitable support for TBW in organizations offers the certainty of major improvements in productivity, effectiveness and innovativeness of teams. The agenda for the changes necessary are clearly presented in this chapter and, if followed, will lead to considerable improvements in team and organizational performance.

Key Revision Points

- What are the six stages of introducing team-based working and what are the tasks of each stage?
- What are the three patterns of external communication in teams and which combinations best promote team effectiveness and cohesiveness?

- What six sources of support do teams need from their organizations?
- Describe the role of the HRM department in developing team-based working
- What reward systems will be best for team-based organizations?
- What methods can leaders employ to reduce inter-team and interdepartmental hostility in their organizations?

Further Reading

Demoulin, S., Leyens, J-P. and Dovidio, J.F. (2009) *Intergroup Misunderstandings: Impact of Divergent Social Realities*, Psychology Press, London.

Hackman, J.R. (1990) *Groups That Work (and Those That Don't)*, Jossey-Bass, San Francisco.

Harris, C. and Beyerlein, M.M. (2003) Team-based organization: Creating an environment for team success, in *Handbook of Organizational Teamwork and Cooperative Working* (eds M.A. West, D. Tjosvold and K.G. Smith), John Wiley & Sons, Ltd, Chichester.

Hewstone, M., Rubin, M. and Willis, H. (2002) Intergroup bias. *Annual Reviews of Psychology*, 53, 575–604.

Mathieu, J.E., Gildon, L.L. and Ruddy, T.M. (2006) Empowerment and team effectiveness: An empirical test of an integrated model. *Journal of Applied Psychology*, 91, 97–108.

Mathieu, J.E., Marks, M.A. and Zaccaro S.J. (2001) Multi-team systems, in *International Handbook of Work and Organizational Psychology* (eds N. Anderson, D. Ones, H.K. Sinangil and C. Viswesvaran), Sage, London, pp. 289–313.

Mohrman, S., Cohen, S. and Mohrman, L. (1995) *Designing Team-based Organizations*, Jossey-Bass, London.

Parker, G., McAdams, J. and Zielinski, D. (2000) *Rewarding Teams: Lessons from the Trenches*, Jossey-Bass, San Francisco.

West, M.A. and Markiewicz, L. (2003) *Building Team-based Working: A Practical Guide to Organizational Transformation*, Blackwell, Oxford.

Web Resources

www.astonod.com for many resources and guidance on developing team-based working and effective team working.

http://www.referenceforbusiness.com/encyclopedia/Str-The/Teams.html (last accessed 11 August 2011).

A very resourceful business encyclopaedia.

http://homepages.inf.ed.ac.uk/jeanc/DOH-glossy-brochure.pdf (last accessed 11 August 2011).

A research by the author and colleagues on team working and effectiveness in healthcare.

13

Virtual Team Working

Electronic aids, particularly domestic computers, will help the inner migration, the opting out of reality. Reality is no longer going to be the stuff out there, but the stuff inside your head. It's going to be commercial and nasty at the same time. (J.G. Ballard)

Every year the progress of advanced capitalist society makes our population consist of more and more isolates. This is because of the infrastructure of the economy, especially electronic communications. (Mary Douglas)

Key Learning Points

- Knowing what is meant by virtual team working and understanding the dimensionality of the concept
- Understanding the dimensions that characterize virtual team working
- The key advantages and disadvantages of virtual team working
- The situations in which virtual team working is most useful and least useful
- How to develop effective virtual team working
- The life cycle of virtual teams

Effective Teamwork: Practical Lessons from Organizational Research, Third Edition.
By M. A. West. © 2012 John Wiley & Sons, Ltd. Published 2012 by John Wiley & Sons, Ltd.,
and the British Psychological Society.

During the last century we have seen seismic shifts in our capacities for communication, including the widespread use of first fixed and now mobile telephony, air travel, the use of email and the Internet, videoconferencing, teleconferencing, fax, podcasts, vodcasts, television and radio as well as a variety of application-sharing devices. All of these developments have influenced the way we work in teams but the pace of change has been far quicker than the pace of our understanding of how these changes affect teamwork. Although our understanding is still limited, we can discern some relatively robust conclusions. This chapter will summarize what we know about virtual team working and offers some prescriptions for how we can integrate the key elements of face-to-face team working with the convenience and benefits of virtual team working. We begin with two case studies:

Case Study

Verifone, Inc.

Verifone, Inc. produces electronic payment solutions – the technology you see when you go to pay at the till in your supermarket or to buy a train ticket at a railway station. Its principal products are point-of-sale, merchant-operated, consumer-facing and self-service payment systems for multiple industries including banks, shops, hotels, petrol stations and pharmacies. Verifone uses virtual teams in every aspect of its operation, whether it is groups of facility managers working to reduce toxins in their offices, manufacturing procurement groups working together to buy semi-conductors, or marketing and development teams developing ideas for new products. Verifone have systematically planned how to make best use of virtual teams and advocate key steps in the process.

- *Define a purpose* for the virtual team. Verifone believes that members of such teams need to know what the purpose is at the outset. They must then identify the information they need to clarify that purpose. The teams also ensure they are clear about the time required for a solution or output – at what point does the organization or its customers expect the team to have delivered? They also agree, as a team, what they will and won't try to achieve as a team, specifying clear boundaries around the task. Team members also discuss what technologies they can use to enable them to work effectively as a team, such as group decision support systems, desktop videoconferencing and email. They discuss in advance which technologies they will use for what purposes. They also specify very precisely what defines success for the team in its work. Every virtual team has a start-up checklist to complete to ensure these issues have all been effectively discussed and decided.

- Through specifying the *duration* of the virtual team's life and the team task, the different types of team are identified:
  - o Short-term teams – these are teams whose task is usually completed within minutes or hours. Typically they would be solving a problem for a customer very quickly. A clear leader ensures the team is focused and effective.
  - o Problem-solving task teams – these are teams of diverse membership focused on responding to specific problems such as technical problems with equipment that perhaps repeatedly malfunction. Engineers from across the world will work together to solve such problems.
  - o Process improvement teams – these teams may be involved in finding ways of dramatically improving the efficiency and effectiveness of processes within the company such as streamlining the sales to order process and reducing turnaround from order to delivery by half. There are at least 60 such teams within the organization at any one time, each with a clear leader, and reporting progress to the company top management team. These virtual process improvement teams underpin a culture of continuous improvement.
  - o Long-term operational teams – an example is the profitability team focused on ensuring continued financial success for the organization. All business unit controllers from around the world are members and they meet for an hour each week by videoconference to review financial forecasts. Company-wide forecasts are distributed in advance to them by email to ensure they have the necessary information to conduct effective financial planning as a team.
- *Recruit members* to the virtual team. At Verifone this is typically no fewer than three and no more than seven team members (consistent with the prescriptions for team size in Chapter 3). Members have a range of experience, knowledge, skills and abilities and in some cases will live in different time zones. This enables the team to work over the course of a much longer day than the typical 9am to 5pm working day.
- *Select technology tools* for the team. Technologies are selected and team members are trained in how to use them. Typically for keeping

in contact, they use beepers, mobile phones and voice mail; for disseminating information, the technologies of choice are fax, email and application sharing over the company intranet; for decision making they rely on email, conference calls and video-conferencing. Marketing teams use remote application sharing to see and comment on slides being presented (using webinar technologies). Problem-solving teams have follow-up conference calls daily to ensure they are on track and on target.

- http://www.inc.com/magazine/19970615/1409.html (last accessed 11 August 2011).

Case Study

Bedrock

In contrast to this planned approach to virtual team working is the case of Bedrock and ChemEng (pseudonyms) who signed a contract for a pan-European data centre and storage service outsourcing. This large order was worth hundreds of millions of euros over a seven-year period to Bedrock. Bedrock aimed to consolidate ChemEng's data centres in several European cities into its own data centre in Copenhagen. The project involved 80 staff from both organizations, working largely virtually, across three countries. After contract signature, the two organizations started several workstreams in parallel. However, there was no joint kick-off meeting between all those involved and issues of teamwork and leadership were not considered in advance in a systematic and thoughtful way. Team members from the various project teams had few face-to-face meetings, ostensibly because of the time pressure and tight financial budget. Conflicts erupted across the organization boundaries between ChemEng and Bedrock. IT staff in ChemEng were resentful of losing their systems to another organization and staged considerable resistance to the project. The lack of teamwork, clear roles, clear goals and structures spawned further conflicts. This manifested in daily email cloudbursts with project managers being deluged by 250 emails a day as people stormed at each other electronically and covered their backs with email trails. The project eventually cost twice as much as planned and took four times as long to complete as originally scheduled. Several burn-out cases occurred, resulting in key staff quitting and morale stagnating. The situation was eventually turned around by courageous and visionary leadership and involved the virtual teams and two organizations coming together in (initially stormy) face-to-face meetings, working out roles, processes and structures and establishing a strong team to identify and sustain trust (including across the organizational boundaries). Bedrock could never recover the business case (the whole project lost money) but the lessons learned from this endeavour – especially about leadership, teamwork and governance within each organization and between both corporations involved – have been adopted as critical success factors for new deals.

These two case studies reveal some of the challenges and benefits of virtual team working. It is not surprising that many otherwise sophisticated organizations struggle with virtuality. Working in this way is relatively new, technologies to facilitate virtual team working are being developed continually and we human beings have to adapt to this way of working and its associated technologies very quickly. Consequently, people respond with varying degrees of alacrity or resistance. The technologies we are using to work virtually have been invented relatively recently whereas we have been developing our skills of face-to-face team working for tens of thousands of years. Research into virtual team working is also, inevitably, in its infancy with research really taking off in the last 10 to 15 years. Consequently, the state of our knowledge is still limited so prescriptions and interventions are often tentative. Nevertheless, we have made progress and in this chapter we can say what is known about which strategies are likely to help virtual team working and which approaches are likely to lead to major problems. We begin by considering what is meant by virtual team working.

What is Virtual Team Working?

People at work in modern workplaces are often separated by time and distance and yet still have to work effectively in teams. Moreover, the use of technologies to communicate, such as email, videoconferencing, shared applications and teleconferencing is now ubiquitous. We are all working virtually and increasingly so in teams. At one extreme, members of a team may be distributed geographically in six different countries while being collectively responsible for developing the global marketing strategy for a new cosmetic product.

At the other extreme, a team of six people is distributed in a building such that four of them share an office and two others are located in two separate offices on a lower floor of the building. Both teams are virtual to an extent but we tend to think of the former as a virtual team and the latter as a co-located team. It immediately becomes clear that virtual team working is not a dichotomous category (you are or are not in a virtual team) but a continuous dimension – or most teams work virtually to some extent. Team members may communicate by email or by telephone at times, for example. The question we need to answer is how working virtually affects team performance and how we can intervene to promote more effective virtual team working.

How is virtual team working distinct from virtual working generally and how does virtual team working differ from traditional team working? Virtual team working involves members communicating predominantly by electronic media such as email, telephone, videoconferencing in order to achieve their shared objectives. Other types of virtual working that do not involve virtual teamwork include *teleworking,* where organizational staff members work outside the main company workplace, largely alone, using telecommunication services; and *virtual group working,* where several teleworkers work in parallel probably reporting to the same manager, such as staff in a call centre. *Virtual team working* by contrast sees members working towards shared objectives and using electronic media to a great extent for their interdependent interactions (Hertel, Geister and Konradt, 2005). Virtual teams differ from more traditional 'co-located teams' in two key ways. First, members are distributed geographically or spatially and second, they rely relatively heavily on technology to manage their team communications.

Virtual team working can be measured by the number of different sites at which team members work, the concentration of people at each site (relatively equally dispersed or with a concentration of members at one or more sites), the relative isolation of team members, degree of separation (at a great distance) or overlap of time zones – all in Western Europe versus all in different time zones (Axtell, Fleck and Turner, 2004). While these different ways of cutting the virtual team working cake make sense and invite intriguing questions, there is simply too little research to tell us which categories are theoretically and practically of most use in understanding virtual team working.

Theory development in this area is still relatively limited but one approach (Kirkman and Mathieu, 2005) proposes that virtuality can be described by three core dimensions: teams that make more use of *virtual tools,* make less use of *synchronous communication* (members communicating with each other simultaneously as in face-to-face conversations rather than asynchronously, picking up each other's emails at different times) and require less *informational richness* in their communication are *more* virtual. The theory also proposes three input factors that further determine the level of virtuality: the *number of boundaries* to be crossed, *proportion of co-located members* and *team size.* The more boundaries to be crossed (organizational, geographic, time zones); the lower the proportion of co-located members; and the greater the number of team members, the more likely teams are to work virtually.

Working virtually necessitates less synchronous communication, less informational richness and greater use of virtual tools. Why might organizations be inclined to encourage virtual team working? Some challenges are organization-wide projects that involve several or all major departments, perhaps spread across sites and national boundaries, such as implementing a culture change programme. Alliances with other organizations are increasingly commonplace within and between economies, requiring teams to be constituted from members of different organizations. In multinational organizations particularly there is a need to work across countries. Mergers and acquisitions both involve intensive negotiation and collaboration across organizational boundaries. More of us want to telecommute at least part of our working week rather than waste time and money travelling to and from work every day, when much work can be accomplished as or more efficiently from home. And in the hugely competitive and global economy that is the context for work, emerging markets are often in other parts of the world rather than the home country of an organization. With increased integration of economies, business travel requires supportive technologies and communication capabilities while people are on the move. Indeed, businesspeople in airports seem to spend more of their time on their mobile phones and laptops now than they do engaging with the immediate world around them. Virtual teamwork can also reduce costs for organizations of travel to meetings (we can use videoconferencing instead), office space (if people are working at home part of the time, space is less pressured) and utilities such as heating and lighting. At a societal level, virtual working can enable those who are often excluded from the workforce to participate, such as people with disabilities and carers (e.g., those caring for elderly and infirm relatives). There are many disadvantages too such as the increased invasion of non-work time that emails, text messages and intranet applications can represent.

Advantages and Disadvantages of Virtual Teams

Table 5 describes some of the advantages and disadvantages of virtual team working and gives examples from four different levels – for individuals, teams, organizations and society as a whole.

Thus far we have explored what is meant by virtual team working, considered the variety of ways in which we can analyse virtuality, explored some of the benefits and disadvantages of virtual team working and asked why organizations would develop virtual teams, given the challenges created by working across physical or geographical distance. Now we turn to explore how to ensure that virtual team working is effective.

Table 5   Advantages and disadvantages of virtual teams (adapted from Hertel, Geister and Konradt, 2005).

	Benefits of virtuality	*Disadvantages of virtuality*
Individual	Flexibility	Isolation
	More control over when to perform particular tasks	Decreased interpersonal contact with team members
	Work–non-work life balance	Interferences in work–non-work life balance
	Motivation that comes from autonomy	Misunderstandings
	Empowerment	Conflicts
Team	Flexibility	Conflicts
	Short-term teams can easily be formed	Poor decision making
	Selection of team members on basis of KSAs not location	Communication problems
		Less productive and effective than co-located
	Bigger skill pool	teams for some tasks
Organization	Around the clock working	Difficulties of supervision
	Speed	Costs of technologies
	Flexibility	Data security
	Reduced travel costs	Loss of organizational citizenship
	Close connection to suppliers	Additional training required
	Close connection to customers	
Society	Development of poorer regions by creating virtual teams in those areas (e.g., rural)	Increase of isolation and alienation
		Invasion of work into home and family time
	Integration of disabled people into the workforce	Use of technology to increase monitoring and
	Integration of carers into the workforce who would otherwise not be able to participate	control of staff
	Reduction in traffic congestion and air pollution	
	Decrease in commuting time	

How to Develop Effective Virtual Team Working

Physical distance between team members is a key characteristic of virtual teams. Research on proximity demonstrates that distance or proximity affects behaviour in many ways (Kiesler and Cummings, 2002). Proximity is associated with greater liking and better communication. This is at least partly because when people are working together in the same room, they can see each other's facial expressions, hand gestures, judge their emotions more accurately and look at material on a flip chart. Research comparing co-located and virtual teams reveals that, as a consequence, co-located teams complete twice as much work as virtual teams (Olson and Olson, 2000). Moreover, people are more likely to collaborate with others if they work in close proximity because it is easier to start conversations and maintain them when you can see others. Some research suggests that if you work more than 50 metres away from another person, communication becomes limited and collaboration much less likely. Moreover, email usage increases as distance (30 metres, 40 metres, 50 metres) increases (Hertel *et al.*, 2005). What then are the challenges of virtual team working and how can these be overcome? We consider first the key inputs and then the processes that are likely to be affected by virtual team working.

Inputs

Some virtual team tasks require the use of synchronous and some asynchronous technologies. Asynchronous technologies are those that do not require team members to use them at the same point in time. Email is an example of asynchronous technology; videoconferencing is a synchronous technology since team members must use it simultaneously. In a study of six virtual teams (Riopelle *et al.*, 2003), the one team with a low complexity, independent (as opposed to interdependent) task used more asynchronous technology and held face-to-face meetings only once a year. A low complexity, independent task might be team members dealing with customer complaints in their geographic region and exchanging information about key complaints and ways of dealing with them. The other five teams, which had more complex interdependent tasks, made much more use of synchronous technology and regular face-to-face meetings. More complex tasks might be designing a new petrol pump system that prevents motorists from putting the wrong fuel in their cars and developing plans for marketing and distribution. Complexity of tasks is therefore an important input. A meta analysis (summarizing a number of different research studies) of virtual team working showed that complex problem solving or conflict resolution groups performed worse using computer-mediated technologies than those which performed the same tasks face to face (Baltes *et al.*, 2002). Thus, such groups should rely less on virtual working – if they place too much reliance on virtual team working, they will be less effective.

Virtual team working also presents challenges to team composition. We know (see Chapter X) that diversity in teams is challenging – diversity implies the potential for greater conflict, particularly early in a team's life.

Add diversity into the mix of boundaries, low proximity and greater use of technologies and the challenge of team working becomes yet more complex. Diverse team working in contexts where members are not in face-to-face contact makes it more likely that differences in use of language, orientation, customs and expressions will lead to misunderstandings and conflict. In Chapter X, we describe diversity fault lines as being particularly problematic for effective team functioning – diversity differences exist along two or more dimensions such as all engineers in the team being men and all marketing people being women. When team members are separated by physical distance, diversity fault lines are more likely to appear. In an alliance between two organizations, such as an engineering company in the United Kingdom and a power generating company in Korea, a diversity fault line is created, comprised of nationality/culture, first language and organization membership. Such fault lines are particularly prevalent in virtual teams because people of the same functional background (HR, marketing, R&D, etc.) are often grouped together in the same location. Functional and location fault lines are therefore created. Language differences are particularly likely to create such fissures in combination with other diversity dimensions. Recognizing the potential in virtual teams for the negative impact of such fault lines is a first step to limiting their negative impact. Having clear team objectives, high levels of reflexivity and good communication is an important way of ensuring team effectiveness in this context (van Knippenburg *et al.*, 2011).

Another compositional challenge is the proportion of members in a virtual team, for whom working in that team is their primary role. The smaller the proportion of such members, the more difficult it will be for the team to be effective. I worked, until recently, in several teams including the management team of a business school, which I led, the management team of a university, and a research team focused on improving the effectiveness of health services. In each of them we used varied means of communication including away days, regular meetings, all-member emails, teleconferences (with as many as five or six people joining), videoconferencing and shared documents. The more teams we are members of, however, the harder it is to be a full-time member of any team. A key input to virtual teams is the proportion of full-time versus part-time members. A particular challenge for me was to be an effective member of the research team when so much of my time was spent on management responsibilities. Consequently, I worked more virtually with the research team than I did with the other teams. The extent to which team membership involves fitting in the team's work around the team members' main jobs affects both team virtuality and effectiveness. The more a team is composed of members whose main job is not the team's work, the more likely it is the team will work virtually and therefore the less complex the team's task must be.

Virtual working often means more use of text-based (asynchronous) communication rather than face-to-face or other forms of synchronous communication. We know that the greater the level of text-based communication, the poorer is team decision making (Baltes *et al.*, 2002). The exception to this, which almost never occurs in the workplace, is where team members have unlimited time and their contributions to the decision-making process are anonymous.

In summary, virtual team working is more difficult the greater the task complexity, the larger the team size (above eight or nine members), the more the number of boundaries to be crossed, the greater team member diversity, and the greater the proportion of 'part-time' members. Almost all of these characteristics were present in the Bedrock Inc. case study described at the beginning of the chapter and explain why success was so difficult to achieve. Therefore leaders have to consider carefully the nature of the task a team is required to do and match virtual technologies and working methods to ensure that the task is effectively completed. They also have to ensure that teams adapt their processes to maximize their effectiveness when working virtually and compensate for the absence of face-to-face interactions. In the next section of the chapter, we identify the team processes that are most critical to consider in managing virtual team working and consider how these processes can be nurtured.

Processes

Trust. The ability to work together in a team is underpinned in any context by trust between team members. Teams with higher levels of trust have more effective group processes (communication, support, backing up), less conflict and more positive climates. In one respect, virtual team working requires even higher levels of trust – particularly from team leaders – since there is no (or at least much less) physical oversight of people's work. Therefore team members have to trust other team members to pull their weight and be effective team players. Team leaders must understand that dispersed teams have to be managed more by motivating and trusting them than by control since knowledge of each member's contribution is necessarily reduced. It is helpful to understand trust in this context by distinguishing between affective and cognitive trust. The latter is related to perceptions of team members' reliability and competence. Do they provide prompt and helpful answers to email questions for example? There is some evidence that cognitive trust can be developed relatively quickly in virtual team working but that affective trust is less likely to develop (Rocco *et al.*, 2000). In a study of 50 members of an IT department who worked virtually, predictors of trust were knowledge of local customs and culture, a sense of shared identity with virtual co-workers (a sense of the valued identity of the team), and communication frequency. The latter applied particularly to non-work-related communication, the sort of friendly chatting or 'social grooming' that builds relationships between friends and acquaintances. So trust can be built if team members are urged to respond to requests within a maximum agreed turnaround time; a strong team identity is established and there is good shared understanding of organizational context and culture. Team members should also be encouraged to get to know each other and chat about non-work-related activities, perhaps at the start of teleconference meetings, for example. One useful device is to ask team members to report on 'what's the best moment in your last 24 hours?'

Cohesion. Sociotechnical systems theory emphasized the importance of a fit between the social system requirements and technical or technological systems of an organization. If the technology disrupts social relationships, it is likely to be resisted by workers and morale and cohesion fall – typical in many poorly run call centres (see Chapter X). Consistent with this, there is evidence of a negative relationship between the extent of virtual team working and liking, friendship and cohesiveness in teams (Axtell *et al.,* 2004). How can virtual teams ensure cohesion when technology and distance combine to reduce that valuable element of team working? Communicating frequently helps and there is much evidence that face-to-face meetings lead more quickly to team maturation and thereby effective team functioning and performance (Gluesing *et al.,* 2003). Such devices as weekly audio/teleconferences and quarterly face-to-face meetings aid this process. In a study of rocket engine design teams who had responsibility for clarifying and changing objectives, learning about new concepts in the design process, and understanding the design concerns of other team (Majchrzak *et al.,* 2000), researchers found that collaborative technology worked but only because of the common language and clear norms about ways of doing things developed by team members in face-to-face meetings.

Conflict. Physical proximity between people is associated with lower conflict levels (Hinds and Mortensen, 2002). High diversity and lack of common social identity is associated with higher levels of team conflict. People who work in different contexts with lack of understanding of the constraints in each other's contexts are also more likely to fall out. Dispersion of people who must work interdependently across time zones is associated with frustrations and recriminations, since work is often not completed, simply because other team members are not at work. Reliance on technology means important social cues are filtered out of communications: an apologetic tone may be lost in an email communication; a warm smile as a joke is made is not seen during a teleconference and a shared exasperation with a third party may not be appreciated in the text of a shared document. The deindividuation that inevitably occurs when team members do not meet face to face can lead to reduced politeness and informal social chatting but increasing intolerance, aggression, conflict and 'flaming' (sending angry email messages).

All of these factors affect the levels of conflict and potential conflict in virtual teams (Kiesler and Sproull, 1992) and we have already seen how team conflict undermines team effectiveness (Chapter 11). To reduce conflict, it is vital that team members are clear with each other about the context of their work (constraints and strengths), that diversity is celebrated in the team as a source of innovation, that there are clear agreements about how and when to work across boundaries and time zones, and that team members work hard to add in social cues to emails – although we may dismiss their use as irritating, the insertion of icons and smiley faces in emails does make a difference. Taking the time to have fun and share humour during teleconferences is helpful not time wasting (within limits of course).

Attributions. These difficulties of conflict in virtual team working are compounded by the extent to which people make the fundamental attribution error – blaming the individual rather than the situation for difficulties. Thus in virtual working contexts, team members are likely to consider other team members as lazy or rude because of a failure to reply to a message (the explanation could be the message was never received). Indeed, there is a significant positive relationship between physical distance between team members and negative attributions. The greater the distance between team members, the greater is their tendency to make negative attributions in response to broken commitments (Cramton and Wilson, 2002). To prevent such negative attributions, those working virtually in teams need to take time to explain their situation and express concern or regret for the problems (even when they are not at fault). Explaining the situation alone does not seem to be sufficient – understanding the problems caused to the other appears to be a necessary component to reduce or prevent the cementing of negative attributions. This suggests we need to be especially clear and overtly and consciously empathetic when using virtual tools in teams, especially as distances between members become greater.

Mental models. Teams share knowledge, discuss together, build shared understanding of their task, their team working and their environments. They develop transactive knowledge too over time – knowing who in the team knows what. They build trust via non-task communication, chatting about weekend activities, children, sports teams and celebrities. They share knowledge about the constraints they individually and collectively face in their work. And they take time to elaborate on information they give each other about their work. In short, they create shared mental models of their team and its work. In virtual team working, it is much more difficult to do these things and thereby to create shared mental models. At the simplest level, for example, face-to-face dyads have more shared understanding of the same task than do virtual dyads. There are many factors which make it much more difficult for teams working virtually to develop the shared mental models and mutual understanding which are at the basis of team working. These include:

- Failure to communicate and retain contextual information (sharing unique information about own context, e.g., our email systems only let us receive attachments below 750kb);
- Unevenly distributed information (e.g., only some members received an email sent by the leader);
- Difficulty communicating and understanding the salience of information (e.g., it was in the third paragraph of the email so we did not pay close attention to it);
- Differences in speed or timing of communication (e.g., emails arrived after the end of the working day);
- Interpreting the meaning of silence (e.g., team members did not reply so this was assumed to indicate support for the proposal, although an indication of support or opposition was not requested in the message) (Cramton, 2002).

Other factors include:

- Site differences – team members working at different locations in the organization will have taken for granted knowledge about the way things are done at the site that others will lack. Such differences in customs in particular locations may be even more important than differences between functions within an organization (e.g., sales and production; or radiologists and A&E doctors). Culture – the way we do things around here – is often unspoken but is a hugely powerful influence on team behaviour (Sole and Edmondson, 2002).
- As we saw in Chapter X, groups tend to focus on commonly held information (Stasser and Titus, 2003) leading to 'hidden profiles'. This phenomenon is likely to be exacerbated in virtual teams and because so much virtual working involves slow communication by text, the problem is made even more challenging.
- There is less efficient exchange of information via synchronous or asynchronous text-based technology than there is face to face.
- Some research suggests that team members, working virtually, are more likely to contradict each other in electronic groups but are less able to resolve the resulting conflicts.

Process assistance. Effective virtual team working will benefit from skilled process assistance and coordination. For example, a meta-analysis of group decision support systems showed that having facilitation greatly increases decision quality on complex tasks (Dennis and Wixom, 2002). The team leader can therefore play a critical role in providing or securing appropriate process assistance. He or she should provide mentoring, understanding and empathy. The leader should also ensure that team members develop shared transactive memory, knowing who knows what, ideally in the form of a system to encode, store and retrieve information. And there must be tacit and explicit coordination of virtual team working – much more explicit coordination than would be necessary for face-to-face teams.

Summary. While new technologies have created many new opportunities for working together, they sometimes exact a price on effective teamwork. Trust, communication, shared mental models were well developed in craft shops and on farms 200 years ago. They are increasingly difficult to achieve as we develop more distributed forms of work organization. Team members working virtually must therefore make considerable extra effort to communicate both formally and informally; develop good transactive knowledge (who knows what) perhaps by codifying this information; develop a shared identity as a team that evokes pride and commitment; build and sustain mental models of the team, its task and its environment; develop a psychologically safe team environment where blame is not the knee-jerk reaction to difficulties but where an orientation of seeking to learn from errors and problems is; where expectations of team members and the team are clear; and where excellent coordination mechanisms are in place. Above all, team members need to be clear about the team's objectives, clear about their roles and clear about how to work effectively together both virtually and face to face.

Next we consider the lifecycle of virtual teams and offer some practical advice for leading and managing them, drawing upon the work of Hertel, Geister and Konrad (2005).

Lifecycle of Virtual Teams

Hertel and colleagues (2005) believe that virtual teams (those that communicate predominantly via technology rather than face to face) should go through five stages in their lives:

1 *Preparation.* This involves the development of a mission statement and objectives (see Chapter X), vital for any team and no less so for virtual teams. Preparation also requires careful personnel selection, involving a focus on technical and professional KSAs such as expertise but critically also on teamworking KSAs (see Chapter X). Personality characteristics associated with more effective team working in virtual contexts are likely

to include conscientiousness and extraversion. Choosing members with expertise in new media and groupware technology may be important in developing similar skill sets for other members. Self-management skills are necessary since virtual working often means working alone, unmotivated by the presence of others. Particularly important KSAs for virtual team working are interpersonal and cultural sensitivity; interpersonal trust and dependability. We have stressed throughout this book the importance for us all of valuing diversity (van Knippenburg) and this is no less important in virtual team working that often involves working across cultural and national boundaries. In designing the task for a virtual team, it may be helpful to break the task into clear sub-tasks to be taken on by individual members and not to build a high degree of interdependence or complexity into the task. Team idea generation is generally good when managed virtually but complex group decision making is not. To really waste time, try having a virtual team write a document synchronously such as during a video- or teleconference. Using shareware to write documents asynchronously makes much more sense. Negotiation and conflict management generally require face-to-face or at least video- or teleconference meetings. Virtual teams must also agree the technology they will use – tools for information exchange, communication, coordination and shared authoring. These range from collaborative learning from bulletin boards, videoconferencing and electronic data exchange up to high interdependence tools such as group decision systems, electronic brainstorming systems, ranking or voting tools, group authoring software and electronic meeting systems. Virtual teams must also agree the systems they will use for exchanges with other teams within the organization with which they must collaborate and communicate.

2 *Launch*. These should always include face-to-face meetings (Powell *et al.,* 2004) enabling team members to get acquainted, and clarify goals and roles. During the launch phase, team members must also acquire necessary information to do the job and be trained as appropriate in the use of the selected communication technologies. Teams also need to put in place structures for transactive memory – recording who knows what and codifying and storing details of their work and decisions so that it is clear for all to see (without creating unnecessary or overwhelming bureaucracy). Establishing norms of behaviour and rules for teamwork will help the team to build trust, cohesion and create a sense of a valued identity. This phase should lead to increasing cooperation and trust.

3 *Performance management*. Team leaders must provide guidance and managerial support beyond the mere provision of an electronic groupware system for the team, ensuring the processes discussed earlier

in this chapter are nurtured. High levels of communication are important therefore but this communication must be regulated. Disinhibited communication, 'flaming' and conflict eruptions damage team cohesion and effectiveness. Moreover, the virtual team must be coached to find a good fit between the communication media employed and communication content. Email, faxes and phone calls are better for sharing and gathering information; longer phone calls and conference calls are better for solving some problems while face-to-face meetings are generally needed for making comprehensive decisions, solving more complex problems and resolving conflicts. Non-job-related communication should not be discouraged since this will compensate for the loss of face-to-face intimacy and familiarity. Hofner Saphiere (1996), for example, found that global business teams were more productive if they had more personal communication topics during their interactions. The leader needs to maintain motivation and emotion by ensuring each team member is aware of her or his role; contributions of each member should be made explicit with plenty of recognition and positive feedback; and the team and its members should receive frequent feedback on performance. All of these interventions are likely to promote trust in the team. Kirkman *et al.* (2004), examined empowerment in 35 virtual teams providing IT services and found that such trust building correlated with team process improvement and customer satisfaction. The leader must also build a sense of strong and positive team identity since this in turn builds cohesion. Both have been shown to be related to team effectiveness in virtual teams (Geister, 2004). And virtual team members record higher levels of satisfaction when they have more opportunities to meet face to face, have more non-job-related communication and have more constructive rather than destructive conflict management (Hertel *et al.*, 2005). At this stage the leader must also ensure that shared knowledge is well managed in the team, promoting shared mental models and continuing to build transactive memory.

4 *Training and development.* As the team develops, training should continue. This includes training for the team leader, for individual team members (e.g., in the use of technology or the management of conflict) and for the team as a whole unit. Sports teams are coached to work as a team and virtual teams also need to be coached and trained to work effectively as a whole team. The team also needs to repeatedly clarify team goals, review and improve their use of communication media, further develop intra- and inter-team processes to ensure they are improving their functioning and performance.

5 *Disbanding and reintegration.* This phase is generally honoured more in the breach by organizations than in reality and is something of a good

idea that academics or practitioners came up with. Given that teams fulfil important social needs for people at work, it may be wise to note their passing or ending as social entities, recognizing and celebrating their contributions and the ties that have been established. This is prelude to the team members reintegrating into the organization (if the team was temporary) or joining a new team if the transition involves such a move. There is virtually no research evidence to inform our thinking about this proposed phase or how important it really is. However, our knowledge of human behaviour, attachment and disruptions to relationships suggest the value of recognizing such transitions and acknowledging some of the emotions that go with them. End-of-project dinners, parties or other events make sense in that regard.

Conclusion

The huge changes in our ability to communicate over distances have outstripped our understanding of how to adapt our ways of working effectively around these changes. We have to undertake more research and try out more ways of working virtually in teams to enable that catch-up process to take place. Meanwhile some things are clear. Virtual team working offers a variety of benefits and challenges and everyone in modern organizations should be trained to understand these and respond appropriately. Virtual team working requires more effort to establish trust, build cohesion and promote both careful and thoughtful communication. The overall challenge is to build clear shared mental models of the team, its work and its environment. The set-up and launch process for virtual team working is vital to this and kick-off meetings can be especially important to get the processes right at the outset. Leaders and managers should take responsibility for ensuring that virtual team working enables organizations to reap the benefits and not be shackled by the disadvantages. That requires knowledge and awareness and the courage to show the way. Hertel and his colleagues summarize by offering five core prescriptions for virtual team working. Make sure teams have clear goals and roles that are not in conflict with team members' commitments to other work units; make sure there are appropriate and efficient communication and collaboration processes preventing misunderstandings and conflict; provide encouragement to team members to promote team awareness, information communication and sharing of socio-emotional cues; give performance feedback and consider and respond to the individual situations of each team member; create experiences of interdependence, via goal setting and good team task design; and use appropriate kick-off workshops and team training to enable and sustain virtual team working.

This chapter offers key lessons in the direction to go in enabling and sustaining virtual team working but we should be aware that there is also considerable practical working knowledge out there in organizations to be drawn upon to enrich the limited understanding organizational research offers thus far. Further research to elicit that knowledge and apply the lessons for promoting much more effective virtual team working in organizations would be hugely valuable, given the amount of energy and resource wasted on ineffective virtual team working within organizations.

Key Revision Points

- What are the main advantages of virtual team working?
- What are the main disadvantages of virtual team working and how can these be minimized?
- In what circumstances is it appropriate for a team to work predominantly virtually?
- What inputs to team working are most important to consider in a virtual team-working situation?
- How can team processes be improved to ensure effective virtual team working?
- What are the key stages in the life cycle of a virtual team and how can each of these stages best be managed?

Further Reading

Axtell, C.M., Fleck, S.J. and Turner, N. (2004) Virtual teams: Collaborating across distance, in *International Review of Industrial and Organizational Psychology,* Vol. 19 (eds C.L. Cooper and I.T. Robertson), John Wiley & Sons, Ltd, Chichester, pp. 205–248.

Dixon, K.R. and Panteli, N. (2010) From virtual teams to virtuality in teams. *Human Relations,* 63, 1177–1197.

Hambley, L.A., O'Neill, T.A. and Kline, T.J.B. (2007) Virtual team leadership: Perspectives from the field. *International Journal of e-Collaboration,* 3, 40–64.

Hertel, G., Geister, S. and Konradt, U. (2005) Managing virtual teams: A review of current empirical research. *Human Resource Management Review,* 15, 69–95.

Kirkman, B.L. and Mathieu, J.E. (2005) The dimensions and antecedents of team virtuality. *Journal of Management,* 31, 700–718.

Townsend, A.M., De Marie, S.M. and Hendrickson, A.R. (1998) Virtual teams: Technology and the workplace of the future. *Academy of Management Executive,* 12, 17–29.

Web Resources

http://www.seanet.com/~daveg/vrteams.htm (last accessed 11 August 2011)
Virtual teams in organizations.

http://www.dailyfinance.com/story/virtual-teams-bring-widespread-challenges/
19481916/ (last accessed 11 August 2011).

A very resourceful news article on virtual teams and the challenges facing VTW.
http://www.bioteams.com/2005/06/27/virtual_teams.html (last accessed 11 August
2011).
A brief description of the paradigm of virtual teams.

14

Top Management Teams

The leaders who work most effectively, it seems to me, never say "I". And that's not because they have trained themselves not to say "I". They think "we"; they think "team". They understand their job to be to make the team function. They accept responsibility and don't sidestep it, but "we" gets the credit ... This is what creates trust, what enables you to get the task done. (Peter F. Drucker)

Key Learning Points

- What are Top Management Teams (TMTs) and what is their task?
- The role that TMTs play in their organizations
- Prescriptions for creating and maintaining TMTs
- Defining the purpose and objectives of TMT as complementary to organizational objectives
- Inputs for TMT effectiveness that are unique to TMTs
- How to compose and ensure the diversity of TMTs
- TMT processes – participation, conflict, agreement seeking and communication
- Processes unique to TMTs and common to all teams and the importance of clear norms of team functioning
- The role of the CEO in the TMT

Effective Teamwork: Practical Lessons from Organizational Research, Third Edition.
By M. A. West. © 2012 John Wiley & Sons, Ltd. Published 2012 by John Wiley & Sons, Ltd.,
and the British Psychological Society.

Born in the tough landscape of the Bronx in New York City and a passionate leader with strong values, Angelo Mozilo started Countrywide Financial in the late 1960s. Mozilo believed he could enable millions of families to buy homes by building a financial business that was founded on probity and commitment to its customers. Forty years later, CEO Mozilo appeared to have lost the plot, convinced on the one hand that a disastrous financial crisis lay just around the corner – he was right – but stubbornly believing Countrywide Financial would be passed over by the plague of financial collapse. The company was in the forefront of the toxic mortgage business and came disastrously close to bankruptcy before being taken over by Bank of America.

Senior executives in companies like Merrill Lynch and AIG (American International Group) were voicing concerns about the effects of the mortgage markets on their companies back in 2005. They were ignored, sidelined or dismissed because their CEOs did not believe their warnings about the massive dangers being created in the United States, United Kingdom and other Western economies. The head of AIG's financial products division, Joe Cassano, was famous for losing his temper in meetings with other senior executives. He did listen to some Cassandras about the dangers of credit losses (people defaulting on debts and mortgages) but ignored others who told him about the possibility of huge calls on the firm's collateral as the debt crisis unwound. The firm collapsed as a consequence and had to be rescued by the Federal Government.

The head of Merrill Lynch, Stan O'Neill ignored people in his team telling him that the firm was massively over-exposed to the (now) infamous sub-prime market, and was ignorant of the problem until it was simply too late. The company lost $51.8 billion (yes billion) and O'Neill was fired. Goldman Sachs on the other hand survived because the top team paid attention to the concerns, advice and information they were getting from the people dubbed pessimists and risk-avoidant in other companies (for a detailed description of these cases, see McLean and Nocera, 2011).

These case studies of organizational failures which have affected millions of people around the world raise the question of what is wrong with our corporations. Are we hiring CEOs who are too stupid to run organizations, too impulsive to be trusted with key decisions or too arrogant to take the advice of those around them? Or should we look more broadly than these heroic individuals and look at the wider group that runs the organization? And that in turn raises the question of whether it is the top team or the CEO that makes the difference? Research examining TMTs suggests that it is both of course, but the whole team rather than the CEO alone has most influence on an organization's success (Finkelstein and Hambrick, 1996; Hambrick, 1994). How the top team manages itself determines whether executives draw on their diverse experiences and knowledge to make high-quality decisions in uncertain and difficult situations (Carpenter, Gelatkanycz and Sanders, 2004; Edmondson, Roberto and Watkins, 2003; Nadler, 1996) and ensure organizational success. As with all teams, however, there is a chasm between those top teams that achieve their potential and those that fall short as the two case studies above illustrate. This chapter provides guidance on how to help the top team steer the organization to success rather than to the financial disasters these case studies describe.

What is the top management team in an organization? Is it the heads of the different departments that report to the CEO or those closest to the CEO who help her or him with their decision making or is it all of the senior leaders in the organization? This is not a simple question to answer as we will see. Some researchers refer to the 'dominant coalition' as the group of powerful people that span the boundary between the organization and the external environment and make influential decisions (Cyert and March, 1963). Others suggest that titles/positions may not be the best way to identify the top team members (Pettigrew, 1992) and that we should ask the CEO who is in the top team (Bantel and Jackson, 1989). These are the people who formulate and implement strategic decisions; they in turn have considerable symbolic significance and their influence on the organizational culture is powerful and pervasive (Flood, MacCurtain and West 2001). What is presented as the top team may simply be a formal information-sharing body while the real decision making is done by an informal group of the CEO's closest advisors which has no official identity. Whatever the constitution of the TMT the aim in this chapter is to answer the question: 'How can this team ensure that its potential – so vital to the effectiveness of the organization overall – is achieved rather than squandered?' Using an input-process-output model we will consider each of the relevant inputs, processes and outputs of team functioning in turn in order to construct a comprehensive understanding of how to ensure that the peculiar challenges of the top team can be met. Such an understanding is vital if organizations are to be steered to success rather than onto the rocks of insolvency, criminality or ineffectiveness. We begin with considering inputs of task design, team effort and skills and organizational support.

Task Design

Good team task design includes having a complete task that is relevant to organizational aims, requires team members to work interdependently, where team members have a high degree of autonomy in going about their work and receive good feedback on team performance. The task of the TMT in any organization seems self-evident. It is to ensure the organization is effective and successful. That requires that the team takes responsibility for ensuring there is an appropriate strategy in place that enables the organization to adapt to and succeed in its environment, that the competing demands of stakeholders are effectively managed, and that what constitutes success and effectiveness is clearly defined. The team must also ensure that the strategy is implemented and that the conditions are in place within the organization to ensure that all its resources are appropriately targeted towards ensuring effectiveness and success. In that sense, TMTs have a complete and clear task that is challenging and ultimately measurable – the conditions for motivating goals (Locke and Latham, 1990).

As the team at the 'strategic apex' of the organization, the TMT has considerable autonomy. They are answerable to stakeholders and board members (where non-executive members are appointed), but they are at the top of the hierarchical heap, enjoying both power and freedom. Their roles are challenging for sure, but combined with freedom, this can be an exhilarating cocktail, producing high levels of engagement and a sense of efficacy. Moreover, the task of the top team is self-evidently relevant (we hope) to achieving the organization's overall goals so motivation is further enhanced. Teams at lower levels within the organization may not enjoy the same sense of relevance and the satisfaction of seeing the powerful consequences of their team working. The debt collection team in a service centre for photocopying machines may sometimes feel as though they are simply turning the same old handle rather than making a significant difference to the organization's performance or the level of customer satisfaction. For the TMT, engaged in surfing the waves of competition, change and strategy development and implementation, the sense of relevance and consequence of their work is high. Moreover, they are likely to see the results of their efforts in share price performance, sales figures, employee opinion surveys, profits, health and safety statistics, customer satisfaction ratings and patents produced. There is feedback in abundance for TMTs since the whole organization is geared towards providing the information on performance an effective TMT is constantly hungry for. We explore the finer details of the top team task later in this chapter when we explore the top team's purpose and how its objectives should be determined.

But what about interdependence – that crucial and fundamental element of team work? The TMT members are usually those who have risen or fought their way to the top of their functional areas. In a manufacturing organization, they might include the head of production (possibly an engineer), the head of sales (a marketeer), the head of R&D (possibly a high-flying chemist), the heads of Finance, HR and possible Estates, along with the MD him- or herself. These individuals have often succeeded through their individualism, competitive energies and abilities to manage the political processes in organizations which win them preferment. There is also the added complication of the succession tournament where team members may be competing amongst themselves for the position of CEO. Bring them together to work in a team and what we often see is a competitive and dysfunctional group of silverback gorillas beating their chests rather than a cooperative, integrated and supportive team. Achieving interdependent working is therefore a particular challenge for many TMTs. Crucially, many TMT members assume their tasks are to fulfil the objectives for their functional areas. If that were the case of course, there would be little need for a team. We form teams to work together collectively to achieve objectives that they could not achieve working alone or in parallel. This is a crucial distinction we will come back to when considering the purpose and objectives of TMTs. The failure to identify what they need to work on together is at the root of the failure of many TMTs to perform as teams.

Team Effort and Skills

The TMT is likely to be constituted of people with high levels of motivation, given their backgrounds, experience and career success. However, a crucial issue for the top team is the extent to which their motivations are focused on the achievement of success in their functional areas (finance, production, sales) rather than on supporting the achievement of success of their fellow team members and the organization as a whole. Of course there will be some degree of interdependence among top team members focused on their own areas (production and sales functions must cooperate to some extent). But silo working by members of the top team can create the opposite of synergy with members competing for resources and seeking to undermine each other rather than committing to ensuring the success of the team and organization as a whole.

What skills do top team members need and who should be members of the team? The CEO must choose the members of his or her top team to fulfil the purpose of that team. That presupposes clarity of purpose and objectives. Imagine the purpose of the top team is to enable their organization to provide outstanding customer service. They see the way to achieve this is by creating an outstandingly positive culture and climate and by working effectively in partnership with suppliers. The key tasks of the top team then become clearer. In addition to ensuring the effective achievement of targets in their areas (production, sales, R&D, HR) they must ensure that all departments are working together to provide the customer with joined-up service which is speedy, effective and reassuring. All departments have to keep each other informed in order to do that effectively and to have in place well-worked-out and integrated procedures for responding to customer concerns. Moreover, creating a positive culture requires all to ensure staff feel valued, respected and supported and to share best practice and approaches for achieving that. Building strong partnerships with suppliers requires all departments to ensure there is frequent contact, a sense of stability and long-term continuity, a commitment to resolving conflicts quickly and fairly and a sense of mutuality in the partnership relationship – a mutual concern with helping each other. These strategies require the top team to work closely, cooperatively, congruently and creatively to achieve these outcomes – in short, to work interdependently. Skills therefore must include the KSAs of teamwork we explored in Chapter 2. Performing well in their individual functional areas is not sufficient to justify top team membership.

This way of understanding that the top team must focus on the team tasks – the added value the team can uniquely bring to the organization – makes it clear that top team membership is then dependent on who has the skills to work together with others to achieve these outcomes. This may mean the HR Director, the CEO, the Marketing Director and the Chief Financial Officer are on the team and not the Production, R&D or Sales Directors. The thoughtless option of having all direct reports to the CEO become top team members makes no sense if they are not the right people to achieve the team purpose. Of course if the purpose is not clearly stated it becomes even more difficult to identify who should be on the top team and what skills they need. Other common mistakes are for the new CEO just to run with the existing top team members, to create an entirely new team or to create a large team of all the senior leaders in the organization. Particular skill sets or orientations for top team membership also include a desire to be not just a function leader (Production Director) but a member of the leadership team of the organization. That requires also someone who can think at a sophisticated conceptual level and take a systems approach to understanding the organization and understanding the relationship between the organization and its environment. Such individuals also require empathy to be able to engage in the robust but respectful debate top teams require without offending or alienating other team members. They also require integrity to ensure that they build rather than undermine trust. This includes raising issues that affect the functioning of the whole organization even though this may undermine their own area of the organization. Integrity of course also involves keeping confidential the content of discussions held by the senior team and implementing decisions agreed by the senior team. We return later to consider some of the behaviours that undermine teams when we discuss top team conflict but these skills of empathy, integrity, leadership orientation and conceptual sophistication are particularly salient for top team membership (Wageman *et al.*, 2008).

What about team member diversity? Much has been written about the representation of various groups on TMTs such as women, black and minority ethnic groups, people with disabilities and older and younger people. Upper echelons (UE) theory proposes that the make-up of the top team in terms of age, education level and tenure significantly influences organizational outcomes. Hambrick (2005) argues that UE theory offers an information-processing understanding of top team functioning and helps to explain how the executive's orientation affects the selection, perception and interpretation of information presented to the team. This in turn affects organizational outcomes such as innovation and company performance. For example, Smith *et al.* (1994) found the greater the diversity of top team members in experience the worse the organization's performance. Research reveals that the higher the level of education of top team members, the more receptive to creative solutions and innovation they are (Bantel and Jackson, 1989; Hambrick, Cho and Chen, 1996; Smith *et al.,* 1994). Research on top team age diversity suggests negative outcomes as a result of conflict rooted in ineffective communication due to the absence of a shared language (Pfeffer, 1983; Zenger and Lawrence, 1989). The less team members share a similar worldview or mental model of their team task, the harder it is to communicate, collaborate and coordinate their strategies as a team (Flood *et al.,* 2001). A number of studies have found that functional diversity (people coming from different functional backgrounds – engineering, production, sales, marketing, HR) is associated with clearer corporate strategies, market share and profit growth, return on assets, and innovation (Bantel, 1993; Bantel and Jackson, 1989; Hambrick *et al.,* 1996; (Horwitz and Horwitz, 2007; Korn, Milliken and Lant, 1992). Diversity in team tenure seems to be associated with lower levels of cohesion and trust (Lawrence, 1997) but also with higher levels of strategic change, market share and profit growth (Boeker, 1997; Hambrick *et al.,* 1996).

What are we to make of this jumble of findings? Psychologists offer two ways of understanding diversity in groups (Harrison and Klein, 2007). One is an information-processing perspective that sees diversity of all forms as providing richness of information to groups, enabling better quality decision making and more comprehensive analysis of the environment (van Knippenberg and Schippers, 2007). The second perspective, based on social identity or social categorization theory, proposes that diverse groups fail to function effectively because of the clash between people who see themselves as belonging to different and potentially competing groups. We create our sense of self and our identity partly from our membership of groups – male, psychologist, from Wales, cyclist, parent, meditation practitioner, white, Sheffield Wednesday supporter, older adult, etc. To bolster our self-image we think about the groups we are members of in positive ways. By inference we may come to think of groups we are not members of in less positive ways or even in negative ways. Consequently, we tend to think more positively about members of our in-groups (those groups we identify with) and less positively about members of out-groups (female, engineer, younger person, Sheffield United supporter). This creates the conditions in diverse groups for low levels of cooperation and potentially for conflict. Differences in mental models and communication may exacerbate social identity processes also. Both perspectives have considerable empirical support suggesting both are highly relevant to our understanding of the functioning of TMTs. Greater functional diversity in teams is likely to lead to more diverse and relevant information being considered by teams in their decision making. On the other hand having minority groups such as one or two women on the top team (still astonishingly rare in many teams – Sealy, Vinnicombe and Singh, 2008; Welbourne, Cycyota and Ferrante, 2007) or people from very different age backgrounds, may create the conditions for conflict or rejection of views by members of different sub-groups (van Knippenberg and Schippers, 2007).

Research suggests that heterogeneity or diversity in groups can produce higher levels of productivity, innovation and effectiveness in top teams but that important conditions need to be in place to overcome the negative effects of diversity. Van Knippenberg *et al.* (2004) proposed the Categorization-Elaboration Model (CEM). First, team members need to collectively and consciously value the differing perspectives diversity brings and the team leader or CEO must model this orientation and overtly and passionately require her or his team to recognize the value of diversity in the team. Second, research shows that the problems of fault lines (where gaps open up between sub-groups in teams – particularly likely where we have a combination of sub-groups such as female HR directors and male engineers) in teams can be overcome by ensuring the team has a clear purpose and clear objectives. Social categorization effects are reduced because team members focus on their shared goals, increasing a collective sense of in-group identity, and reducing the effects of fault lines. The value of such clarity of purpose for converting diversity into top team innovation, and inhibiting the effects of fault lines has been clearly demonstrated in a study of 42 TMTs in the United Kingdom (van Knippenburg *et al.,* 2011).

Organizational Supports

For the top team to respond appropriately and rapidly, the team needs information that tells its members about the environment, the organization's functioning and their progress towards achieving their objectives. Management information systems are the primary means by which this is accomplished. Figure 4 shows the Key Performance Indicators used by a UK business school, to provide the management team with the information needed to ensure the team could sculpt strategy, focus organizational attention on key issues and ensure progress towards objectives. Using a system of red, green and amber 'traffic lights' the KPIs tell the top team

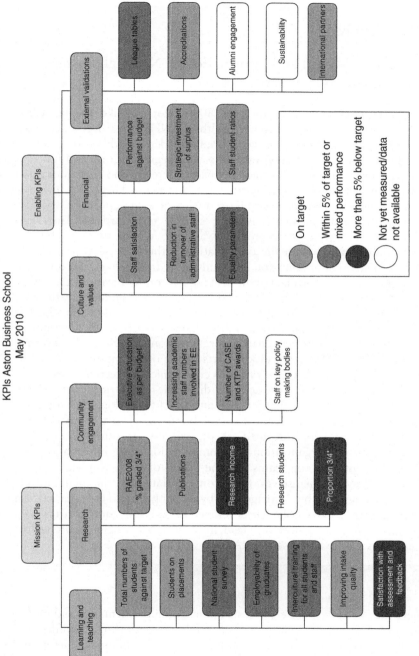

KPIs Aston Business School
May 2010

Mission KPIs

Learning and teaching
- Total numbers of students against target
- Students on placements
- National student survey
- Employability of graduates
- Intercultural training for all students and staff
- Improving intake quality
- Satisfaction with assessment and feedback

Research
- RAE2008 % graded 3/4*
- Publications
- Research income
- Research students
- Proportion 3/4*

Community engagement
- Executive education as per budget
- Increasing academic staff numbers involved in EE
- Number of CASE and KTP awards
- Staff on key policy making bodies

Enabling KPIs

Culture and values
- Staff satisfaction
- Reduction in turnover of administrative staff
- Equality parameters

Financial
- Performance against budget
- Strategic investment of surplus
- Staff student ratios

External validations
- League tables
- Accreditations
- Alumni engagement
- Sustainability
- International partners

Legend:
- On target
- Within 5% of target or mixed performance
- More than 5% below target
- Not yet measured/data not available

Figure 4 Organizational supports for top teams.

Case Study

Communication and information in Nottinghamshire Healthcare NHS Trust

In managing an organization of 8000 people, Mike Cooke, Chief Executive of Nottinghamshire Healthcare NHS Trust, has a top team of highly motivated and very bright leaders working together to deliver mental health services over a wide region. In order to function effectively as a team, they need to ensure there is good communication from the whole organization up to the top team. They need to know about successes, errors, near misses, quality of service, productivity, staff concerns, areas of ineffectiveness, serious untoward incidents and ideas for new and improved ways of doing things. Effective communication within the organization is therefore vital for the top team. Those communication lines must flow upward and the top team must be clear and prudent about seeking the communications they need. Communications that enable them to sculpt strategy continually through repeated conversations with their staff and that ensure they can adjust as necessary in reaction to inevitable changes (such as in government policy, reconfigurations of partner organizations, economic downturns). The top team also requires key parts of the organization that need to work together to deliver services to communicate effectively with each other and to signal successes and difficulties in intra-organizational, cross-departmental communication and effective working. The top team is charged with ensuring effective collaboration across the organization and must be kept informed of the success or otherwise of that collaboration. Organizational communication and information are therefore vital for top teams and the failure of many top teams lies in them allowing themselves to become isolated in the high-altitude domains they inhabit. Management by walking around the organization is a strategy Mike Cooke has developed to ensure he and his team keep in close touch with those they lead. http://www.nottinghamshirehealth-care.nhs.uk/ (last accessed 11 August 2011)

where they need to focus efforts, sustain existing performance and innovate. The organization as a whole is responsible for providing this information to ensure there is continuous adjustment and alignment between the organization and its environment.

Just like team members in any team, top team members need to have developed the KSAs for effective team working but given the particular challenges they face, it is even more important that they understand how to communicate effectively within the team, to share information, set goals, give feedback, manage conflicts, engage in joint planning and task coordination, and solve problems collaboratively. It is the collective responsibility of team members to deal with 'derailers' on the team – those who are so aggressive or undermining that they damage the team's ability to achieve its goals. Such skills need to be honed to a high level by members of TMTs and this requires training. Many managers are promoted to the top team without any training in team working during their careers and find themselves in a highly pressured situation without the skills to ensure collective team success. Given the difficulties top teams face and the often strong personalities of those promoted to this position, providing training and coaching for individuals on the teams is a necessity in most cases. The CEO must take responsibility for coaching members of the team and this can be augmented by having team coaches observe the team's functioning, setting goals for individual team members in relation to their team-working skills and providing feedback on performance. Many of the examples of dysfunctional TMTs illustrate how some team members lacked the skills that enabled them to function effectively in that situation. In one study of strategic business unit teams in a large information-processing corporation (Losada and Heaphy, 2004), the importance of having positivity among team members was clearly illustrated. The team meetings of 60 teams were observed. In those where the ratio of positive to negative interactions between team members was around 5 : 1 or greater, subsequent financial performance of the organization was much better. Moreover, the best-functioning teams had a healthy balance of team member interactions with at least as many interventions in team meetings being information seeking or questioning rather than advocacy or pressing one's opinion. Team meetings characterized by positivity and an orientation of seeking understanding seem to be more effective for top teams than aggressive, assertive and combative meetings.

So far we have considered the inputs to TMTs. Now we turn to examine the processes – objectives, participation, support for innovation, reflexivity, task focus and conflict management.

Top Management Team Processes

The starting point for consideration of any team's work is understanding the nature of the task. The point of having a team is because there is a task that requires a team. Once we are clear about the task we can then decide what skills are needed and which individuals have those skills. Team selection can then occur. The objectives of the TMT derive from but are not the same as the objectives of the organization. The organization's objectives are the responsibility of the whole organization. The objectives of the TMT team are to add value to the organization's activities in ways that enable the organization to achieve its objectives. If the organizational objective is to provide high-quality and safe healthcare, the TMT might add value by identifying and implementing systems for monitoring quality, training staff and ensuring effective error reporting. It is obviously not the job of top team members to provide the healthcare direct to patients themselves. Many TMTs make the mistake of assuming the objectives of the organization and of the top team are the same. Consequently, the top team ends up having over-large agendas, is drawn in too many directions, offers only superficial input in important areas, interferes inappropriately in operational activities in other areas and fails to achieve a clear sense of purpose that unites the team and capitalizes on their interdependent working. Remember teamwork is about interdependence – how team members work *together* to achieve shared goals. The lifeboat crew must communicate, coordinate, back members up and coach performance constantly to achieve effective teamwork. So too must the top management team. When TMT members focus on achieving targets in their own functional areas and are not focused on their collective responsibilities as a team, the organization becomes fractionated and ineffective. A study of 120 TMTs around the world showed that all too frequently CEOs over-challenged individual members but under-challenged the team, resulting in team members neglecting top team work and focusing their energies on their individual areas (Wageman *et al.*, 2008). Instead, they should be involved primarily in:

- exchanging strategic information such as sharing knowledge about the actions of competitors, legislative changes, market shifts;
- coordinating enterprise-wide initiatives such as ensuring all staff have effective appraisals, have high-quality first-line supervision or implementing team-based working across the organization;
- making vital decisions on behalf of the organization such as deciding on new product launches, making acquisitions of companies or opening new plants abroad.

Once the appropriate purposes of the team are identified, clear objectives can then be set. And, consistent with earlier considerations of team vision and objectives (Chapter 6), the objectives of the team must be clear, challenging and few in number – no more than about 7 or 8.

Case Study

Business School top management team

In my role as Executive Dean of a leading UK Business School with a £37 million turnover, I focused on working with the team to set clear, challenging and measurable objectives that ensured we were focused appropriately and worked effectively as a TMT. This required first and foremost a focus on the key stakeholders (students) and effectiveness at working within the wider university setting of which we were a part. The objectives in 2010 were therefore:

- Increase significantly levels of student satisfaction with their experience and improve the student–staff ratio
- Improve collaboration with university central services (finance, HR, estates) and the other schools of study within the university
- Manage university initiatives of culture change and leadership development effectively
- Balance the budget and ensure strategic investment ambitions are met by achieving a significant surplus
- Significantly increase staff satisfaction
- Ensure effective development of technology-assisted learning throughout all learning programmes
- Ensure successful accreditation from the European Foundation for Management Development in 2011.

These objectives do not emphasize the targets of individual team members (research, student numbers, executive education, corporate connections, marketing) but areas of activity where team members needed to work together to address vital strategic objectives.

The research referred to earlier (Wageman *et al.,* 2008) demonstrated that many CEOs assume that if team members know the organization's mission statement, they can work out the team's purpose and objectives. But the mission statement does not offer guidance for what team members should do as a group. Second, the research found that top team members did not share a common understanding of the organization's strategy – even if they knew the words. They need a shared understanding of what the strategy will look like translated into practice and what their role as a team is in achieving that. Third, clarity of purpose is only achieved when team members have the courage to work through the inevitable differences between bright and forceful team members in their judgements, opinions and preferences (Wageman *et al.*, 2008) about the direction the organization should pursue. Only in this way can a strong sense of purpose, forged through the heat of intelligent and visionary debate about differences produce a purpose that aligns the whole organization in a wise direction. That takes courage.

Top Team Participation

In Chapter 7 we explored themes of participation in teams and the key issues identified there apply no less to top team processes. In addition, there are aspects of the unique challenges for top teams that affect how they manage their interactions, information sharing and influence over decisions. There are three important considerations that affect participation in the top team – their tasks, norms and team size.

In a comprehensive study of 120 TMTs around the world, Wageman and her colleagues had consultants rate the success of those teams in meeting the needs of their stakeholders, how effectively they were developing their ability to sustain effective team working in the future and the extent to which team members were learning and growing as a result of their top team membership. They found that the best teams had 'genuinely meaningful tasks'; had clear norms of conduct that enabled the team to be successful; and were typically no more than eight members. The best top teams undertook tasks that required them to work together, engaging with complex, conceptually challenging tasks that would make a real difference to the success of the organization. This included tasks such as acquisitions, succession planning, moves to new geographical locations and moving corporate headquarters. The less successful teams engaged with large numbers of trivial, simple, inappropriate and undemanding tasks. Their agendas were packed with items that really did not shift the needle of organizational success and they had little time available to focus on the big stuff. Top teams are about the worst place to discuss the design of web sites, parking problems and the wording of documents.

Successful teams moreover, had clear, agreed norms of conduct. These are the ground rules of how the team members will behave and provide important and overt pointers to the expectations of top team members' role performance. Wageman *et al.* (2008, p. 129), describe four universally useful TMT norms:

Commitment: Treat the role of team member as seriously as your individual leadership role

Transparency: If it affects more than one of us, put it on the team table

Participation: Each member's voice is welcomed on issues affecting the enterprise

Integrity:　What you say and what you do when you are with the team is what you say and do when you're outside the team.

They also give the example of Applebee's, a global dining room grill and bar franchiser of over 2000 restaurants, with headquarters in Kansas, USA (http://en.wikipedia.org/wiki/Applebee's (last accessed 11 August 2011)). Their top team had the following norms: build trust, be decisive, be accountable (see it, own it, fix it), hold great meetings, deliver results, demonstrate work/life balance, have fun.

Corporate Social Responsibility

The top team also bears responsibility for ensuring that their organization contributes to the betterment of society, community and the environment rather than exploits the community or ravages the world it is embedded in. Inter-connectedness implies responsibility and the profit motive must always be subservient to responsibility for sustaining communities and environments. This is fundamental to the concept of organization and to the concept of society but has been neglected as a core orientation by many TMT. Corporate social responsibility is central to the task of any TMT. Rosabeth Moss Kanter, an outstanding management theorist of the last 50 years, has championed this principle (see Kanter, 2009). She asserts that clearly expressed values must guide organizations of the future if organizations are to contribute to not undermine community. She calls companies that are already moving in this direction 'the vanguard' and says that, in such companies, values, principles and attention to society are at the centre of business strategy.

- IBM, in 2003, conducted a 'values jam' – a 72-hour web meeting, involving over 15 000 contributors, focused on identifying what IBM should stand for in the world. The CEO at the time, Sam Palmesano, said 'Management is temporary, returns are cyclical. The values are the connective tissue that has longevity.' The meeting produced three values statements: dedication to every client's success; innovation that matters for the company and the world; and trust and personal responsibility in all relationships.

Kanter's other examples include:

- Proctor and Gamble dedicated their strategy to improving the lives of the world's consumers 'for now and for generations to come'. This led to breakthroughs in water purification via a not-for-profit company that saved many lives in the aftermath of the Asian tsunami.

- Cemex, a building materials firm, in one of the most polluting industries, made a strategic commitment to improving working conditions and community development. Its exploration of alternative fuels and environmental clean-up helped it win a World Environment Centre Gold Medal for International Corporate Achievement in Sustainable Development.
- Omron, a Japanese electronics company, has the motto 'at work for a better life, a better world for all' which drives innovations including one of the world's first ATMs, a system to increase safety in laundries, and a blood pressure monitor for women.
- Banco Real's strategy (Brazil) has made social and environmental responsibility its top priority. Its commitment to the environment led the World Bank's International Finance Corporation to write the Equator Principles in 2003 (and revised in 2006). This is a set of benchmarks for managing environmental and social issues in financing development projects globally. The Equator Principles commit participating banks and financial institutions to only financing projects that follow the processes defined by the Principles.

Such explicit norms provide a set of anchors that ensure team members are not drifting too far from the team focus and reinforce the principles that

---

Case Study

Top team norms

The management team of Aston Business School agreed a list of three things we must always and three things we must never do. These included:

THREE THINGS WE MUST ALWAYS DO
1 Work as a team not a committee
2 Challenge – focus on the difficult/ important
3 Say what we think but within the team

THREE THINGS WE MUST NEVER DO
1 Talk the School/University or its people down
2 Intentionally mislead each other or anyone in the organization
3 Start and not finish major projects

Our team functioning against these norms was reviewed at each meeting and a new set generated annually to ensure they remained fresh.

enable top teams to cope with the complexity, competing demands and very great challenges they face.

The larger a top team gets, the more difficult it is to ensure effective participation. In team meetings, for example, when teams rise above 8 or 9 in number, team conversations mutate into serial broadcasts. Members make speeches rather than converse with the team. Moreover, non-productive conflicts are much more likely the larger the team becomes. The top team is not a representative committee – it is the group of people charged with clarifying and supporting the implementation of the organization's strategy and responding to the inevitable surprises that require alignment of the organization to changes in its environment.

Having sat on TMTs varying in size from 14 to 7 members, it is clear to me that we should ensure that the team is no bigger than necessary to accomplish its task and never more than 8 or 9 members. CEOs simply get it wrong when they create leadership teams representing all the major areas of the organization – such groupings can be helpful as information-sharing or coordinating groups but they do not function effectively as TMTs. Related to this is the boundedness of the team.

Top team members need to be clear about who is and who is not on the team if they are to function effectively. In their study of 120 teams, Wageman and her colleagues found that only 11 of the teams agreed on who was on the team. On one team, the CEO reported that there were 11 members on the team, while the team members he identified varied in their reports of between 7 and 84 members of the team. In a smaller team which the CEO said had 5 members, the members themselves varied in their reports from 5 to 9. Where the boundaries of teams are not clear – who is and is not a member of the team – the effectiveness of top teamwork will be undermined.

Top Team Meetings

Despite what those in the wider organization imagine, top team meetings can range from the deadeningly boring where team members are desperately trying to keep awake and wondering how many more of these meetings they can survive to meetings that are so tense and unpleasant that the possibility of wise decision making has long flown out of any open windows. Given the expertise in the room and the importance of their task, ensuring team meetings are effective is at least as important a challenge for the top team members as those of members in the rest of the organization. I discovered early in my top team leadership that having individual team members report on their areas of responsibility at every meeting was a less than useful strategy. Long PowerPoint presentations or self-congratulatory reports that no one really listened to consumed precious TMT time. Such presentations tended to focus on the past rather than the future.

Thinking through the agenda is key. One approach is to ask all team members what they would like on the agenda. This is a recipe for far too many items of varying relevance resulting in inadequate time to discuss the key issues. Another solution is to have the top team objectives (remember there should be no more than six or seven) as the core items on the top team agenda. That way there is focus and other items are only included at the end if they are essential. Roche Canada only allow items on the top team agenda if they are strategic, mission critical and only the top team can decide/ address them. Agendas should be short – as few items as possible. Items that have always appeared historically should not be on the agenda unless there is a very good reason – every agenda item must be there by virtue of its importance. And team members must understand what it is they are required to achieve by the time an item has been dealt with – a decision, actions identified, information shared that will influence their subsequent actions. And team members must agree on how the outcomes arising from the decisions they take can be monitored and measured to ensure change (for example) has really occurred. From their study of 120 TMTs, Wageman *et al.* (2008) give the following additional guidance:

- *Start with the most important issues* – teams need most time to discuss those issues that will make most difference to the organization. Rushing them at the end of the meeting is obviously unwise.
- *Face the future not the past* – top teams must steer the organization forward not spend all their time reviewing past performance. There is learning to be had from past difficulties and successes but the way ahead needs to be anticipated and navigated successfully.
- *Prepare and participate* – team members must prepare for meetings effectively by reading key documents, gathering the information they need, talking with other top team members in advance, consulting their staff and ensuring they are prepared to contribute to the decision-making process. All the more reason to ensure the agenda is short in terms of number of items.
- *Challenge questionable tasks* – everyone on the team must take responsibility for proposing to skip over inappropriate items that have appeared on the agenda (even if the CEO put the item on). Such items can be delegated.
- *Delegate* – many tasks dealt with by TMTs should be delegated to empowered individuals and teams at other levels in the organization.
- *Keep the large tasks large* – Separating out the large tasks into small pieces can feel like progress but it stops the team working as a team in dealing with a big picture issue. Deciding to open another office in Asia

might include finding out more about property prices, market demands, political stability in different countries. Having individual members take responsibility for those activities can result in the top team not being engaged sufficiently *as a team* in making the big decisions, so it is effectively side stepped.

Team members also require appropriate information to help them function effectively and education, training and resources to enable them to respond to new challenges. The TMT is an information-hungry beast since the team needs information that will advance their understanding of the complex environment and enable them to achieve their objectives as a team. However, in many TMT meetings information is presented and team members simply passively accept the data. The role of the top team is to collectively interrogate, make sense of and creatively explore data in order to achieve an accurate and sophisticated understanding of their environment and challenges. Then they are in a better position to make decisions that will take the organization in the right directions. This requires that they are prudent about the information they request – getting helpful information, not drowning in data and reports and ensuring the data are both relevant and accurate. Then they need to have sufficient time to review the data together, discuss its implications and agree how to move forward. In effect, their analysis of data is a team effort.

And contrary to what we like to believe about the capability of our leaders, few of them are outstanding practitioners of effective teamwork. Many of them have risen to become members of the top team as a result of competitive rather than cooperative interactions with colleagues. Education of top team members should be an on-going process. That includes training top team members in outstanding leadership skills, team-working skills and strategy development. CEOs often assume that outstanding people have the skills they need to be a member of a top team or that they will quickly acquire them once they are thrown in the water. Drowning people often bring down those around them too. Ensuring that individuals take time to identify their training needs, find outstanding courses or experiences where they can acquire those skills and take the time to do the training is vital. Effective TMTs are those whose members continue to learn and grow and those in which team working continues to evolve towards maximum effectiveness. Providing the best quality and most stretching education and training possible for top team members makes sense, given their level of responsibility and such teams, as we have seen earlier, are characterized by high levels of innovation and team member engagement.

Top team members cannot be experts in all areas. When the top team is faced with a new task, such as opening an operation in a new country, they will need advice and input. Developing a marketing strategy for a new product may be outside the capabilities of team members. In that situation, the CEO or top team member must seek outside help in the shape of those within the organization with such skills or external consultants. Ensuring top team members have the advice, skills, knowledge and expertise available to enable them to operate effectively is vital for the functioning of the organization as a whole. Economies achieved by deciding we'll have a go ourselves as a top team, even though none of us knows much about marketing, are usually false.

A central theme in our understanding of team working is the importance of reflexivity – teams taking time out to review their objectives, processes and performance, and how they can be improved. For the top team, such reflection, planning and action, are of critical importance. Regular away days to review directions, processes, environment and strategies enable the team to take stock, to have time to step back from their immediate busy agendas and to refocus. I recommend that TMTs have full away days at least every three months – based on my experience of leading such a team in a medium-sized enterprise (Aston Business School) with 200+ employees and £37 million turnover and being part of a university top team with 1000+ employees and a turnover of over £100 million. The complexities of such organizations and their environments require more frequent reflection and 'time outs' to ensure wisdom, prudence and innovation characterize the workings of the top team.

The CEO bears the responsibility for ensuring that such periods of reflection are built in to the team's work since the tendency will always be to postpone or avoid such intermissions in the face of the workload top team members face. Evidence from our research is that such reflexivity is associated with increased productivity and innovation rather than the reverse in a wide variety of settings and sectors (West and Anderson, 1996). The CEO can also play a lead role in encouraging reflexivity 'in play'. Effective top teams need to carefully review their fine-textured performance also, taking the time at the end of meetings to consider what went well, what did not go well, what could be improved in terms of their use of meetings and use of time in meetings. Such reflexivity in action can also be applied to specific projects, the management of crises and difficulties, and in other situations where an 'after action review' might provide valuable learning.

As one top team member warned us, the failure to reflect can be costly: 'We do not review and by not doing that we have bad experiences with failure – everyone has a different assessment of what went wrong when something fails. If you don't review, there is no collective memory – everyone has his or her own version. With time each version becomes fact. You end up having four different factual versions about what went right and what went wrong. We implement – but do not typically get together to question or review as we cannot afford the time.' And such failures to reflect caused many of the difficulties in the financial sector described at the outset of this chapter.

The CEO's role is also to coach the team to focus on the big issues – the mission-critical activities and to avoid becoming mired in operational, tactical and trivial pursuits. Such coaching is a key part of the CEO's role both in and out of meetings. Coaching the team to work as a team is central. Many CEOs do good work coaching their individual team members but neglect the higher order and more powerful role of coaching the team to work as a team. That means ensuring team members are collectively taking responsibility for a key challenge such as making an acquisition, or refocusing staff to deliver integrated patient care or encouraging innovation throughout the organization. For a CEO to ask one team member to take responsibility for managing a culture change process (for example) ignores the fact that culture change will only be accomplished if the whole top team bears collective responsibility for its implementation. The CEO's role is then to help the team set objectives, monitor performance against those objectives, and collectively take responsibility for implementing culture change initiatives across the organization. That requires collective goal setting, planning and actions as well as reviews, under the eyes of the coach – just as a sports team is coached by the manager.

Another approach, that can augment the CEO's efforts, is to engage the services of an external coach to provide team coaching. Such a coach would typically take time to understand the team's business and strategy, interview team members, use a robust and rigorous instrument such as the ATPI, to measure top team performance and observe team meetings. She or he would then provide feedback, goal setting facilitation and conceptually sophisticated insights into the team's functioning. The consequence would be sling-shot progress for the team, enabling them to radically improve their level of teamwork and thereby provide a rocket boost for their work in the organization. Many coaches believe they have the capacity to do this but few can operate at the strategic apex of the organization, working effectively with the top team. That requires a knowledge of strategy development, the complexity of top team work, an ability to use systems thinking, humility, observational skills and courage to confront dysfunctional behaviours such as the CEO losing his or her temper in meetings. There is no evidence that teamwork is improved by the administration and feedback of questionnaire surveys using instruments such as the Belbin Team Roles Inventory, the MBTI or other personality questionnaires. The issue is not individual personalities but team functioning and the ability of the team to engage collectively with the conceptual and practical challenges they face in steering their organization. How to find such a coach amongst the surfeit of well-meaning practitioners who believe they have the abilities to coach a top team is a challenge. Seeking out qualified practitioners (such as – in the

United Kingdom, Chartered Occupational Psychologists) and checking how much experience they have in working with top teams is one way. This should be augmented by seeking recommendations from other reliable CEOs or seeking recommendations from CEOs the person has worked with previously. And the focus of coaching must always be improving teamwork in facing the organization's challenges. White-water rafting is fun and may build a sense of cohesion in the team but it is not directly addressing the vitally important issues the top team faces. And yes, social events that build camaraderie among team members are helpful, including dining out together or holding away days in inspiring locations. This is well worth doing but it is no substitute for a hard focus on the issues the team must address as a team.

Conflict

Top teams are generally composed of forceful, bright and experienced individuals. Such people tend to hold strong views and if we bring them together it is possible that their engagement with issues can spill over into high levels of conflict about key decisions in the organization or, worse, can lead to entrenched interpersonal conflict which destroys effective teamwork. The evidence is unequivocal. High levels of interpersonal conflict where some or all top team members neither trust each other nor get on begets an ineffective or worse downright dangerous TMT. A study of the TMTs of software companies in Ireland revealed a recognition among team members that what sometimes passed for task conflict in theory (e.g., questioning of ideas etc.) was intended (or perceived as intended) as a personal attack in order to question a team member's credibility or damage their reputation. In contrast, though much more rarely, what appeared to be interpersonal conflict was actually an indication of high trust. One particularly close-knit team reported that they frequently expressed frustration with each other and voices were sometimes raised but that it cleared the air and was quickly resolved because they trusted each other (Flood *et al.*, 2001). Consistent with this is the finding that, in a study of 76 TMTs in high-technology firms, diverse teams with low levels of interpersonal conflict and high levels of agreement-seeking achieved higher levels of strategic consensus (Knight *et al.*, 1999). Of course too much consensus can lead to 'groupthink' where harmony and adherence to the groups norms become more important than team effectiveness – although this is typically only where there is a very dominant CEO leading the top team.

There is considerable empirical evidence suggesting that levels of trust, conflict and cooperation in the TMT affect the wider organizational climate. High levels of trust breed more learning within the team (Edmondson, 1999) and this in turn facilitates the transfer of information across the organization. This diffuses downwards throughout each of the different functions (Zand, 1972). Farrell *et al.* (2004) found that affective tone and levels of trust within the top team influenced how employees outside the top team perceived the organizational climate. The higher the levels of trust between top team members, the more employees perceived the climate as one supportive of innovation, risk taking and experimentation (see also Albrecht and Travaglione, 2003).

Top team members' behaviour will directly create trust or mistrust. Members who always disagree strongly with others' views, who agree in team meetings but disagree outside, who 'talk down' their fellow team members in the wider organization, who are cynical about every vision or initiative, who are aggressive or back biting, who take a supportive position in meetings but undermine in practice, who set their part of the organization against other parts (subtly or openly) or who seek to ingratiate themselves with the CEO by undermining the reputations of their colleagues – all of these top team members undermine the ability of the team to explore differences of opinion in a mutually respectful, empowering and engaging way. And are these endangered species in TMTs? Far from it. In my work in every sector, be it healthcare, manufacturing, software, oil and gas, or education, such behaviours are commonly in evidence in the majority of teams. There is much scope for improving the functioning of TMTs, which is why many top team members desperately need training, coaching and above all, good leadership.

CEO Leadership

Hambrick (1994) noted that '… everyday observations and a wealth of related literature indicates that the top group leader has a disproportionate, sometimes nearly dominating influence on the group's various characteristics and outputs' (p.180). Peterson *et al.*'s (2003) study suggests that a CEO's personality has a significant influence on how top team members work together interacts. For example, they found that CEO conscientiousness was related to team-level concern for legality of their decisions, and CEO emotional stability to team cohesion and intellectual flexibility. CEO agreeableness was significantly associated with team cohesion, decentralization of power and concern for legality. Top team intellectual flexibility and cohesiveness predicted significant income growth suggesting that CEO personality can indirectly affect organizational outcomes through top team dynamics.

In contrast, paranoid, neurotic and narcissistic leaders create suspicion, pessimism and anxiety in the top team; the team in turn then creates such emotional climates in the wider organization. This is particularly the case in smaller organizations where the top managers are more visible and salient in the organization (Miller and Toulouse, 1986). Hodgkinson and Wright (2002) draw on psychodynamic theory to explain the failure of a process intervention in a publishing company by suggesting that 'the participants adopted a series of defensive avoidance strategies amplified by a series of psychodynamic processes initiated by the Chief Executive Officer (CEO)'. The researchers observed the recognition by team members of their divergent views of the organization's strategy and their roles. This divergence was threatening to the team and the CEO in particular, creating high levels of stress, cynicism and withdrawal from the intervention. The CEO resorted to cynicism, ridicule, intimidation and control, further undermining top team functioning.

Kets de Vries and Miller (1984) explore how dysfunctional leaders (e.g., narcissistic, paranoid and controlling leaders) stoke TMT anxiety and decision making based on irrational and unconscious processes rather than rational considerations. In a study I conducted with colleagues in Ireland (Flood *et al.*, 2001), many top managers cited the CEO's ego as one of their biggest challenges. Many encountered the darker side of charismatic leaders who were 'adept at spotting vulnerability and playing on that'. Such leaders can charm those above them and bully those below them.

What competencies must the CEO have therefore and what strategies must the CEO pursue to effectively lead the top team in an organization?

1 *Understanding organizations.* In order to enable effective decision making of the top team, the CEO must have a good understanding of what organizations are all about – models of organizational structure, strategy, culture, finances, marketing, operations, and business models. For example, a CEO who understands organizations will know that changes to culture are far more powerful in organizations than structural change – and far more difficult.
2 *Conceptual skills.* The CEO has to cope with and communicate a high level of complexity and information. This requires that the CEO has both an eye for detail (variations between departments over time in customer satisfaction) and an ability to see the big picture (the changes in demographics and government legislation and how that will affect markets). At the same time the CEO should have the intuitive insight to understand what is at the core of issues and problems within the organization, to discern themes and patterns and have the courage to choose a way forward.
3 *Ability to decide.* The CEO must have the courage to make decisions when they need to be made, particularly in crises, and the courage sometimes not to make a decision, to allow events to unfold a little or for

protagonists in an organizational conflict to work through their disagreement (albeit with encouragement from the CEO). And courage is often required in making tough decisions such as pursuing a new venture, firing a colleague or meeting with a dissatisfied customer. And sometimes it is deciding what to do when the CEO does not know what to do – seeking advice, taking time to meet with an executive coach or taking the team for a weekend into the hills to retreat and reflect. All of these qualities are necessary if the CEO is to provide a good model for and enable the effective functioning of the top team. The CEO has to enable the top team to surf the waves of decision making rather than being drowned in them. And the CEO has to know which waves to surf and which to let pass by.

4   *Ability to listen and consult.* A key behavioural skill that CEOs have to learn in order to enable the top team is to shut up. Imagine the CEO says to the team: 'We have a big challenge with this customer and we must make a decision. I want to hear what each of you thinks – here's what I think first.' Of course, compliant team members will then simply go along with the CEO's view and he or she will have squandered the opportunity to get the diverse views and perspectives from all the team's members that would enable a more comprehensive and sophisticated analysis of the situation. CEOs must take time to elicit and explore top team members' views on important issues before offering their own. Otherwise team meetings become dull affairs where members simply nod their heads in agreement with the CEO – particularly likely where the CEO is dominating, aggressive or intimidating.

5   *Giving autonomy and trust.* If the CEO has selected outstanding members to be part of the team (his or her responsibility) then they should be given trust and the autonomy needed to do their jobs. Excessively controlling and interfering CEOs undermine the ability and confidence of the team to work together. CEOs are often simply wrong when they think they know their top team members' operational needs better than the team members themselves. The CEO must agree overall aims and targets with their top teams, provide appropriate support and set them free to achieve and excel.

6   *Emotional intelligence.* Our discussion above about the emotional context of top team working surely makes it clear that top team members need high levels of emotional intelligence. This includes self-awareness, the ability to understand others' emotions, the ability to manage one's own emotions (CEOs who often lose their tempers or snap at their team members invariably lead dysfunctional teams). Given the potential tensions and the demands on the top team, emotional intelligence is an especially important quality for a CEO. The myth of the dominant, usually male, aggressive CEO who takes companies to success is based

on an outmoded understanding of team and organizational functioning. Yes, there are examples of people who achieve success in that way but for each of these there are scores of examples of CEOs in that mould who lead their companies and teams to disaster.

7   *Humility*. The CEO sits in a privileged position with a group of highly competent individuals deferring to him or her and the whole organization responding to their requirements. Being in such a position carries the danger that adulation goes to the CEO's head and he or she loses that humility that is essential to leadership. Recognizing realistically one's strengths, weaknesses and inadequacies is vital. One of mine is being too opportunistic as a leader and pursuing too many initiatives. I need my top team members to admonish me when I am pursuing too many or inappropriate opportunities for the organization. That requires humility – an orientation every leader should ensure they cultivate. The position carries with it the seductive dangers of power and humility is a potent antidote. Top teams led by arrogant, narcissistic or closed leaders are doomed to failure. CEOs must practice being open, curious (eager to learn), real (genuine and sincere in their behaviour), kind and appreciative in working with their top team and the whole organization.

8   *Ability to inspire*. The CEO must have the ability to inspire the top team to pursue a vision and that takes both the top team's courage and courage from the CEO to discover, articulate and then embody that vision. Moreover, CEOs will inspire their teams by constantly and overtly recognizing and publicly appreciating the contributions made by top team members. Regardless of seniority, people want their contributions to be valued; they want to feel respected and to experience a sense of support from the CEO. It is a big mistake to think one's top team colleagues somehow do not need the positive feedback on their contribution and performance that all crave. Helping the top team conjure a vision and ensuring that there is a team climate of appreciation and gratitude is therefore a vital component of CEO top team leadership.

Conclusions

Top team visions, strategies, missions and objectives have to be underpinned by values. We started this chapter describing the collapse of financial services organizations that subsequently had an enormous detrimental impact on millions of people's lives, partly because their leadership teams lost touch with such core human values as courage, wisdom and justice. Given the power wielded by top teams, it is important that they embody the values held dear by all human societies and ensure their organizations contribute to the development of those values in society rather than undermine them. Peterson and Seligman (two US psychologists) have researched the fundamental human values in human communities cross-culturally, surveying more than a million people, and have identified six core areas of values – Wisdom, Courage, Justice, Humanity, Prudence and Wonder (for a detailed description of these values see Peterson and Seligman, 2004). If there is one thing we have learned from the collapse of the financial services sectors in 2008, it is that TMTs and organizations as a whole must act from values rather than greed in their responsibilities as custodians of large parts of our economies.

Four themes have repeatedly emerged in this book, intersecting to form a single repeated pattern. First, in today's highly uncertain organizations characterized by high levels of work demands and rapidly changing structures and cultures, we can enhance performance by team members taking time away to reflect quietly upon their functioning. This allows them to adapt courageously in order to achieve new evolutionary forms that fit their circumstances better. Secondly, teams need to find creative ways of working which challenge existing orthodoxies and offer alternatives to the status quo if they are to contribute substantially to organizational and societal development. Such creativity only comes from constructive conflict, and a preparedness to tolerate and even encourage uncertainty and ambiguity. In this way, those who work in teams can experience the excitement and mutual appreciation generated by real breakthroughs because of human collaboration. Thirdly, in demanding, changing and uncertain environments people must support one another to create climates of safety, confidence and empowerment. Fourth, teams exist within organizations that will either provide nourishing and stimulating environments or prove anoxic and starve them of the means of survival. People form teams and we must understand the human issues involved in teamwork. If the team is to dance creatively and in synchrony, they have to practise and reflect, practise and reflect.

If the motivation and commitment of people are to be engaged in the work of their teams, there must be a strong sense of the value of the work they do. This may be in promoting health, conserving the environment, helping others to learn, supporting those in need, producing high-quality goods for people, ensuring safety, promoting understanding, confronting injustice or contributing to the community. Vision is derived from values and our values determine our motivation. Reflexivity helps to clarify for team members the values they hold about both team social functioning and task performance. Such focus and clarity may also make salient the differences between team members' views and those of senior management or the organization as a whole. This in turn may lead to conflict. But such conflict is necessary for organizational adaptability, and successful innovation ensures that organizations reflect rather than eclipse the diversity of values in society. Through the development of the evolutionary and revolutionary reflective teams described throughout this book, organizations may better serve the societies of which they are a part.

Key Revision Points

- What is the overarching purpose of a top management team in an organization?
- How should members of a TMT be selected?
- How does the composition and diversity of TMT influence its effectiveness?
- What are the roles and tasks of TMTs, and how should the team's objectives be formulated?
- What team inputs are unique to TMTs?
- What competencies must the CEO have?
- What strategies should the CEO pursue to effectively lead the top team?

Further Reading

Crane, A., McWilliams, A., Matten, D. and Moon, J. (eds) (2009) *The Oxford Handbook of Corporate Social Responsibility,* Oxford University Press, Oxford.

Kanter, R.M. (2009) Bringing values back to the boardroom. *RSA Journal,* Summer, 30–33.

McLean, B. and Nocera, J. (2011) *All the Devils are Here: The Hidden History of the Financial Crisis,* Viking Press.

Peterson, C. and Seligman, M.E.P. (2004) *Character Strengths and Virtues: A Handbook and Classification,* Oxford University Press, New York/American Psychological Association, Washington, DC.

Wageman, R., Nunes, D.A., Burruss, J.A. and Hackman, J.R. (2008) *Senior Leadership Teams: What it Takes to Make Them Great,* Harvard Business School Press, Boston.

Web Resources

http://www.yourofficecoach.com/Topics/building_an_effective_mgmt_team.htm (last accessed 11 August 2011).

Building an effective management team.

References

Agarwal, R. (2003) Teamwork in the netcentric organization, in *International Handbook of Organizational Teamwork and Cooperative Working* (eds M.A. West, D. Tjosvold and K.G. Smith), John Wiley & Sons, Ltd, Chichester, pp. 443–462.

Ahearn, K.K., Ferris, G.R., Hochwarter, W.A. *et al.* (2004) Leader political skill and team performance. *Journal of Management,* 30(3), 309–327.

Ainsworth, M.D.S. (1982) Attachment: Retrospect and prospect, in *The Place of Attachment in Human Behavior* (eds C.M. Parkes and J. Stevenson-Hinde), Basic Books, New York, pp. 3–30.

Albrecht, S.L. and Travaglione, A. (2003) Trust in public senior management during times of turbulent change. *International Journal of Human Resource Management,* 14, 1–17.

Amabile, T.M. (1997) Motivating creativity in organizations: On doing what you love and loving what you do. *California Management Review,* 40, 39–58.

Ancona, D. and Caldwell, D.F. (1992) Demography and design: Predictors of new product team performance. *Organization Science,* 3, 321–341.

Anderson, N. and Sleap, S. (2004) An evaluation of gender differences on the Belbin Team Role Self-Perception Inventory. *Journal of Occupational and Organizational Psychology,* 77(3), 429–437.

Anderson, N. and Thomas, H.D.C. (1996) Work group socialization, in *Handbook of Work Group Psychology* (ed. M.A. West), John Wiley & Sons, Ltd, Chichester, pp. 423–450.

Anderson, N. and West, M.A. (1998) Measuring climate for work group innovation: Development and validation of the Team Climate Inventory. *Journal of Organizational Behavior,* 19, 235–258.

Andrews, F.M. (1979) *Scientific Productivity,* Cambridge University Press, Cambridge.

Effective Teamwork: Practical Lessons from Organizational Research, Third Edition.
By M. A. West. © 2012 John Wiley & Sons, Ltd. Published 2012 by John Wiley & Sons, Ltd.,
and the British Psychological Society.

Applebaum, E. and Batt, R. (1994) *The New American Workplace,* ILR Press, Ithaca, NY.

Argyris, C. (1978) *Organizational Learning: A Theory of Action Perspective,* Addison Wesley, Reading, MA.

Argyris, C. (1990) *Overcoming Organizational Defences: Facilitating Organizational Learning,* Allyn and Bacon, Boston.

Argyris, C. (1993) *Knowledge for Action: A Guide to Overcoming Barriers to Organizational Change,* Jossey-Bass, San Francisco.

Asch, S. (1956) Studies of independence and conformity: A minority of one against a unanimous majority. *Psychological Monographs,* 70, (Whole No. 416.)

Ashford, S.J. and Tsul, A.S. (1991) Self-regulation for managerial effectiveness. The role of active feedback seeking. *Academy of Management Journal,* 34(2), 251–280.

Axtell, C.M., Fleck, S.J. and Turner, N. (2004) Virtual teams: Collaborating across distance, in *International Review of Industrial and Organizational Psychology,* Vol. 19 (eds C.L. Cooper and I.T. Robertson), John Wiley & Sons, Ltd, Chichester, pp. 205–248.

Bacon, N. and Blyton, P. (2000) High road and low road teamworking: perceptions of management rationales and organizational and human resource outcomes. *Human Relations,* 53, 1425–1458.

Baltes, B.B., Dickson, M.W., Sherman, M.P. *et al.* (2002) Computer-mediated communication and group decision making: A meta-analysis. *Organizational Behavior and Human Decision Processes,* 87(1), 156–179.

Bantel, K.A. (1993) Top team, environment and performance effects on strategic planning formality. *Group and Organization Management,* 18(4), 436–458.

Bantel, K.A. and Jackson, S.E. (1989) Top management and innovations in banking: Does the composition of the top team make a difference? *Strategic Management Journal,* 10, 107–124.

Barchas, P. (1986) A sociophysiological orientation to small groups, in *Advances in Group Processes,* Vol. 3 (ed. E. Lawler), JAI Press, Greenwich, CT, pp. 209–46.

Barrick, M.R. and Mount, M.K. (1991) The big five personality dimensions and job performance: A meta-analysis. *Personnel Psychology,* 44, 1–26.

Barrick, M.R., Stewart, G.L., Neubert, M.J. and Mount, M.K. (1998) Relating member ability and personality to work-team processes and team effectiveness. *Journal of Applied Psychology,* 83, 377–391.

Barsade, S. and Gibson, D.E. (1998) Group emotion: A view from the top and bottom, in *Research on Managing Groups and Teams* (eds D. Gruenfeld *et al.*), JAI Press, Greenwich, CT, pp. 81–102.

Bass, B.M. (1985) *Leadership and Performance Beyond Expectations,* The Free Press, New York.

Batchelor, M. (2001) *Meditation for Life,* Wisdom Publications, Boston.

Baumeister, R.F. and Leary, M.R. (1995) The need to belong: Desire for interpersonal attachments as a fundamental human motivation. *Psychological Bulletin,* 117, 497–529.

Baumeister, R.F., Wotman, S.R. and Stillwell, A.M. (1993) Unrequited love: on heartbreak, anger, guilt, scriptlessness and humiliation. *Journal of Personality and Social Psychology,* 64, 377–394.

Beal, D., Cohen, R.R., Burke, M.J. and McLendon, C.L. (2003) Cohesion and performance in groups: a meta-analytic clarification of construct relations. *Journal of Applied Psychology,* 88, 989–1004.

Belbin, R.M. (1981) *Management Teams: Why They Succeed or Fail,* Butterworth-Heinemann, Oxford.

Belbin, R.M. (1993) *Team Roles at Work: A Strategy for Human Resource Management,* Butterworth-Heinemann, Oxford.

Bell, S.T. (2007) Deep-level composition variables as predictors of team performance: A meta-analysis. *Journal of Applied Psychology,* 92, 595–615.

Bennett, N., Harvey, J.A., Wise, C. and Woods, P.A. (2003) *Desk Study Review of Distributed Leadership,* National College for School Leadership/Centre for Educational Policy & Management, Nottingham.

Billig, M. and Tajfel, H. (1973) Social categorization and similarity in intergroup behavior. *European Journal of Social Psychology,* 3, 27–52.

Boeker, W. (1997) Executive migration and strategic change: The effect of top manager movement on product-market entry. *Administrative Science Quarterly,* 42, 213–236.

Bond R. and Smith P.B. (1996) Culture and conformity: a meta-analysis of studies using Asch's (1952b, 1956) line judgment task. *Psychology Bulletin,* 119, 111–137.

Boning, B., Ichniowski, C. and Shaw, K. (2001) *Opportunity Counts: Teams and the Effectiveness of Production Incentives.* NBER Working Paper No. 8306, National Bureau of Economic Research, Cambridge, MA.

Borrill, C., West, M., Shapiro, D. and Rees, A. (2000) Team working and effectiveness in the NHS. *British Journal of Health Care Management,* 6, 364–371.

Brewer, P.R. (2001) Value words and lizard brains: Do citizens deliberate about appeals to their core values? *Political Psychology,* 22, 45–64.

Brodbeck, F.C. and Greitemeyer, T. (2000) A dynamic model of group performance: Considering the group member's capacity to learn. *Group Processes and Intergroup Relations,* 2, 159–182.

Brown, R. (2000). *Group Processes,* 2nd edn, Blackwell, Oxford.

Bryman, A., Collinson, D., Grint, K. *et al.* (2011) *The Sage Handbook of Leadership,* Sage, London.

Bunderson, J.S. and Sutcliffe, K.M. (2002) Comparing alternative conceptualizations of functional diversity in management teams: Process and performance effects. *Academy of Management Journal,* 45, 875–894.

Burke, S.S., Stagl, K.C., Klein, C. *et al.* (2006) What type of leadership behaviors are functional in teams? A meta-analysis. *Leadership Quarterly,* 17, 288–307.

Byrne, D. (1971) *The Attraction Paradigm,* Academic Press, New York.

Cameron, K.S., Dutton, J.E., Quinn, R.E. (2003) *Positive Organizational Scholarship: Foundations of a New Discipline,* Berrett-Koehler, San Francisco.

Carli, L.L. and Eagly, A.H. (2011) Gender and leadership, in *The Sage Handbook of Leadership* (eds A. Bryman, D. Collinson, K. Grint *et al.*), Sage, London, pp. 103–117.

Carpenter, M.A., Geletkanycz, M.A. and Sanders, G.M. (2004) Upper echelons research revisited: Antecedents, elements and consequences of top management team composition. *Journal of Management,* 30, 749–778.

Carson, J.B., Tesluk, P.E. and Marrone, J.A. (2007) Shared leadership in teams: An investigation of antecedent conditions and performance. *Academy of Management Journal,* 50, 1217–1234.

Carter, A.J. and West, M.A. (1999) Sharing the burden – teamwork in healthcare settings, in *Stress in Health Professionals* (eds J. Firth-Cozens and R. Payne), John Wiley & Sons, Ltd, Chichester, pp. 191–202.

Chen, Z., Lam, W. and Zhong, J.A. (2007) Leader–member exchange and member performance: a new look at individual-level negative feedback-seeking behaviour and team-level empowerment climate. *Journal of Applied Psychology,* 92, 202–212.

Chhokar, J.S., Brodbeck, F.C., House, R.J. (eds) (2007) *Culture and Leadership, Across the World: The GLOBE Book of In-depth Studies,* Lawrence Erlbaum, Mahwah, NJ.

Claxton, G.L. (1998a) *Hare Brain Tortoise Mind – Why Intelligence Increases When You Think Less,* Fourth Estate Ltd, London.

Claxton, G.L. (1998b) Knowing without knowing why: Investigating human intuition. *The Psychologist,* 11, 217–220.

Clouse, R.W. and Spurgeon, K.L. (1995) Corporate analysis of humor. *Psychology: A Journal of Human Behaviour,* 32, 1–24.

Cohen, S. and Wills, T.A. (1985) Stress, social support, and the buffering hypothesis. *Psychological Bulletin,* 98, 310–357.

Cohen, S.G. and Bailey, D.E. (1997) What makes teams work: Group effectiveness research from the shop floor to the executive suite. *Journal of Management,* 23, 239–290.

Cooke, N.J., Kiekel, P.A., Salas, E. and Stout, R. (2003) Measuring team knowledge: a window to the cognitive underpinnings of team performance. *Journal of Applied Psychology,* 7, 179–199.

Cotton, J.L. (1993) *Employee Involvement: Methods for Improving Performance and Work Attitudes,* Sage, Newbury Park, CA.

Cramton, C.D. (2002). Attribution in distributed work groups, in *Distributed Work: New Ways of Working Across Distance Using Technology* (eds P. Hinds and S. Kiesler), MIT Press, Cambridge, MA, pp. 191–212.

Cramton, C.D. and Wilson, J.M. (2002) Explanation and judgment in distributed groups: An interactional justice perspective. Paper presented at the Academy of Management annual meeting, Denver.

Cyert, R. and March, J.G. (1963) *A Behavioral Theory of the Firm,* 2nd edn (1992), Blackwell, Oxford.

Day, D.V., Gronn, P. and Salas, E. (2004). Leadership capacity in teams. *Leadership Quarterly,* 15, 857–880.

De Cremer, D., van Dick, R, and Murnighan, K.K. (2011) *Social Psychology and Organizations,* Routledge, London.

De Dreu, C.K.W. and van de Vliert, E. (eds) (1997) *Using Conflict in Organizations,* Sage, London.

De Dreu, C.K.W. and Van Vianen, A.E.M. (2001) Responses to relationship conflict and team effectiveness. *Journal of Organizational Behaviour,* 22, 309–328.

De Dreu, C.K.W. and West, M.A. (2001) Minority dissent and team innovation: The importance of participation in decision making. *Journal of Applied Psychology,* 86, 1191–1201.

De Dreu, C.K.W. and Weingart, L.R. (2003) Task versus relationship conflict and team effectiveness: A meta-analysis. *Journal of Applied Psychology,* 88, 741–749.

Delarue, A., van Hootegem, G., Procter, S. and Burridge, M. (2008) Teamworking and organizational performance: a review of survey-based research, *International Journal of Management Reviews,* 10(2), 127–148.

Demoulin, S., Leyens, J-P. and Dovidio, J.F. (2009) Interactions and divergent realities, in *Intergroup Misunderstandings: Impact of Divergent Social Realities* (eds S. Demoulin, J-P. Leyens and J.F. Dovidio), Psychology Press, New York.

Dennis, A. and Wixom, B. (2002) Investigating the moderators of the group support systems use with meta-analysis. *Journal of Management Information Systems,* 18(3), 235–257.

Deutsch, M. (1973) *The Resolution of Conflict: Constructive and Destructive Processes,* Yale University Press, New Haven.

Devine, D.J. and Philips, J.L. (2001) Do smarter teams do better: A meta-analysis of cognitive ability and team performance. *Small Group Research,* 32, 507–532.

Diehl, M. and Stroebe, W. (1987). Productivity loss in brainstorming groups: Towards the solution of a riddle. *Journal of Personality and Social Psychology,* 53, 497–509.

Dunbar, K. (1997) How scientists think: On-line creativity and conceptual change in science, in *Creative Thought: An Investigation of Conceptual Structures and Processes* (eds T.B. Ward, S.M. Smith and J. Vaid), American Psychology Association, Washington, DC, pp. 461–493.

Dunlop, J.T. and Weil, D. (1996) Diffusion and performance of modular production in the U.S. apparel industry. *Industrial Relations,* 35, 334–355.

Earley, P.C. (1993) East meets West meets Mid East: further explorations of collectivistic and individualistic work groups. *Academy of Management Journal,* 36, 319–348.

Edmondson, A.C. (1996) Learning from mistakes is easier said than done: group and organizational influences on the detection and correction of human error. *Journal of Applied Behavioural Science,* 32, 5–28.

Edmondson, A.C. (1999) Psychological safety and learning behaviour in work teams. *Administrative Science Quarterly,* 44, 350–383.

Edmondson, A.C., Roberto, M.R. and Watkins, M. (2003) A dynamic model of top management team effectiveness: managing unstructured task streams. *Leadership Quarterly,* 219, 1–29.

Edwards, B.D., Day, E.A., Arthur, W. and Bell, S.T. (2006) Relationships among team ability composition, team mental models, and team performance. *Journal of Applied Psychology,* 91, 727–736.

Egan, G. (1986) *The Skilled Helper,* 3rd edn, Brooks/Cole, Pacific Grove, CA.

Ellis, A.P.J., Hollenbeck, J.R., Ilgen, D.R. *et al.* (2003) Team learning: Collectively connecting the dots. *Journal of Applied Psychology,* 88, 821–835.

English, A., Griffith, R.L. and Steelman, L.A. (2004) Conscientiousness and team performance: The moderating influence of task type. *Small Group Research,* 35, 643–665.

Farrell, J.B., Flood, P.C., MacCurtain, S. *et al.* (2004) CEO leadership, top team trust and the combination and exchange of information. *Irish Journal of Management,* 26, 22–40.

Finkelstein, S. and Hambrick, D.C. (1996) *Strategic Leadership: Top Executives and Their Effects on Organizations,* West Publishing, St. Paul, MN.

Fisher, R., Ury, W. and Patton, B. (1999) *Getting to Yes: Negotiating an Agreement Without Giving In,* Random House, London.

Flood, P., MacCurtain, S. and West, M.A. (2001) *Effective Top Management Teams,* Blackhall Press, Dublin, Ireland.

Fontana, D. (1989). *Managing Stress,* Blackwell, Oxford.

Ford, C.M. and Gioia, D.A. (eds) (1995) *Creative Action in Organizations: Ivory Tower Visions and Real World Voices,* Sage, London.

Fredrickson, B.L. (2009) *Positivity: Groundbreaking Research Reveals How to Embrace the Hidden Strength of Positive Emotions, Overcome Negativity, and Thrive,* Crown, New York.

Furnham, A., Steele, H. and Pendleton, D. (1993) A psychometric assessment of the Belbin Team Role Self-perception Inventory. *Journal of Occupational and Organizational Psychology,* 66, 245–257.

Ganster, D.C., Fusilier, M.R. and Mayes, B.T. (1986) Role of social support in the experience of stress at work. *Journal of Applied Psychology,* 71, 102–110.

Geister, S. (2004). Development and evaluation of an Online-Feedback-System for virtual teams. Unpublished dissertation, University of Kiel.

Gersick, C.J.G. (1988) Time and transition in work teams: Toward a new model of group development. *Academy of Management Journal,* 31, 9–41.

Gersick, C.J.G. (1989) Marking time: Predictable transitions in task groups. *Academy of Management Journal,* 32, 274–309.

Gersick, C.J.G. (1994) Pacing strategic change. *Academy of Management Journal,* 9–45.

Glassop, L.I. (2002) The organizational benefits of teams. *Human Relations,* 55, 225–249.

Gluesing, J.C., Alcordo, T.C., Baba, M.L. *et al.* (2003) The development of global virtual teams, in *Virtual Teams that Work: Creating Conditions for Virtual Team Effectiveness* (eds C.B. Gibson and S.G. Cohen), Jossey-Bass, San Francisco, pp. 353–380.

Goleman, D. (1995) *Emotional Intelligence: Why it Can Matter More Than IQ,* Bloomsbury, London.

Goleman, D. (2002) *The New Leaders: Emotional Intelligence at Work,* Little, Brown, London.

Goleman, D., Boyatzis, R. and McKee, A. (2002) *The New Leaders: Transforming the Art of Leadership into the Science of Results,* Little, Brown, London.

Gollwitzer, P.M. and Bargh, J.A. (eds) (1996) *The Psychology of Action: Linking Cognition and Motivation to Behaviour,* Guilford Press, New York.

Graen, G. and Cashman, J. (1975) A role making model of leadership in formal organizations: a developmental approach, in *Leadership Frontiers* (eds J.G. Hunt and L.L. Larson), Kent State University Press, Kent, OH.

Graen, G.B. and Scandura, T.A. (1987) Toward a psychology of dyadic organizing, in *Research in Organizational Behavior,* Vol. 9 (eds L.L. Cummings and B.M. Staw), JAI Press, Greenwich, CT, pp. 175–208.

Gully, S.M., Incalcaterra, K.A., Joshi, A. and Beaubien, J.M. (2002) A meta-analysis of team efficacy, potency, and performance: Interdependence and level of analysis as moderators of observed relationships. *Journal of Applied Psychology,* 87, 819–832.

Guzzo, R.A. (1996) Fundamental considerations about workgroups, in *Handbook of Work Group Psychology* (ed. M.A. West), John Wiley & Sons, Ltd, Chichester.

Hackman, J.R. (ed.) (1990) *Groups That Work (and Those That Don't): Conditions for Effective Teamwork,* Jossey-Bass, San Francisco.

Hackman, J.R. (2002) *Leading Teams: Setting the Stage for Great Performances,* Harvard Business School Press, Boston.

Hackman, J.R. and Morris C.G. (1975) Group tasks, group interactions process, and group performance effectiveness: A review and proposed integration, in *Advances in Experimental Social Psychology,* Vol. 8 (ed. L. Berkowitz), Academic Press, New York.

Hackman, J.R. and Oldham, G.R. (1976) Motivation through the design of work: Test of a theory. *Organizational Behaviour and Human Performance,* 15, 250–279.

Hackman, J.R. and Wageman, R. (2005) A theory of team coaching. *Academy of Management Review,* 30, 269–287.

Hambrick, D.C. (1994) Top management groups: A conceptual integration and reconsideration of the team label, in *Research in Organizational Behavior* (eds B.M. Staw and L.L. Cummings), JAI Press, Greenwich, CT, pp. 171–214.

Hambrick, D.C. (2005) Upper echelons theory: Origins, twists and turns, and lessons learned. *Great Minds in Management: The Process of Theory Development,* 14(3), 109–127.

Hambrick, D.C., Cho, T.S. and Chen, M.J. (1996) The influence of top management team heterogeneity on firms' competitive moves. *Administrative Science Quarterly,* 41(4), 659–684.

Harris, C. and Beyerlein, M.M. (2003) Team-based organization: Creating an environment for team success, in *Handbook of Organizational Teamwork and Cooperative Working* (eds M.A. West, D. Tjosvold and K.G. Smith), John Wiley & Sons, Ltd, Chichester, pp. 187–210.

Harrison, D.A. and Klein, K.J. (2007) What's the difference? Diversity constructs as separation, variety, or disparity in organizations. *Academy of Management Review,* 32, 1199–1228.

Heller F., Pusić E., Strauss G. and Wilpert B. (1998) *Organizational Participation: Myth and Reality,* Oxford University Press, New York.

Henry, J. (2001). *Creativity Management,* Sage, London.

Hertel, G., Geister, S. and Konradt, U. (2005) Managing virtual teams: A review of current empirical research. *Human Resource Management Review,* 15, 69–95.

Hewstone, M., Rubin, M. and Willis, H. (2002) Intergroup bias. *Annual Reviews of Psychology,* 53, 575–604.

Hill, G.W. (1982) Group versus individual performance: Are N+1 heads better than one? *Psychological Bulletin,* 91, 517–539.

Hinds, P. and Mortensen, M. (2002) *Understanding Antecedents to Conflict in Geographically Distributed Research and Development Teams.* Proceedings of the International Conference on Information Systems (ICIS), Association for Information Systems, Atlanta, GA.

Hirschfeld, R.R., Jordan, M.H., Feild, H.S. *et al.* (2005) Teams' female representation and perceived potency as inputs to team outcomes in a predominantly male field setting. *Personnel Psychology,* 58, 893–924.

Hodgkinson, G.P. and Wright, G. (2002) Confronting strategic inertia in a top management team Learning from failure. *Organization Studies,* 23(6), 949–977.

Hofner Saphiere, D.M. (1996) Productive behaviors of global business teams. *International Journal of Intercultural Relations,* 20, 2.

Horwitz, S.K. and Horwitz, I.B. (2007) The effects of team diversity on team outcomes: A meta-analytic review of team demography. *Journal of Management,* 33, 987–1015.

Howell, J.M. and Avolio, B.J. (1993) Transformational leadership, transactional leadership, locus of control and support for innovation: Key predictors of consolidated business-unit performance. *Journal of Applied Psychology,* 78, 891–902.

Hu, J. and Liden, R.C. (2011) Antecedents of team potency and team effectiveness: an examination of goal and process clarity and servant leadership. *Journal of Applied Psychology,* 96(4), 851–862.

Ingham, A.G., Levinger, G., Graves, J., Peckham, V. (1974) The Ringelmann effect: studies of groupsize and group performance. *Journal of Experimental Social Psychology,* 10(4), 371–384.

Isen, A.M. (1993) Positive affect and decision making, in *Handbook of Emotions* (eds M. Lewis and J.M. Haviland), Guilford Press, New York, pp. 261–278.

Isen, A.M. (1999) Positive affect, in *The Handbook of Cognition and Emotion* (eds T. Dalgleish and M.J. Power), John Wiley & Sons, Inc., New York, pp. 521–539.

Jackson, S.E. (1996) The consequences of diversity in multidisciplinary work teams, in *Handbook of Work Group Psychology* (ed. M.A. West), John Wiley & Sons, Ltd, Chichester, pp. 53–75.

Janis, I.L. (1982) *Victims of Groupthink,* Houghton Mifflin, Boston.

Jehn, K. (1997) A qualitative analysis of conflict types and dimensions in organizational groups. *Administrative Science Quarterly* 42, 430–457.

Judge, T.A. and Piccolo, R.F. (2004) Transformational and transactional leadership: A meta-analytic test of their relative validity. *Journal of Applied Psychology,* 89, 755–768.

Judge, T.A., Piccolo, R.F., and Illies, R. (2004) The forgotten ones? The validity of consideration and initiating structure in leadership research. *Journal of Applied Psychology,* 89, 36–51.

Kabat-Zinn, J. (2004) *Wherever You Go, There You Are: Mindfulness Meditation for Everyday Life,* Piatkus Books.

Kanter, R.M. (2009) Bringing values back to the boardroom. *RSA Journal,* Summer, 30–33.

Karau, S.J. and Williams, K.D. (1993) Social loafing: A meta-analytic review and theoretical integration. *Journal of Personality and Social Psychology,* 65, 681–706.

Kets de Vries, M.F. and Miller, D. (1987) *Unstable at the Top,* New American Library, New York.

Kiesler, S. and Cummings, J.N. (2002) What do we know about proximity and distance in work groups? A legacy of research, in *Distributed Work* (eds P. Hinds and S. Kiesler), MIT Press, Cambridge, MA, pp. 57–82.

Kiesler, S. and Sproull, L. (1992) Group decision making and communication technology. *Organizational Behavior & Human Decision Processes*, 52, 96–123.

Kilduff, M., Angelmar, R. and Mehra, A. (2000) Top management-team diversity and firm performance: Examining the role of cognitions. *Organization Science*, 11, 21–34.

Kirkman, B.L. and Mathieu, J.E. (2005) The dimensions and antecedents of team virtuality. *Journal of Management*, 31(5), 700–718.

Kirkman, B.L., Benson R., Paul, E.T. and Cristina B.G. (2004) The impact of team empowerment on virtual team performance: the moderating role of face-to-face interaction. *Academy of Management Journal*, 47, 2.

Knight, D., Pearce, C.L., Smith, K.G. *et al.* (1999) Top management team diversity, group process, and strategic consensus. *Strategic Management Journal*, 5, 445–465.

Korn, H.J., Milliken, F.J. and Lant, T.K. (1992) Top management team change and organizational performance: The influence of succession, composition, and context. Paper presented at the 52nd Annual Meeting of the Academy of Management, Las Vegas, Nevada.

Korsgaard, M.A., Brodt, S.E. and Sapienza, H.J. (2003) Trust, identity, and attachment: Promoting individuals' cooperation in groups, in *Handbook of Work Group Psychology* (ed. M.A. West), John Wiley & Sons, Ltd, Chichester.

Kozlowski, S.W.J. and Ilgen, D.R. (2006) Enhancing the effectiveness of work groups and teams. *Psychological Science in the Public Interest*, 7, 77–124.

Kozlowski, S.W.J., Watola, D.J., Jensen, J.M. *et al.* (2009) Developing adaptive teams: A theory of dynamic team leadership, in *Team Effectiveness in Complex Organizations: Cross-disciplinary Perspectives and Approaches* (eds E. Salas, G.F. Goodwin and C.S. Burke), Routledge, New York, pp. 113–155.

Kravitz, D.A. and Martin, B. (1986) Ringelmann rediscovered: The original article. *Journal of Personality and Social Psychology*, 50(5), 936–941.

Lam, S.S.K. and Schaubroeck, J. (2000) The effects of group decision support systems on pooling of unshared information during group discussion. *Journal of Applied Psychology*, 85(4), 565–573.

Landy, F.J., Rastegary, H., Thayer, J. and Colvin, C. (1991) Time urgency: the construct and its measurement. *Journal of Applied Psychology*, 76, 644–657.

Latané, B. and Darley, J.M. (1970) *The Unresponsive Bystander: Why Doesn't He Help?*, Appleton-Century-Crofts, New York.

Latané, B., Williams, K.D., Harkins, S.G. (1979) Many hands make light the work: the causes and consequences of social loafing. *Journal of Personality and Social Psychology*, 37(6), 822–832.

Latham, G.P. and Yukl, G.A. (1975) Assigned versus participative goal setting with educated and uneducated wood workers. *Journal of Applied Psychology*, 60, 299–302.

Latham, G.P. and Yukl, G. (1976) Effects of assigned and participative goal setting on performance and job satisfaction. *Journal of Applied Psychology*, 61, 166–171.

Lauderdale, P., Smith-Cunnien, P., Parker, J. and Inverarity, J. (1984) External threat and the definition of deviance. *Journal of Personality and Social Psychology*, 46, 1058–1068.

Lawrence, B.S. (1997) The black box of organizational demography. *Organizational Science*, 8, 1–22.

Leung, K., Lu, L. and Liang, X. (2003) When East meets West: Effective teamwork across cultures, in *International Handbook of Organizational Teamwork and Cooperative Working* (eds M.A. West, D. Tjosvold and K.G. Smith), John Wiley & Sons, Ltd, Chichester, pp. 551–72.

Locke, E. (1990) The motivation sequence, the motivation hub, and the motivation core. *Organizational Behaviour and Human Decision Making Processes*, 50, 288–99.

Locke, E. and Latham, G. (1990) *A Theory of Goal Setting and Task Motivation*, Prentice-Hall, Englewood Cliffs, NJ.

Locke, E. and Latham, G. (2002) Building a practically useful theory of goal setting and task motivation, *American Psychologist*, 57, 705–17.

Locke, E.A., Shaw, K.N., Saari, L.M. and Latham, G.P. (1981) Goal setting and task performance. *Psychological Bulletin*, 90, 125–52.

Losada, M. and Heaphy, E. (2004) The role of positivity and connectivity in the performance of business teams: A nonlinear dynamics model. *American Behavioural Scientist*, 47(6), 740–765.

Macy, B.A. and Izumi, H. (1993) Organizational change, design and work innovation: A meta analysis of 131 North American field studies 1961–1991, in *Research in Organizational Change and Design*, Vol. 7, (eds R.W. Woodman and W.A. Passmore), JAI Press, Greenwich, CT.

Maier, N.R.F and Solem, A.R. (1962) Improving solutions by turning choice situations into problems. *Personnel Psychology*, 15(2), 152–157.

Majchrzak, A., Rice, R.E., Malhotra, A. *et al.* (2000) Technology adaptation: The case of a computer-supported inter-organizational virtual team. *MIS Quarterly*, 24(4), 569–600.

Manning, M.R., Jackson, C.N. and Fusilier, N.R. (1996) Occupational stress, social support and the cost of healthcare. *Academy of Management Journal*, 39, 750–783.

March, J.G. (1994) *A Primer on Decision Making*, Free Press, New York.

Marmot, M., Siegrist, J., Theorell, T. and Feeney, A. (1999) Health and the psychosocial environment at work, in *Social Determinants of Health* (eds M. Marmot and R.G. Wilkinson), Oxford University Press, Oxford, pp. 105–131.

Martin, R. and Hewstone, M. (eds) (2010) *Minority Influence and Innovation: Antecedents, Processes and Consequences*, Psychology Press, London.

Martin, R., Hewstone, M. and Martin, P.Y. (2008) Majority versus minority influence: The role of message processing in determining resistance to counter-persuasion. *European Journal of Social Psychology*, 38(1), 16–34.

Mathieu, J.E. and Schulze, W. (2006) The influence of team knowledge and formal plans on episodic team process→performance relationships. *Academy of Management Journal*, 49(3), 605–619.

Mathieu, J.E., Gilson, L.L. and Ruddy, T.M. (2006) Empowerment and team effectiveness: an empirical test of an integrated model. *Journal of Applied Psychology*, 91, 97–108.

Mathieu, J.E., Marks, M.A. and Zaccaro, S.J. (2001) Multi-team systems, in *International Handbook of Work and Organizational Psychology* (eds N. Anderson, D. Ones, H.K. Sinangil, and C. Viswesvaran), Sage, London, pp. 289–313.

Mathieu, J., Maynard, M.T., Rapp, T. and Gilson, L. (2008) Team effectiveness 1997–2007: A review of recent advancements and a glimpse into the future. *Journal of Management*, 34, 410–476.

Mathieu, J.E., Heffner, T.S., Goodwin, G.F. *et al.* (2005) Scaling the quality of teammates' mental models: Equifinality and normative comparisons. *Journal of Organizational Behavior*, 26, 37–56.

Maznevski, M.L. (1994) Understanding our differences: Performance in decision-making groups with diverse members. *Human Relations*, 47, 531–552.

McDaniel, M.A., Morgeson, F.P., Finnegan, E.B. *et al.* (2001) Use of situational judgment tests to predict job performance: A clarification of the literature. *Journal of Applied Psychology*, 86, 730–740.

McGrath, J.E. (1984) *Groups: Interaction and Performance*, Prentice Hall, Englewood Cliffs, NJ.

McGrath, J.E. and Kelly, J.R. (1986) *Time and Human Interaction: Toward a Social Psychology of Time*, Guilford Press, New York.

McLean, B. and Nocera, J. (2011) *All the Devils are Here: The Hidden History of the Financial Crisis*, Viking Press.

Milgram, S. (1963) Behavioral study of obedience. *Journal of Abnormal and Social Psychology*, 67(3), 371–378.

Milgram, S. (1965a) Liberating effects of group pressure. *Journal of Personality and Social Psychology*, 1, 127–134.

Milgram, S. (1965b) Some conditions of obedience and disobedience to authority. *Human Relations*, 18, 57–75.

Miller, D. and Toulouse, J. (1986) Chief executive personality and corporate strategy, and structure. *Management Science*, 32, 1389–1409.

Mohrman, S., Cohen, S. and Mohrman, L. (1995) *Designing Team Based Organizations*, Jossey-Bass, San Francisco.

Moscovici, S., Mugny, G. and van Avermaet, E. (eds) (1985) *Perspectives on Minority Influence*, Cambridge University Press, Cambridge.

Mount, M.K., Barrick, M.R. and Stewart, G.L. (1998) Five-factor model of personality and performance in jobs involving interpersonal interactions. *Human Performance*, 11, 145–165.

Mullen, B. and Copper, C. (1994) The relation between group cohesiveness and performance: An integration. *Psychological Bulletin*, 115, 210–222.

Mumford, M.D. and Gustafson, S.B. (1988) Creativity syndrome: Integration, application and innovation. *Psychological Bulletin*, 103, 27–43.

Myers I.B. and McCaulley M.H. (1985) Manual: A guide to the development and use of the Myers-Briggs Type Indicator, Consulting Psychologists Press, Palo Alto, CA.

Nadler, D.A. (1996) Managing the team at the top. *Strategy and Business*, 2, 42–51.

Nemeth, C.J. and Nemeth-Brown, B. (2003) Better than individuals? The potential benefits of dissent and diversity for group creativity, in *Group Creativity* (eds P. Paulus and B. Nijstad), Oxford University Press, Oxford.

Nemeth, C. and Owens, P. (1996) Making work groups more effective: the value of minority dissent, in *Handbook of Work Group Psychology* (ed. M.A. West), John Wiley & Sons, Ltd, Chichester, pp. 125–141.

Nemeth, C.J., Rogers, J.D. and Brown, K.S. (2001) Devil's advocate versus authentic dissent: Stimulating quantity and quality. *European Journal of Social Psychology*, 31, 707–720.

Nicholson, N. (2000) *Managing the Human Animal*, Texere, London.

Nicholson, N. and West, M.A. (1988) *Managerial Job Change: Men and Women in Transition*, Cambridge University Press, Cambridge.

Oldham, G.R. and Cummings, A. (1996) Employee creativity: Personal and contextual factors at work. *Academy of Management Journal*, 39, 607–634.

Olson, G.M. and Olson, J.S. (2000) Distance matters. *Human-Computer Interaction*, 15, 139–178.

Parker, G., McAdams, J. and Zielinski, D. (2000) *Rewarding Teams: Lessons from the Trenches*, Jossey-Bass, San Francisco.

Paul, A.K. and Anantharaman, R.N. (2003) Impact of people management practices on organizational performance: analysis of a causal model. *International Journal of Human Resource Management*, 14, 1246–1266.

Paulus, P.B. (2000) Groups, teams and creativity: The creative potential of idea-generating groups. *Applied Psychology: An International Review*, 49, 237–262.

Paulus, P.B., Nakui, T., Putman, V.L. and Brown, V.R. (2006) Effects of task instructions and brief breaks on brainstorming. *Group Dynamics: Theory, Research and Practice*, 10, 206–219.

Peterson, M.F. and Hunt, J.G. (1997) International perspectives on international leadership. *Leadership Quarterly*, 8, 203–231.

Peterson, C. and Seligman, M.E.P. (2004) *Character Strengths and Virtues: A Handbook and Classification*, Oxford University Press, Oxford/American Psychological Association, Washington, DC.

Peterson, R.S., Smith, D.B., Martorana, P.V. and Owens, P.D. (2003) The impact of chief executive officer personality on top management team dynamics. *Journal of Applied Psychology*, 88, 795–808.

Peterson, N.G., Mumford, M.D., Borman, W. C. *et al.* (2001) Understanding work using the occupational information network (ONET): Implications for practice and research. *Personnel Psychology*, 54, 451–92.

Pettigrew, A. (1992) On studying managerial elites. *Strategic Management Journal*, 13, 163–182.

Pfeffer, J. (1983) Organizational demography, in *Research in Organizational Behavior*, Vol. 5 (eds L.L. Cummings and B.M. Staw),) JAI Press, Greenwich, CT, pp. 299–357.

Pinto, J.K. and Prescott, J.E. (1987) *Changes in Critical Success Factor Importance Over the Life of a Project*. Proceedings of the National Academy of Management annual conference, Chicago, IL, pp. 328–332.

Pondy, L. (1967) Organizational conflict: Concepts and models. *Administrative Science Quarterly*, 17, 296–320.

Powell, A., Piccoli, G. and Ives, B. (2004) Virtual teams: A review of current literature and directions for future research. *Database for Advances in Information Systems*, 35(1), 6–36.

Pritchard, R.D., Jones, S.D., Roth, P.L. *et al.* (1988) Effects of group feedback goal setting, and incentives on organizational productivity. *Journal of Applied Psychology*, 73, 337–358.

Procter, S. and Burridge, M. (2004) Extent, intensity and context: teamworking and performance in the 1998 UK Workplace Employee Relations Survey (WERS 98) *IIRA HRM Study Group Working Papers in Human Resource Management*, No. 12.

Rasmussen, T.H. and Jeppesen, H.J. (2006) Teamwork and associated psychological factors: A review. *Work & Stress*, 20, 105–128.

Richter, A.W., Dawson, J.F. and West, M.A. (2011) The effectiveness of teams in organizations: a meta-analysis, The *International Journal of Human Resource Management*, 22, 2749–2769.

Riopelle, K., Gluesing, J.C., Alcordo, T.C. *et al.* (2003) Context, task, and the evolution of technology use in global virtual teams, in *Virtual Teams that Work: Creating Conditions for Virtual Team Effectiveness* (eds C.B. Gibson and S.G. Cohen), Jossey-Bass, San Francisco, pp. 239–264.

Rocco, E., Finholt, T.A., Hofer, E.C., Herbsleb, J.D. (2000) *Designing as if Trust Mattered*, Collaboratory for Research on Electronic Work (CREW) Technical Report, University of Michigan, Ann Arbor, MI.

Rogelberg, S.G., Barnes-Farrell, J.L. and Lowe, C.A. (1992) The stepladder technique: An alternative group structuring facilitating effective group decision making. *Journal of Applied Psychology*, 77, 730–737.

Romanov, K., Appelberg, K., Honkasalo, M. and Koskenvuo, M. (1996) Recent interpersonal conflict at work and psychiatric morbidity: A prospective study of 15,530 employees aged 24–64. *Journal of Psychosomatic Research*, 40, 169–76.

Runco, M.A. and Pritzker, S.R. (1999a) *Encyclopaedia of Creativity, Vol. 1, A–H*, Academic Press, London.

Runco, M.A. and Pritzker, S.R. (1999b) *Encyclopaedia of Creativity, Vol. 2, I–Z*, Academic Press, London.

Rutte, C.G. (2003) Social loafing in teams, in *International Handbook of Organizational Teamwork and Cooperative Working* (eds M.A. West, D. Tjosvold, and K.G. Smith), John Wiley & Sons, Ltd, Chichester, pp. 361–378.

Sacramento, C.A., Chang, S.M.W. and West, M.A. (2006) Team innovation through collaboration, in *Innovation through Collaboration* (eds M.M. Beyerlein, S.T. Beyerlein and F.A. Kennedy), Elsevier, pp. 81–112.

Salas, E., Nichols, D.R. and Driskell, J.E. (2007) Testing three team training strategies in intact teams: A meta-analysis. *Small Group Research*, 38, 471–488.

Salas, E., Rosen, M.A., Burke, C.S. and Goodwin, G.F. (2009) The wisdom of collectives in organizations: An update of competencies, in *Team Effectiveness in Complex Organizations: Cross-disciplinary Perspectives and Approaches* (eds E. Salas, G.F. Goodwin and C.S. Burke), Routledge, London, pp. 39–79.

Salas, E., Wilson, K.A., Burke, C.S. and Wightman, D.C. (2006a) Does crew resource management training work? An update, an extension, and some critical needs. *Human Factors*, 48, 392–412.

Salas, E., Wilson, K.A, Burke, C.S. *et al.* (2006b) Crew resource management training: research, practice, and lessons learned, in *Reviews of Human Factors and Ergonomics*, Vol. 2 (ed. Robert C. Williges), Human Factors and Ergonomics Society, Santa Monica, CA.

Salas, E., Wilson, K.A., Burke, C.S. *et al.* (2006c) A checklist for crew resource management training. *Ergonomics in Design,* 14(2), 6–15.

Schmidt, F. and Hunter, J. (1998) The validity and utility of selection methods in personnel psychology: Practical and theoretical implications of 85 years of research findings. *Psychological Bulletin,* 124, 262–274.

Schneider, B., Goldstein, H.W. and Smith, D.B. (1995) The ASA framework: An update. *Personnel Psychology,* 48, 747–773.

Schutz, W.C. (1967) *The FIRO Scales,* Consulting Psychologists Press, Palo Alto, CA.

Sealy, R., Vinnicombe, S. and Singh, V. (2008) The pipeline to the board finally opens: Women's progress in FTSE 100 boards in the UK, in *Women on Corporate Boards of Directors: International Research and Practice* (eds S. Vinnicombe, V. Singh, R.J. Burke *et al.*), Edward Elgar, Cheltenham, pp. 37–46.

Seligman, M.E.P. (1998) *Learned Optimism: How to Change Your Mind and Your Life,* 2nd edn, Pocket Books, New York.

Semini, G. and Glendon, A.I. (1973) Polarization and the established group. *British Journal of Social and Clinical Psychology,* 12, 113–21.

Shaw, M.E. (1932) A comparison of individuals and small groups in the rational solution of complex problems. *American Journal of Psychology,* 44, 491–504.

Sherif, M., Harvey, O.J., White, B.J. *et al.* (1961) *Intergroup Conflict and Co-operation: The Robber's Cave Experiment,* Institute of Group Relations, Norman, OK.

Shore, L.M. and Barksdale, K. (1998) Examining degree of balance and level of obligation in the employment relationship: A social exchange approach. *Journal of Organizational Behaviour,* 19, 731–744.

Slavin, R.E. (1983) When does cooperative learning increase student achievement? *Psychological Bulletin,* 94(3), 429–445.

Smith, K.G., Smith, K.A., Olian, J. *et al.* (1994) Top management team demography and process: The role of social integration and communication. *Administrative Science Quarterly,* 39, 412–438.

Smith, P.B. and Bond, M.H. (1993) *Social Psychology Across Cultures: Analysis and Perspectives,* Harvester Wheatsheaf, New York.

Sole, D. and A. Edmondson (2002) Bridging knowledge gaps: learning in geographically dispersed cross-functional development teams, in *The Strategic Management of Intellectual Capital and Organizational Knowledge: A Collection of Readings* (eds C.W. Choo and N. Bontis), Oxford University Press, New York.

Stasser G. and Stewart D. (1992) Discovery of Hidden Profiles by Decision-Making Groups: Solving a Problem Versus Making a Judgment. *Journal of Personality and Social Psychology,* 63(3), 426–434.

Stasser, G and Titus, W. (2003) Hidden profiles: A brief history. *Psychological Inquiry,* 3–4, 302–311.

Stevens, M.J. and Campion, M.A. (1994) The knowledge, skill, and ability requirements for teamwork: Implications for human resource management. *Journal of Management,* 20, 503–530.

Stevens, M.J. and Campion M.A. (1999) Staffing work teams: Development and validation of a selection test for teamwork settings. *Journal of Management,* 25, 207–228.

Stein, A.A. (1976) Conflict and cohesion: A review of the literature. *Journal of Conflict Resolution*, 20, 143–72.

Steiner, I.D. (1972) *Group Process and Productivity*, Academic Press, New York.

Sternberg, R.J. (2003) *Wisdom, Intelligence, and Creativity Synthesized*, Cambridge University Press, New York.

Sternberg, R.J. and Lubart, T.I. (1996) Investing in creativity. *American Psychologist*, 51, 677–688.

Stroebe, W., Stroebe, M. and Zech, E. (1996) The role of social sharing in adjustment to loss. Paper presented at the 11th General Meeting of the European Association of Experimental and Social Psychology, Gmunden, Austria.

Sy, T., Cote, S. and Saavedra, R. (2005) The contagious leader: Impact of the leader's mood on the mood of group members, group affective tone, and group processes. *Journal of Applied Psychology*, 90, 295–305.

Tajfel, H. (1970) Experiments in intergroup discrimination. *Scientific American*, 223, 96–102.

Tajfel, H. and Billig, M. (1974) Familiarity and categorization in intergroup behaviour. *Journal of Experimental Social Psychology*, 10, 159–170.

Tannenbaum S.I., Salas, E. and Cannon-Bowers, J.A. (1996) Promoting team effectiveness, in *Handbook of Work Group Psychology* (ed. M.A. West), John Wiley & Sons, Ltd, Chichester, pp. 503–529.

Tata, J. and Prasad, S. (2004) Team self-management, organizational structure, and judgments of team effectiveness. *Journal of Managerial Issues*, 16, 248–265.

Tjosvold, D. (1991) *Team Organisation: An Enduring Competitive Advantage*, John Wiley & Sons, Ltd, Chichester.

Tjosvold, D. (1998) Co-operative and competitive goal approaches to conflict: accomplishments and challenges. *Applied Psychology: An International Review*, 47, 285–342.

Tubbs, M.E. (1986) Goal setting: A meta-analytic examination of the empirical evidence. *Journal of Applied Psychology*, 71, 474–483.

Tuckman, B.W. and Jensen, M.C. (1977) Stages of small group development revisited. *Group and Organizational Studies*, 2, 419–427.

Turner, J.C. (1985) Social categorization and the self concept: A social cognitive theory of group behavior, in *Advances in Group Processes: Theory and Research*, Vol. 2 (ed. E.J. Lawler), JAI Press, Greenwich, CT, pp. 77–122.

Tziner, A. and Eden, D. (1985) Effects of crew composition on crew performance: does the whole equal the sum of its parts? *Journal of Applied Psychology*, 70, 85–93.

VanGundy, Jr, A.B. (1988) *Techniques of Structured Problem Solving*, Van Nostrand Reinhold, New York.

van Knippenburg, D. and Schippers, M.C. (2007) Work group diversity. *Annual Review of Psychology*, 58, 515–541.

van Knippenberg, D., De Dreu, C.K.W. and Homans, A.C. (2004) Work group diversity and group performance: An integrative model and research agenda. *Journal of Applied Psychology*, 89, 1008–1022.

van Knippenberg, D., Haslam, S.A. and Platow, M.J. (2007) Unity through diversity: Value-in-diversity beliefs as moderator of the relationship between work group diversity and group identification. *Group Dynamics: Theory, Research, and Practice*, 11, 207–222.

van Knippenberg, D., Dawson, J.F., West, M.A. and Homan, A.C. (2011) Diversity faultlines, shared objectives, and top management team performance. *Human Relations*, 64, 307–336.

Vinokur, A., Burnstein, E., Sechrest, L. and Wortman, P.M. (1985) Group decision-making by experts: Field study of panels evaluating medical technologies. *Journal of Personality and Social Psychology*, 49, 70–84.

Wageman, R., Nunes, D.A., Burruss, J.A. and Hackman, J.R. (2008) *Senior Leadership Teams: What it Takes to Make Them Great*, Harvard Business School Press, Boston.

Walker, T.G. and Main, E.C. (1973) Choice shifts and extreme behaviour: Judicial review in the federal courts. *Journal of Social Psychology*, 91(2), 215–221.

Watson, W.E., Kumar, K. and Michaelsen, L.K. (1993) Cultural diversity's impact on interaction process and performance: Comparing homogenous and diverse task groups. *Academy of Management Journal*, 36, 590–602.

Webber, S.S. and Donahue, L.M. (2001) Impact of highly and less job-related diversity on work group cohesion and performance: A meta-analysis. *Journal of Management*, 27, 141–162.

Welbourne, T.M., Cycyota, C.S. and Ferrante, C.J. (2007) Wall Street reaction to women in IPOs: An examination of gender diversity in top management teams. *Group & Organization Management*, 32, 524–547.

Weldon, E. and Weingart, L.R. (1993) Group goals and group performance. *British Journal of Social Psychology*, 32, 307–334.

West, B.J., Patera, J.L. and Carsten, M.K. (2009) Team level positivity: investigating psychological capacities and team level outcomes. *Journal of Organizational Behavior*, 30, 249–267.

West, M.A. (1996) *Developing Creativity in Organizations*, Blackwell/British Psychological Society, Oxford.

West, M.A. (2000) Reflexivity, revolution and innovation in work teams, in *Product Development Teams: Advances in Interdisciplinary Studies of Work Teams* (ed. M. Beyerlein), JAI Press, Greenwich, CT, pp. 1–30.

West, M.A. (2002) Sparkling fountains or stagnant ponds: An integrative model of creativity and innovation implementation in work groups. *Applied Psychology: An International Review*, 51(3), 355–387.

West, M.A. (2003) *Effective Teamwork: Practical Lessons from Organizational Research*, Blackwell/British Psychological Society, Oxford.

West M.A. and Allen, N.A. (1997) Selecting for teamwork, in *International Handbook of Selection and Assessment* (eds N. Anderson and P. Herriot), John Wiley & Sons, Ltd, Chichester, pp. 493–506.

West, M.A. and Anderson, N. (1996) Innovation in top management teams. *Journal of Applied Psychology*, 81, 680–693.

West, M.A. and Markiewicz, L. (2003) *Building Team-based Working: A Practical Guide to Organizational Transformation*, Blackwell, Oxford.

West, M.A., Borrill, C.S. and Unsworth, K.L. (1998) Team effectiveness in organizations, in *International Review of Industrial and Organisational Psychology*, Vol. 13 (eds C.L. Cooper and I.T. Robertson), John Wiley & Sons, Ltd, Chichester, pp. 1–48.

West, M.A., Brodbeck, F.C. and Richter, A.W. (2004) Does the "romance of teams" exist? The effectiveness of teams in experimental and field settings. *Journal of Occupational and Organizational Psychology*, 77, 467–473.

West, M.A., Markiewicz, L. and Dawson, J.F. (2006) *Aston Team Performance Inventory: Management Set*, ASE, London.

West, M.A., Patterson, M.G. and Dawson, J. (1999) A path to profit?: Teamwork at the top. *Centre Piece: the Magazine of Economic Performance*, 4(3), 7–11.

West, M.A., Tjosvold, D. and Smith, K.G. (eds) (2003) *The International Handbook of Organizational Teamwork and Cooperation*, John Wiley & Sons, Ltd, Chichester.

Widmer, P.S., Schippers, M.C. and West, M.A. (2009) Recent developments in reflexivity research: A review. *Psychology of Everyday Activity*, 2, 2–11.

Wiersema, M.F. and Bantel, K.A. (1992) Top management team demography and corporate strategic change. *Academy of Management Journal*, 35, 91–121.

Williams, J.G. and Solano, C.H. (1983) The social reality of feeling lonely: friendship and reciprocation. *Personality and Social Psychology Bulletin*, 9, 237–242.

Woods, S.A. and West, M.A. (2010) *The Psychology of Work and Organizations*, CENGAGE, London.

Worchel, S., Lind, E.A. and Kaufman, K.H. (1975) Evaluations of group products as a function of expectations of group longevity, outcome of competition and publicity of evaluations. *Journal of Personality and Social Psychology*, 31, 1089–1097.

Worchel, S., Rothgerber, H., Day, E.A. *et al.* (1998) Social identity and individual productivity within groups. *British Journal of Social Psychology*, 37, 389–413.

Yukl, G. (1998) *Leadership in Organizations*, 4th edn, Prentice Hall, London.

Yukl, G. (2010) *Leadership in Organizations*, 7th edn, Prentice Hall, London.

Zaccaro, S.J., Heinen, B. and Shuffler, M. (2009) Team leadership and team effectiveness, in *Team Effectiveness in Complex Organizations: Cross-disciplinary Perspectives and Approaches* (eds E. Salas, G.F. Goodwin and C.S. Burke), Routledge, London, pp. 83–111.

Zand, D.E. (1972) Trust and managerial problem solving. *Administrative Science Quarterly*, 17, 229–239.

Zenger, T.R. and Lawrence, B.S. (1989) Organizational demography: The differential effects of age and tenure distributions on technical communication. *Academy of Management Journal*, 32, 353–376.

Zwick, T. (2004) Employee participation and productivity. *Labour Economics*, 11(6), 715–740.

Author Index

Agarwal, R., 125
Ahearn, K.K., 60
Ainsworth, M.D.S., 131
Albrecht, S.L., 263
Allen, N.A., 49
Amabile, T.M., 157, 170
Anantharaman, R.N., 20
Ancona, D., 54, 205–6
Anderson, D., 220
Anderson, N.R., 46, 58, 97, 156, 260
Andrews, F.M., 54, 157
Angelmar, R., 56
Applebaum, E., 19
Argyris, C., 69–70, 140, 153, 159
Asch, S., 138
Ashford, S.J., 81
Avolio, B., 81
Axtell, C.M., 226, 232, 239

Bacon, N., 20, 153
Bailey, D.E., 17–32
Ballard, J.G., 221
Baltes, B.B., 229, 231
Bantel, K.A., 53, 243, 247
Barchas, P., 173
Barksdale, K., 184
Barnes-Farrel, J.L., 129

Barrick, M.R., 43, 44, 127
Barsade, S., 186
Bass, B., 81
Batchelor, M., 80
Batt, R., 19
Baumeister, R.F., 15, 172, 174
Beal, D., 186, 187
Belbin, R.M., 45–8
Bell, B.S., 134
Bell, S.T., 44, 59
Bennett, N., 84
Beyerlein, M.M., 12, 202, 220
Billig, M., 216
Blyton, P., 20
Boeker, W., 247
Bond, R., 138, 139
Boning B., 20
Borrill, C., 17, 53, 56, 121
Boyatzis, R., 85, 186, 187
Brewer, P.R., 216
Brodbeck, F.C., 16, 26, 27, 57
Brodt, S.E., 133
Brown, K., 145, 153
Brown, R., 20, 127, 137, 217
Bunderson, J.S., 54
Burke, C.S., 60, 61, 85, 86, 102
Burke, M.J., 187

Effective Teamwork: Practical Lessons from Organizational Research, Third Edition.
By M. A. West. © 2012 John Wiley & Sons, Ltd. Published 2012 by John Wiley & Sons, Ltd.,
and the British Psychological Society.

Burridge, M., 20
Burruss, J.A., 59
Burton, R., 172
Byrne, D., 52

Caldwell, D., 54, 205–6
Cameron, K., 11, 18
Campion, M.A., 49–50
Cannon-Bowers, J.A., 88, 102, 153
Carli, L.L., 56
Carpenter, M.A., 243
Carson, 84
Carsten, M.K., 90, 102
Cashman, J., 175
Chang, S.M.W., 18
Channing, W.E., 188
Chen, M.J., 60, 247
Chhokar, J.S., 27
Cho, T.S., 247
Claxton, G., 168, 170, 171
Clouse, R.W., 186
Cohen, R.R., 187
Cohen, S., 174, 202, 220
Cohen, S.G., 17, 32
Cooke, N.J., 50
Copper, C., 45, 89, 186
Côté, S., 61, 86
Cotton, J.L., 19
Covey, S.R., 201
Cramton, C.D., 233, 234
Cummings, A., 170, 182
Cummings, J.N., 228
Cycyota, C.S., 248
Cyert, R., 243

Dalai Lama, 187
Dante, A., 135
Darley, J.M., 128
Dawson, J., 17, 19, 56
Day, E.A., 84
De Cremer, D., 15, 37
De Dreu, C.K.W., 58, 99, 150, 188,
    189, 195, 198
Delarue, A., 19
Demoulin, S., 217, 220
Dennis, A., 235
Deutsch, M., 188, 198

Devine, D.J., 43
Diehl, M., 24, 128
Donahue, L.M., 56
Douglas, M., 221
Dovidio, J.F., 217, 220
Driskel, J.E., 88
Drucker, P.F., 241
Dunbar, K., 53
Dunlop, J.T., 20
Dutton, J.E., 11, 187

Eagly, A.H., 56
Earley, P.C., 27
Eden, D., 43
Edmondson, A.C., 133, 157, 234,
    243, 262
Edwards, B.D., 120
Einstein, A., 41, 155
Ellis, A.J.P., 43
English, A., 44

Farrell, J.B., 263
Ferrante, C.J., 248
Finklestein, S., 242
Fisher, R., 99, 190
Fleck, F.J., 226, 239
Flood, P.C., 243, 247, 262, 264
Ford, C.M., 156, 171
Fredrickson, B., 6, 11, 61
Freire, P., 188
Furnham, A., 46
Fusilier, M.R., 174

Ganster, D.C., 174, 181
Garcea, N., 11, 187
Geister, S., 226, 228, 235, 239
Gelatkanycz, M.A., 243
Gersick, C.J.G., 66, 91
Gibson, D.E., 186
Gilson, L.L., 20, 38, 59, 220
Gioia, D.A., 156, 171
Glassop, L.I., 20
Glendon, A.I., 128
Gluesing, J.C., 232
Goethe, J., 107
Goldstein, H.W., 52
Goleman, D., 80, 85, 132, 186, 187

Graen, G., 71, 175
Greitemeyer, T., 26
Griffith, R.L., 44
Gronn, P., 84
Gully, S.M., 151, 153
Gustafson, S.B., 157
Guzzo, R.A., 32, 92, 102, 134, 153

Hackman, J.R., 56, 59, 61, 67, 71, 72,
　77–8, 85, 182, 196, 207, 220, 268
Hambrick, D.C., 242, 247
Harkins, S., 12
Harrington, S., 11, 187
Harris, C., 202, 220
Harrison, D.A., 247
Haslam, S.A., 58
Heaphy, E., 123, 251
Heinen, B., 22, 76, 84, 86
Heller, F., 25, 157, 215
Henry, J., 156
Hertel, G., 226, 228, 229, 235,
　237–8, 239
Hewstone, M., 148, 153, 214,
　218, 220
Hill, M., 45
Hinds, P., 232
Hirschfield, R.R., 50
Hodgkinson, G.P., 264
Hofner Saphiere, D.M., 237
Horwitz, I.B., 247
Horwitz, S.K., 247
House, R.J., 27
Howell, J., 81
Hu, J., 66, 85
Hunt, J.G., 138

Ichniowski, C., 20
Ilgen, D.R., 37, 134, 151, 153
Illies, R., 82
Ingham, A.G., 22
Isen, A.M., 157
Izumi, H., 19

Jackson, C.N., 174
Jackson, S., 52
Jackson, S.E., 243, 247
Janis, I., 128, 136–8

Jefferson, T., 119
Jehn, K., 189, 198
Jensen, M.C., 89
Jeppesen, H.J., 173, 187
Judge, T.A., 82

Kabat-Zinn, J., 72, 80
Kanter, R.M., 255–6, 268
Karau, S.J., 25–6, 128
Kaufman, K.H., 89
Kelly, J.R., 91
Kets de Vries, M.F., 264
Kiesler, S., 228, 233
Kilduff, M., 56
Klein, K.J., 247
Knight, D., 262
Konradt, U., 226, 228, 235, 239
Korn, H.J., 247
Korsgaard, M.A., 133
Kozlowski, S.W.J., 37, 84, 86, 89,
　134, 151
Kravitz, D.A., 21
Kumar, K., 56–7

Lam, S.S.K., 129
Landy, F.J., 55
Lant, T.K., 247
Latané, B., 22, 128
Latham, G.P., 33, 64, 76, 108, 111,
　117, 244
Lauderdale, P., 217
Lawrence, B.S., 247
Leary, M.R., 15, 172
Leung, K., 57
Lewin, K., 13
Leyens, J-P., 217, 220
Liang, X., 57
Liden, R.C., 66, 85
Lind, E.A., 89
Linley, A., 187
Linley, P.A., 11, 187
Locke, E., 33, 64, 76, 108, 111,
　117, 244
Losada, M., 123, 251
Lowe, C.A., 129
Lu, L., 57
Lubart, T.I., 157

Macy, B.A., 19
Maier, N.R.F., 22
Main, E.C., 128
Majchrzak, A., 232
Manning, M.R., 174, 181
March, J.G., 243
Markiewicz, L., 17, 68, 79, 202, 220
Marmot, M., 170
Marrone, 84
Martin, B., 21
Martin, P.Y., 148, 153
Martin, R., 148, 153, 214
Mathieu, J.E., 20, 38, 42, 53, 55, 56,
    59, 84, 101, 120, 134, 202, 219,
    220, 226, 239
Mayes, B.T., 174
Maynard, M.T., 38, 59, 134
Maznevski, M.L., 53
McAdams, J., 211, 220
McCaulley, M.H., 44
McCurtain, S., 243
McDaniel, M.A., 50
McGrath, J.E., 23, 91
McKee, A., 85, 186, 187
McLean, B., 242, 268
McWilliams, A., 268
Mead, M., 1
Mehra, A., 56
Michaelson, L.K., 56–7
Miligram, S., 139
Miller, D., 264
Milliken, F.J., 247
Mohrman, L., 202, 220
Mohrman, S., 202, 220
Morris, C.G., 71
Mortensen, M., 232
Moscovici, S., 148, 153, 214
Mount, M.K., 43, 44
Mugny, G., 148, 153
Mullen, B., 45, 89, 186
Mumford, M.D., 157
Murnighan, K.K., 15, 37
Myers, A.P., 44

Nadler, D.A., 243
Nakui, T., 38
Nemeth, C., 148, 150, 159

Nemeth, C.J., 145, 148, 150
Nemeth-Brown, B., 150, 153
Nichols, D.R., 88
Nicholson, N., 60, 75, 169
Nocera, J., 242, 268
Nunes, D.A., 59

Oldham, G.R., 67, 170, 182
Olson, G.M., 229
Olson, J.S., 229
Owens, P., 148, 150, 159

Parker, G., 211, 220
Pater, J.L., 90, 102
Patterson, M.G., 56
Patton, B., 99, 190
Paul, E.T., 20
Paulus, P.B., 24, 25, 38, 55, 171
Pendleton, D., 46
Peterson, C., 267, 268
Peterson, M.F., 138
Peterson, N.G., 49
Peterson, R.S., 263
Pettigrew, A., 243
Pfeffer, J., 247
Philips, J.L., 43
Piccolo, R.F., 82
Pinto, J.K., 157
Platow, M.J., 58
Powell, A., 236
Prasad, S., 20
Prescott, J.E., 157
Pritzker, S.R., 156, 171
Procter, S., 20
Putnam, V.L., 38

Quinn, R.E., 11, 187

Rapp, T., 38, 59, 134
Rasmussen, T.H., 173, 187
Richter, A.W., 16, 19, 20
Ringlemann, M., 21
Riopelle, K., 229
Roberto, M.R., 243
Rocco, E., 231
Rogelberg, S.G., 129
Rogers, C., 131–2

Rogers, J.D., 145, 153
Romanov, K., 189
Rubin, M., 218
Ruddy, T.M., 20, 220
Runco, M.A., 156, 171
Rutte, C.G., 21

Saavedra, R., 61, 86
Sacramento, C.A., 18
Salas, E., 31–2, 84, 86, 88, 97–8, 101, 102, 134, 153
Sanders, G.M., 243
Sapienza, H.J., 133
Scandura, T.A., 71
Schaubroeck, J., 129
Schippers, M.C., 5, 11, 18, 38, 57, 59, 122, 247, 248
Schneider, B., 52
Schulze, W., 42
Schutz, W.C., 45
Sealy, R., 248
Seligman, M.E.P., 80, 187, 267, 268
Semin, G., 128
Shaw, K.N., 20
Shaw, M.E., 21
Sherif, M., 216–17
Shore, L.M., 184
Shuffler, M., 22, 76, 84, 86
Singh, V., 248
Slavin, R.E., 17
Sleap, S., 46
Smith, D.B., 52
Smith, K.G., 16, 38, 142, 153, 198, 247
Smith, P.B., 139
Solano, C.H., 175
Sole, D., 234
Solem, A.R., 22
Sproull, L., 233
Spurgeon, K.L., 186
Stasser, G., 127, 234
Steele, H., 46
Steelman, L.A., 44
Stein, A.A., 216
Steiner, I.D., 22
Sternberg, R., 70, 157

Stevens, M.J., 49–50
Stewart, D., 127
Stewart, G., 44
Stillwell, A.M., 174
Stroebe, W., 24, 128
Sutcliffe, K.M., 54
Sy, T., 61, 86

Tajfel, H., 216
Tannenbaum, S.I., 88, 102
Tata, J., 20
Tesluk, 84
Thomas, H.D.C., 58
Titus, W., 234
Tjosvold, D., 16, 38, 55, 129, 142, 153, 159, 198
Toulouse, J., 264
Travaglione, A., 263
Tsui, A.S., 81
Tuckman, B.W., 89, 91
Turner, J.C., 216
Turner, N., 226, 239
Tznier, A., 43

Unsworth, K.L., 56
Ury, W., 99, 190

van Avermaet, E., 148, 153
Van de Vliert, E., 99, 188, 189
van Dick, R., 15, 37
van Knippenburg, D., 18, 38, 57–8, 59, 230, 236, 248
Van Vianen, A.E.M., 189, 195
VanGundy, A.B. Jr., 162
Vinnicombe, S., 248
Vinokur, A., 137

Wageman, R., 56, 59, 72, 246, 252–4, 257–8, 268
Walker, T.G., 128
Watkins, M., 243
Watson, W.E., 56–7
Webber, S.S., 56
Weil, D., 20
Weingart, L.R., 17, 189
Welbourne, T.M., 248

Weldon, E., 17
West, B.J., 90, 102
West, M.A., 5, 11, 16–20, 28, 38, 49, 55, 56, 68, 71, 75, 79, 86, 97, 122, 142, 150, 153, 156, 162, 167–9, 173, 174, 176, 198, 202, 213, 220, 243, 260
Whitman, W., 135
Widmer, P.S., 5, 11, 122
Wiersma, M.F., 53
Williams, J.G., 175
Williams, K., 22
Williams, K.D., 25–6, 128
Willis, H., 218
Wills, T.A., 174
Wilson, J.M., 233

Wilson, K.A., 102
Wixom, B., 235
Woods, S.A., 28, 176
Worchel, S., 26, 89
Wotman, S.R., 174
Wright, G., 264

Yukl, G.A., 81, 86, 112, 176

Zaccaro, S.J., 22, 76, 84, 86, 220
Zand, D.E., 263
Zech, E., 26
Zenger, T.R., 247
Zielinski, D., 211, 220
Zwick, T., 20

Subject Index

ability, 43–4, 49–52
achievement-orientated leadership
    style, 83
action and performing teams, 28
action plans, 108
affection, 44–5
age, 56
aggressive approach, 194
agreeableness, 43
ambassadorial activities, 205
appraisal support 181
Aston Organization Development
    (AOD), 115–17, 204
Aston Team Performance Inventory
    (ATPI), 97
Assertiveness, 194
asynchronous technologies, 229
attraction-selection-attrition model
    (ASA), 52
authority, 65, 77
    obedience to, 139
autonomy, 30–31, 77–8, 182,
    243–3, 265
away days, 93–4

baseball, 23–4
basketball, 23–4

Bay of Pigs invasion, 136–7, 142
blame cultures, 140
brain-netting, 164
brainstorming, 23–5, 161–5
    negative, 146, 164
    techniques, 162–7
brainwriting pool, 163–4

Categorization-Elaboration Model
    (CEM), 248
Challenger space shuttle disaster, 142
change, 1, 5, 18–20, 91, 146–8, 151–2,
    155–8, 169, 214–16
    see also innovation; team innovation
charisma, 83, 84
coaching, 64, 72–3, 197
    agreeing goals, 76
    giving feedback, 75–6
    listening, 72–4
    recognizing and revealing feelings,
        74–5
cohesiveness, 89, 135–6, 137
Combat Games Ltd., 87
commitment to excellence
    see task focus
communication skills, 127
company worker/implementer, 47

Effective Teamwork: Practical Lessons from Organizational Research, Third Edition.
By M. A. West. © 2012 John Wiley & Sons, Ltd. Published 2012 by John Wiley & Sons, Ltd.,
and the British Psychological Society.

complacent team, 8–10
completer finishers, 48
conflict, 188
   see also team conflict
conformity, 138–9
conscientiousness, 43
constructive controversy, 142–5
control, 44–5
coordinator, 46
Countrywide Financial, 242
creativity, 20, 23–5, 69, 155
   techniques, 162–7
Crew Resource Management Training
   (CRM), 97–8
cross-functional teams, 18, 213
Cuba, 136–7, 145
culture, 26–7
   diversity, 56–7
customer needs, 113–14

decision making, 22–3, 125–9
defensive routines, 139–40
devil's advocacy, 145
differentiators, 115–16
diversity, 18, 43, 52–9, 229–30, 246–8
   demographic diversity, 55–7
   functional diversity, 53–5
   implications, 58–9
   personal diversity, 55
   relations-oriented diversity, 53
   task-related diversity, 52
domains, 115
domination, 127
double-loop learning, 70
driven team, 8–10
dysfunctional team, 8–10

economic logic, 116
education, 208
effectiveness
   see team effectiveness
effort, 21–2, 25–6
egocentrism, 127
egocentrism fallacy, 70
emotional intelligence, 80
emotional support, 177–9
emotions, 174–6, 177

empathy, 80
enacted support, 177
exploration, 161
extraversion, 43

facilitative leadership, 83
fault lines, 230
favouritism, 71
feedback, 75–6
   see also performance feedback
flaming, 233
formal reviews, 92–4
free-riding, 22
fundamental attribution error, 190
fundamental interpersonal relations
   orientations (FIRO), 45

gainsharing, 16
gender, 56
goals, 33, 76, 108–11
   goal orientation, 164
group polarization, 128
groupthink, 128, 136–8

hidden profile, 127
hierarchy effects, 127
home and work life balance, 184
human resource management (HRM),
   19, 20, 203, 209–10
humility, 84
humour, 185–6

Ideation, 161
Implementation, 162
Inclusion, 44
information sharing, 124–5, 126
information, from organizations, 208
informational support, 179–80
innovation, 7, 9, 15–16, 18, 69, 156–60,
   168, 213
instrumental support, 180
interaction, 120–122
interdependence, 244–6
interpersonal conflict, 189, 193–5
interpersonal KSAs, 50
inter-team relations/cooperation, 3, 7,
   69, 110, 210

introversion, 44
intuition, 44
invulnerability fallacy, 70

job enrichment, 182–4
judging, 44

Kennedy, Bobby, 137, 145
Kennedy, President, 136–7, 145
Key Performance Indicators (KPIs), 248, 249
knowledge, skills and attitudes (KSAs), 49–52, 235–6
    questionnaire, 51–2

leadership styles, 83
leading, 63–6
    see also team leaders
learning, 18
listening
    active, 72
    drawing out, 73
    open, 73
    reflective, 73–4
Loxley Engineering Ltd., 149

managing, 64, 67–71
mediation, 195
meetings, 122–3, 166–7
    top team, 257–9
mining, 16–7
minority group influence, 148–50, 214–15
mission statements, 108–10
monitor evaluator, 48
multi-team systems (MTS), 202
Myers-Briggs Type Indicator, 44–5

National Health Service (NHS), 14–15, 250
negative brainstorming, 146, 164
neuroticism, 43

obedience to authority, 139
objectives
    see organizational objectives; team objectives

omnipotence fallacy, 70
omniscience fallacy, 70
openness to experience, 43
organizational objectives, 18, 113, 207, 213
organizations, 201
    HRM department, 19, 20, 203, 209–10
    innovation, 155–6
    relationship with teams, 205–7
    requirements from teams, 213–16
    support for teams, 78, 159, 248–50
    team-based working, 17–20, 27–8, 202

Participation, 119–25, 135–6, 157
passive approach, 194
passive-aggressive approach, 194
perceiving, 44
performance feedback
    individuals, 75–6
    team, 33, 51, 75–6, 205–6, 208–9
personality factors, 43–6, 127
piggy-backing, 163
plants, 47
problem solving, 22–3, 160–162
process gains, 25–7
process losses, 22
production blocking effect, 24, 128
production teams, 28
project and development teams, 28
pseudo teams, 14–15
psychology of inevitability, 193–4

Quality, 17–18, 113

Reflexivity, 5, 10, 260, 267
    see also social reflexivity; task reflexivity
relations-orientated diversity, 53
resilient team, 8–10
resource investigator, 47
resources, 208
responsibility, 128
    corporate social, 255–7
reward systems, 211–13
Robber's Cave studies, 216–17

role clarification and negotiation, 32, 100–101
Rusk, Dean, 137

safety in teams, 131–3, 157
selection, 161–2
satisficing, 129
scouting activities, 206
self-awareness, 80
self-discipline, 43
self-management, 80
  self-management KSAs, 50
self-managing teams, 84–5
sensing, 44
servicer receiver needs, 113
service teams, 28
shaper, 47
similarity-attraction theory, 52
size, 27, 65
skill mix, 53
skill variety, 182
skills, 49–52, 182
social awareness, 80
social climate, 184–6
social conformity, 127
social laboring, 25–7
social loafing, 21, 25–7, 31–4, 128
social process interventions, 89, 98–9
social reflexivity, 6–12
social skills, 49
social support, 176–81, 186
specialist, 48
Springwood primary healthcare team, 109–11
stakeholder analysis, 146–7, 147–8, 161–2, 166
statisticized groups, 23
status effects, 127
stepladder technique, 129–31, 141
strategy, 115–17
  differentiators, 116
  domains, 115
  economic logic, 116
  sequences and stages, 116–17
  vehicles, 115–16
strategy and policy teams, 28

support
  appraisal, 176–7, 181
  emotional, 176–9
  informational, 176, 179
  for innovation, 156, 157, 159
  instrumental, 176, 180
  from organizations, 207–9
  supportive leadership style, 83
synchronous technologies, 229
synergy, 15, 22

table of elements, 165–6
targets, 207
task conflict, 189
task coordinator activities, 205–6
task design, 243–5
task effectiveness, 6–7
task feedback, 182
task focus, 142–5
  and team innovation, 155, 159
task identity, 182
task performance, 174
task reflexivity, 6–12, 69, 101–2
task significance, 182
task-related diversity, 52–3
task-related problems, 95–7
tasks, 6, 29–31
  design, 78
  and team effectiveness, 30, 31
  and team leaders, 65
team bridging, 216–17
team building, 87
Team Climate Inventory, 97
team climate relationships, 114
team conflict
  organizational causes, 191–3
  resolving, 189–91
  top teams, 262–3
  types, 189
team decision making
  see decision making
team defence mechanisms, 139–40
team development, 89
  stages, 89–91
team effectiveness, 6–8
  building, 31–4
  measuring, 34–5

team functioning, task and social
    elements, 6–8
team innovation, 7, 69, 156–60,
    168, 210
  influences, 167–8
  questionnaire, 158
team leaders, 58–9, 60
  coaching, 62, 72–6
  decision making, 128
  developing skills, 79–81
  effective, 66
  emotional intelligence, 80
  fallacies, 70
  favouritism, 71
  and groupthink, 137–8
  leading, 63–6
  managing, 67–71
  mediation, 195–7
  problems between teams, 217–18
  selection, 203
  self-management teams, 84–5
  styles, 83
  tasks, 61–3
  trip wires, 77–9
  trust, safety and support, 132
  see also transactional leaders;
    transformational leaders
team members
  difficult, 195–7
  emotions, 174–5
  growth and development, 182–4
  reward systems, 211
  selection, 42–3, 203
  well-being, 6–7, 69, 114, 176–7, 210
team objectives, 7–8, 14, 67, 78, 92,
    107–13, 207, 213, 245, 252–3
team outcomes, 68–9
team participation, 119–25,
    135–6, 157
  top team, 254–5
team roles, clarification and
    negotiation, 32, 100–101
team potency, 4, 122, 151
team process conflict, 189
team reflexivity, 5, 10, 260, 267
  questionnaire, 9–10

Team Roles Inventory, 46–8
team safety, 131–3, 157
team size, 27, 65
team start-up, 92
team training
  addressing known task-related
    problems, 96–7
  cross training, 88
  formal reviews, 92–4
  identifying problems, 97
  self-correction, 88
  social process interventions, 98–9
  team coordination and
    adaptation, 88
  team start-up, 92
team viability, 6, 7, 9–10, 69, 176–7
team vision, 107, 113–15, 135–6,
    156, 214
  ability to develop, 112–3
  attainability, 112
  clarity, 111
  defining, 107–11
  elements, 113–15
  motivating value, 111
  sharedness, 112
  and team innovation, 156–8
team worker, 48
team working, 13–5
  benefits, 14–16
  drawbacks, 21–2
  organizational benefits, 17–19
team-based working (TBW), 202–5
technical assistance, 209
teleworking, 226
time-out, 71
Top Management Teams (TMTs), 241
  processes, 251–4
transactional leaders, 81, 82
transformational leaders, 81–2

values, 111–12
vehicles, 115–16
verbal support, 176
Verifone, Inc., 222–4
viability, 6, 7, 69
virtual team processes, 231–5

cohesion, 232
conflict, 232–3
trust, 231–2
virtual team working, 226
virtual teams, 221
  advantages and disadvantages, 227–8
  effectiveness, 228
  lifecycle, 235–8

processes, 231–5
vision
  see team vision

wisdom, 70
work and home life balance, 184
work safety, 16
work team, 27–8